READERS' GUIDES TO ESSENTIAL CRITICISM SERIES

CONSULTANT EDITOR: NICOLAS TREDELL

Published

Thomas P. Adler	Tennessee Williams: *A Streetcar Named Desire/Cat on a Hot Tin Roof*
Pascale Aebischer	Jacobean Drama
Lucie Armitt	George Eliot: *Adam Bede/The Mill on the Floss/Middlemarch*
Simon Avery	Thomas Hardy: *The Mayor of Casterbridge/Jude the Obscure*
Paul Baines	Daniel Defoe: *Robinson Crusoe/Moll Flanders*
Brian Baker	Science Fiction
Annika Bautz	Jane Austen: *Sense and Sensibility/Pride and Prejudice/Emma*
Matthew Beedham	The Novels of Kazuo Ishiguro
Richard Beynon	D. H. Lawrence: *The Rainbow/Women in Love*
Peter Boxall	Samuel Beckett: *Waiting for Godot/Endgame*
Claire Brennan	The Poetry of Sylvia Plath
Susan Bruce	Shakespeare: *King Lear*
Sandie Byrne	Jane Austen: *Mansfield Park*
Sandie Byrne	The Poetry of Ted Hughes
Alison Chapman	Elizabeth Gaskell: *Mary Barton/North and South*
Peter Childs	The Fiction of Ian McEwan
Christine Clegg	Vladimir Nabokov: *Lolita*
Jay Corwin	Gabriel García Márquez
John Coyle	James Joyce: *Ulysses/A Portrait of the Artist as a Young Man*
Martin Coyle	Shakespeare: *Richard II*
Sarah Davison	Modernist Literatures
Sarah Dewar-Watson	Tragedy
Justin D. Edwards	Postcolonial Literature
Michael Faherty	The Poetry of W. B. Yeats
Sarah Gamble	The Fiction of Angela Carter
Jodi-Anne George	*Beowulf*
Jodi-Anne George	Chaucer: The General Prologue to *The Canterbury Tales*
Jane Goldman	Virginia Woolf: *To the Lighthouse/The Waves*
Huw Griffiths	Shakespeare: *Hamlet*
Vanessa Guignery	The Fiction of Julian Barnes
Louisa Hadley	The Fiction of A. S. Byatt
Sarah Haggarty and Jon Mee	William Blake: *Songs of Innocence and Experience*
Geoffrey Harvey	Thomas Hardy: *Tess of the d'Urbervilles*
Paul Hendon	The Poetry of W. H. Auden
Terry Hodgson	The Plays of Tom Stoppard for Stage, Radio, TV and Film
William Hughes	Bram Stoker: *Dracula*
Stuart Hutchinson	Mark Twain: *Tom Sawyer/Huckleberry Finn*
Stuart Hutchinson	Edith Wharton: *The House of Mirth/The Custom of the Country*
Betty Jay	E. M. Forster: *A Passage to India*
Aaron Kelly	Twentieth-Century Irish Literature
Elmer Kennedy-Andrews	Nathaniel Hawthorne: *The Scarlet Letter*
Elmer Kennedy-Andrews	The Poetry of Seamus Heaney
Daniel Lea	George Orwell: *Animal Farm/Nineteen Eighty-Four*
Rachel Lister	Alice Walker: *The Color Purple*

Sara Lodge	Charlotte Brontë: *Jane Eyre*
Philippa Lyon	Twentieth-Century War Poetry
Merja Makinen	The Novels of Jeanette Winterson
Stephen Marino	Arthur Miller: *Death of a Salesman/The Crucible*
Britta Martens	The Poetry of Robert Browning
Matt McGuire	Contemporary Scottish Literature
Timothy Milnes	Wordsworth: *The Prelude*
Jago Morrison	The Fiction of Chinua Achebe
Merritt Moseley	The Fiction of Pat Barker
Pat Pinsent and Clare Walsh	Children's Literature
Carl Plasa	Toni Morrison: *Beloved*
Carl Plasa	Jean Rhys: *Wide Sargasso Sea*
Nicholas Potter	Shakespeare: *Antony and Cleopatra*
Nicholas Potter	Shakespeare: *Othello*
Nicholas Potter	Shakespeare's Late Plays: *Pericles/Cymbeline/The Winter's Tale/The Tempest*
Steven Price	The Plays, Screenplays and Films of David Mamet
Berthold Schoene-Harwood	Mary Shelley: *Frankenstein*
Nicholas Seager	The Rise of the Novel
Nick Selby	T. S. Eliot: *The Waste Land*
Nick Selby	Herman Melville: *Moby Dick*
Nick Selby	The Poetry of Walt Whitman
David Smale	Salman Rushdie: *Midnight's Children/The Satanic Verses*
Enit Steiner	Jane Austen: *Northanger Abbey/Persuasion*
Patsy Stoneman	Emily Brontë: *Wuthering Heights*
Susie Thomas	Hanif Kureishi
Nicolas Tredell	Joseph Conrad: *Heart of Darkness*
Nicolas Tredell	Charles Dickens: *Great Expectations*
Nicolas Tredell	William Faulkner: *The Sound and the Fury/As I Lay Dying*
Nicolas Tredell	F. Scott Fitzgerald: *The Great Gatsby*
Nicolas Tredell	Shakespeare: *A Midsummer Night's Dream*
Nicolas Tredell	Shakespeare: *Macbeth*
Nicolas Tredell	Shakespeare: The Tragedies
Nicolas Tredell	The Fiction of Martin Amis
David Wheatley	Contemporary British Poetry
Martin Willis	Literature and Science
Matthew Woodcock	Shakespeare: *Henry V*
Gillian Woods	Shakespeare: *Romeo and Juliet*
Angela Wright	Gothic Fiction
Michael Whitworth	Virginia Woolf: *Mrs Dalloway*
Andrew Wyllie and Catherine Rees	The Plays of Harold Pinter

Forthcoming

Nick Bentley	Contemporary British Fiction
Kate Watson	Crime and Detective Fiction

Shakespeare
As You Like It

DANA E. ASPINALL

Consultant editor: Nicolas Tredell

BLOOMSBURY ACADEMIC
LONDON • NEW YORK • OXFORD • NEW DELHI • SYDNEY

BLOOMSBURY ACADEMIC
Bloomsbury Publishing Plc
50 Bedford Square, London, WC1B 3DP, UK
1385 Broadway, New York, NY 10018, USA
29 Earlsfort Terrace, Dublin 2, Ireland

BLOOMSBURY, BLOOMSBURY ACADEMIC and the Diana logo
are trademarks of Bloomsbury Publishing Plc

First published by PALGRAVE 2018
Reprinted by Bloomsbury Academic 2023

Copyright © Dana E. Aspinall, 2018

Dana E. Aspinall has asserted her right under the Copyright,
Designs and Patents Act, 1988, to be identified as the author of this work.

For legal purposes the Acknowledgements on p. ix constitute
an extension of this copyright page

All rights reserved. No part of this publication may be reproduced or
transmitted in any form or by any means, electronic or mechanical,
including photocopying, recording, or any information storage or retrieval
system, without prior permission in writing from the publishers.

Bloomsbury Publishing Plc does not have any control over, or responsibility for,
any third-party websites referred to or in this book. All internet addresses given
in this book were correct at the time of going to press. The author and publisher
regret any inconvenience caused if addresses have changed or sites have
ceased to exist, but can accept no responsibility for any such changes.

A catalogue record for this book is available from the British Library.

A catalog record for this book is available from the Library of Congress.

ISBN: HB: 978-1-1374-7049-2
PB: 978-1-1374-7048-5
ePDF: 978-1-1374-7050-8
ePub: 978-1-3503-1685-1

To find out more about our authors and books visit
www.bloomsbury.com and sign up for our newsletters.

CONTENTS

ACKNOWLEDGEMENTS ix

NOTE x

INTRODUCTION xi

Discusses the play's possible dates of composition and production and its sources and analogues, and outlines the rest of the Guide.

CHAPTER ONE 1

1709–1800: "To Breed Me Well": Determinations of Genre and Character

Considers criticism of *As You Like It* in the eighteenth century by Nicholas Rowe, Charles Gildon, William Warburton, Samuel Johnson, Richard Hurd, Francis Gentleman, Elizabeth Griffith, William Richardson and Walter Whiter.

CHAPTER TWO 11

1800–1900: "Dancing Measures": Arriving at Critical Consensus

Traces nineteenth-century criticism of *As You Like It* from Romanticism to the birth of professional literary studies where emphasis shifts toward areas such as the search for a "correct" text as well as textual analysis, although many critics still devote attention to characters, Shakespeare's value as moral exemplar, and genre. Critics discussed include Coleridge, August Wilhelm Schlegel, Hazlitt, William Maginn, Hermann Ulrici, G. G. Gervinus, Taine, H. N. Hudson, Denton J. Snider, Frederick S. Boas and Bernard Shaw. The nineteenth century also ushers in women's accounts of Shakespeare, as the critics Anna Brownell Jameson, Mary Cowden Clarke, and Helena Faucit Martin write about the playwright's women characters as role models for middle class women and these characters' relationships with men.

CHAPTER THREE   31

1906–72: "A Great Reckoning": New Criticism

Concentrates primarily on the origins, establishment, and entrenchment of New Criticism as the dominant approach to *As You Like It*. Critics examined include J. B. Priestley, E. E. Stoll, P. V. Krieder, E. K. Chambers, H. B. Charlton, C. L. Barber, Harold Jenkins, Marco Mincoff, Jay L. Halio, Madeleine Doran, Sylvan Barnet and David Young.

CHAPTER FOUR   45

1948–83: "Not for All Markets": Movements Away from New Criticism and the Authority of the Text

Overlaps much of Chapter 3 chronologically, but gives attention to those critical texts on *As You Like It* that resist or pursue matters left behind by New Criticism. Among the critics considered are Northrop Frye, C. L. Barber, Jan Kott, Anne Barton, Peter Erikson, Terry Eagleton, Brian Gibbons, Martha Ronk, Robert N. Watson and Wolfgang Iser.

CHAPTER FIVE   66

1978–Present: "All the World's a Stage": Cultural Studies

Focuses on Cultural Studies critics writing on *As You Like It* from 1978 until the present. Those discussed include Judy Z. Kronenfeld, Elliott Krieger, Martha Ronk Lifson, Grace Tiffany, Andrew Barnaby, Louise Schleiner, Peter Milward, Nathaniel Strout, Linda Woodbridge and Chris Fitter.

CHAPTER SIX   82

1980–Present: "To Mutiny Against this Servitude": New Historicism

Features critics writing on *As You Like It* who identify or seem aligned with New Historicism, including Stephen Greenblatt, Louis Adrian Montrose,

Richard Wilson, Cynthia Marshall, A. Stuart Daley and Susanne L. Wofford, and also considers key dissenters such as Catherine Belsey, Mary Thomas Crane and Matthew Kendrick.

CHAPTER SEVEN   99

1965–Present: "If I Were a Woman": Feminism and Gender

Explores feminist criticism of *As You Like It* from roughly 1965 until today. Among critics discussed are Nancy K. Hayles, Clara Claiborne Park, Barbara J. Bono, Marjorie Garber, Phyllis Rackin, Jean E. Howard, Carol Rutter, Kay Stanton, Juliet Dusinberre, Penny Gay and Cynthia Lewis.

CHAPTER EIGHT   118

1981–Present: "She Phebes Me": Homoerotics, Queer Theory and Identity

Considers critics of *As You Like It* influenced by Gender Studies and Queer Theory, including Robert Kimbrough, Bruce R. Smith, Valerie Traub, William Kerrigan, Cynthia Marshall, Jessica Tvordi, Carol Thomas Neely and Valerie Rohy.

CONCLUSION   132

Highlights how critical and scholarly studies of *As You Like It* continue to enrich our understanding of this complex and popular play. Contends that discussions that focus on the play's negotiations of gender, male-female relationships, love and loyalty, property rights, and family will continue and will be enriched by performance studies, as in the work of Russell Jackson, Richard Foulkes, Lina Perkins Wilder and Indira Ghose. Other matters embedded in the play may also occupy future critics' and scholars' attention, as witnessed in recent essays on the play's relationship to colonialism by Leah S. Marcus and to utopianism by Ryan Farrar, and on teaching *As You Like It* by Elaine Hobby and Jan Stirm.

NOTES	139
SELECT BIBLIOGRAPHY	163
INDEX	171

ACKNOWLEDGEMENTS

While all writing is difficult, the writing of this text marks an especial challenge: I began my research for it five months before finding out I had leukaemia, and finished it a year and a half after my final round of chemotherapy.

I want to thank Consultant Editor Nicolas Tredell first, since he gave me not only the opportunity to participate in this series, but also showed me real patience as I struggled to get back on my feet. Thanks as well to this volume's editor, Rachel Bridgewater, for her attention and impressive skill.

My library's reference staff deserves thanks, too, for their efforts in gathering for me all the texts I requested: Angie Kelleher, Marcus Richter, and Steven Vest.

Four of my students – some of the best I have had – also assisted me with reading and preparing my manuscript, and I thank them: Jessica Bigelow, Xavier Ivery, Christopher Nolan, and Margaret C. Rausch.

Thanks as well to AMJ, who seems an answer to past years' questions and a welcome part of my future.

Finally, thanks to my son, Richard, who told me, when I needed to hear it, "You are going to be OK, Dad."

NOTE

When a writer or other significant figure is mentioned for the first time in the main text, their dates of birth and (if appropriate) death are usually supplied, but in some cases these were not available.

INTRODUCTION

Writing in the *Farnham, Haslemere & Hindhead Herald* on 15 July 1899, George Bernard Shaw (1856–1950) claimed, "Every man believes himself to be a Hamlet; every woman a Rosalind."[1] Shaw made his pronouncement in order to explain the success his generation's actors and actresses frequently, almost predictably, achieved when they played these parts on London's stages. Shaw believed, in essence, that the players of Hamlet and Rosalind do not "act" these parts during performances: seeing so much of themselves in these characters, rather, the actors "try to do their best selves"[2] as they assume the parts, and these performances of their best selves fill the theatres with appreciative spectators.

Shaw's assertion contrasts with the more commonly held assumption that an actor who plays Macbeth, say, or Imogen or Mistress Quickly, does so by temporarily assuming another persona and rarely blurs the distinctions between the part and the person playing the part. If Shaw is correct, however, in seeing something more personal in Rosalind's character, critics then must consider not only the significance and complexity of Shakespeare's achievement in her, but also ourselves and what we desire in drama. If actors who play Rosalind or Hamlet actually depict the best of themselves, perhaps we should take Shaw's remark one step further and assume that, as readers and spectators, we also see ourselves as we want to be seen in these characters, and thus return again and again to ourselves as represented in the Danish prince or the exiled duchess.

For over 300 years, editors and critics have praised Rosalind's and *As You Like It*'s ability to make us see good in ourselves and others. Some critics attribute the play's optimistic tone to its roots in the pastoral tradition, while others see Christian forgiveness and charity as its driving force, and still others identify the play's emphases on self-reliance, subjectivity, and cooperation as more humanistic constituents of its harmonious conclusion. Even in recent years, when critics consider in more political and gender-conscious terms matters such as Rosalind's silence and submission to Orlando in marriage, and contrast these actions with her prior behaviour as an intelligent, autonomous figure – perhaps even a defiant or resistant one – all acknowledge her as a dominant presence throughout the play, one heretofore not witnessed on the early modern English stage.

No matter where we fall on issues such as Rosalind's autonomy, the fact remains that this play inexhaustibly attracts readers and audiences, as Shaw pointed out so many years ago. The critics' comments summarized in this guide partially explain this attraction, and should inspire responses from current readers, especially as concerns the play's characters, genre, and significance to our own generation. This introduction provides information on the play's possible dates of composition and production, its sources and analogues, and other facts that should help generate these responses.

Date

Taking into account surviving evidence, scholars place *As You Like It*'s composition some time between 1598 and 1600. From 1597 to 1600 and beyond, London's newly reorganized boy playing companies staged several pastorals by John Lyly (c. 1554–1606) and others, many of which took place in forests and pastures and featured characters posing as shepherds and shepherdesses. In 1598 there also appeared two Robin Hood plays, one written by Anthony Munday (c. 1560–1633) and called *The Downfall of Robert, Earl of Huntington*, and the other, also written by Munday and Henry Chettle (c. 1564–1606), titled *The Death of Robert, Earl of Huntington*. The Lord Admiral's Men, Shakespeare's company's rivals, performed both plays at the Rose Theatre. Because of these plays' popularity, and also because in 1598 a new printing of *Rosalynde*, by Thomas Lodge (1558–1625), appeared, during this year Shakespeare may have countered with his own *As You Like It*, which contains an allusion to Robin Hood in 1.1 and in which a forest hosts most of the action.[3]

In September 1598, moreover, Francis Meres (c. 1565–1647) published *Palladis Tamia*, which for the first time provides a list of plays attributed to Shakespeare. While *As You Like It* does not appear in Meres' catalogue, he mentions a comedy called *Loue Labours Wonne*; in the nineteenth century, critics began conjecturing that this play may represent *As You Like It* under an alternate title. If their conjecture proves correct, then *As You Like It* was performed in 1598 or earlier.

In the summer of 1599, the Globe Theatre opened in Southwark, a stone's throw from the Rose Theatre of Philip Henslowe (c. 1550–1616). At 2.7.139 of *As You Like It*, Jacques may echo this new venue's motto, "*Totus mundus agit historionem*", or "All the world plays the actor", when he proclaims "All the world's a stage". Earlier in the play (1.2.74–75), Celia recalls a moment when "the little wit that fools have was silenced", which may refer to the Bishop of London's June 1599 order to ban and burn certain satirical books. Both these possible allusions suggest composition during the latter part of 1599, the date most current scholars agree is most likely.[4]

At the same time that Shakespeare's Lord Chamberlain's Men moved into the Globe, the company also decided upon a significant change in personnel, one that also may confirm our play as written in 1599. Known for his raucous jigs and extemporaneous line additions, comic actor Will Kempe (d. 1603) delighted his audiences at the Theatre and the Curtain, where the Lord Chamberlain's Men played in Shoreditch before their move, but he may have infuriated Shakespeare and his fellow actors with his frequent departures from the script. Whatever the circumstances, Kempe left the company in early 1599 and Robert Armin (c. 1563–1615), a gifted pamphlet writer and singer, replaced him. Armin offered Shakespeare's company a more refined and complicated – not to mention a more reliable – type of humour. Touchstone, a character several critics believe Shakespeare created for Armin's brand of humour, appears in none of the play's sources.

We also should note that, despite its popularity today, no record of the play's performance survives from its Stationers' Register entry in 1600 until the eighteenth century, although King James I may have watched a performance at Wilton House in December 1603.[5] Before its first revival at Drury Lane in 1740 – which ushered in the play's incessant popularity – an alteration appeared on 9 January 1723, written by Charles Johnson (1679–1748) and titled *Love in a Forest*.

Text

On 4 August 1600 "As you like yt/a booke" appears alongside *Henry V, Much Ado about Nothing*, and *Every Man in His Humour* in the Stationers' Register, an event which also marks the latest possible performance date for the play.[6] No evidence of the play's printing, however, exists until 1623, when *As You like It* appeared in the First Folio compiled by Heminges and Condell.

All editions of *As You Like It* follow the 1623 Folio text, and divide the play's acts and scenes according to this text as well. Most scholars assume that the play was copied from a promptbook, a frequently emended and annotated copy of the text in possession of the prompter during performance, while a few contend that it was set from a transcript of Shakespeare's foul papers, or an autograph copy of the play. Stanley Wells and Gary Taylor believe that the part of the First Folio where *As You Like It* appears was set by Compositors B, C, and D.[7] Editors and scholars consider most of the text free of corruption or alteration.

Sources

In writing *As You Like It*, Shakespeare participates in the centuries-old pastoral tradition, where courtly characters flee oppressive or threatening situations, almost always into a less sophisticated, more rural and bucolic, green (or golden) world.[8] Once there, these characters often assume the guise and, on occasion, the responsibilities of shepherds. This rural setting allows the refugees opportunity to contemplate their plights – sometimes through songs and formal debates – and to devise methods of overcoming or circumventing the forces that prompted their exile. Typically, they return to their homes in harmony and hope, but not before recognizing more fully their society's shortcomings and corruptions. Pastoral literature, then, often involves social, religious, and political criticism, and in *As You Like It* Shakespeare, too, employs the tradition to interrogate such social concerns as the varying effects of love – including homoerotic and homosexual love – as well as of gender and identity, primogeniture, patriarchy, friendship, marriage, trust, loyalty, and kindness.

Rosalynde, by Thomas Lodge

For the plot of *As You Like It*, Shakespeare lifts several storylines from *Rosalynde*, written by Thomas Lodge in 1586–87 and published in 1590, with several subsequent reprintings. In *Rosalynde*, for example, the evil king of France, Torismond (Frederick in *As You Like It*), wrests power from the loving monarch Gerismond (Duke Senior), father to Rosalynde (Rosalind), although in Lodge's text the two men are not brothers. Also, a malignant elder brother Saladyne (Oliver) threatens and shackles a morally superior younger brother Rosader (Orlando), who, along with his faithful servant Adam Spencer (Adam) escapes into the Forest of Arden, where Alinda (Celia) and Rosalynde have fled. Again, though, Shakespeare alters this subplot significantly: Saladyne and Rosader's father in *Rosalynde* has not followed the laws of primogeniture as rigidly as does Shakespeare, so Shakespeare's text interrogates more thoroughly than Lodge's the actual disadvantages wrought upon second sons in his culture.

Shakespeare refashions Lodge's storyline involving Rosalynde and Alinda as well: he diminishes Celia's presence significantly, particularly after she and Rosalind abandon Frederick's court. In Ardenne, Rosalynde (now disguised as a boy, Ganymede) and Alinda (disguised as a girl, Aliena) meet and interact with Montanus (Silvius), Phoebe (Phebe), and Corydon (Corin), and a mock marriage between Rosader and Rosalynde still takes place, but Shakespeare brings other characters, including William, Audrey, Sir Oliver Martext, and, more significantly, Jacques and Touchstone into the play. Shakespeare reduces the violence of Lodge's play, furthermore: where Rosalynde's father wins back his position by overcoming his usurper in battle, for example, Shakespeare's Frederick undergoes a religious conversion and returns the realm to Duke Senior. Finally, while Shakespeare and Lodge both identify the forest to which their characters escape as Ardenne, in France, Shakespeare mixes Lodge's French locale with distinctly English allusions, including those to primogeniture as well as to Robin Hood. Shakespeare's reference to Robin Hood evokes associations not only with the "community and brotherhood" indicative of a bygone era, as Jean E. Howard (b. 1948) explains, but also with the "resistance to tyranny" implicit in many peasants' reactions to enclosure laws during Shakespeare's lifetime.[9]

The Tale of Gamelyn

Lodge consulted the medieval *Tale of Gamelyn* – which, incidentally, comprises the story the Cook begins but never finishes in Geoffrey Chaucer's *Cook's Tale* – for the story of the elder brother Johan (Saladyne in Lodge's text and Oliver in Shakespeare's) who cheats his younger brother Gamelyn (Rosader/Orlando) out of his portion of their father's bequest. *Gamelyn* also features the younger brother Gamelyn's escape into the forest, where he meets outlaws who "live like the old Robin Hood of England" (*As You Like It* 1.1.116).

Other sources

One other text may have influenced Shakespeare's plotting of *As You Like It*: the anonymous *Sir Clyomon and Sir Clamydes* (c. 1560–70). In this early Elizabethan drama, Clamydes loses his position as knight when his beloved Juliana's brother Clyomen stands in for him at the dubbing. This play also features the princess Neronis, who disguises herself as a male and escapes into the forest to dwell with shepherds, including one named Corin. Audrey and William also may originate in this text.

Behind these direct sources lurk the indirect influences of Theocritus and Virgil, particularly their eclogues; Ovid's *Metamorphoses*; the Bible, particularly Genesis and Christ's teachings on mercy and love; and the *Arcadia* (1590) of Sir Philip Sidney (1554–86).

Criticism

Chapter 1 of this guide considers the eighteenth century and its critical concerns. For most eighteenth-century critics, Shakespeare became the model for trueness to nature, moral purity, and adherence to classical rules. Eighteenth-century critics also paid close attention to genre, and their viewpoints should help in understanding subsequent generic placements of *As You Like It* and the significance of such distinctions. Chapter 1 also covers an emergent interest in the characters who inhabit *As You Like It*. As we move into the nineteenth century, specific characters become many critics' primary focus: Jacques, for example, generates multiple interpretive responses, as does Rosalind.

In Chapter 2, which explores nineteenth-century criticism, we witness a shift into professionalized discussions of *As You Like It*, largely because examinations of the playwright's works enter into universities, where "correct" methods of interpreting his texts arise. Because literature becomes the domain of professors, emphasis shifts towards other areas, including the search for a "correct" text as well as textual analysis, although many critics still devote attention to characters, Shakespeare's value as moral exemplar, and genre. The nineteenth century also ushers in women's accounts of Shakespeare, as the critics Anna Brownell Jameson (1794–1858), Mary Cowden Clarke (1809–98), and Helena Faucit Martin (1817–98) write about the playwright's women characters as role models for middle-class women and these characters' relationships with men.

Chapter 3 covers the years 1906 to 1972, and concentrates primarily on the origins, establishment, and entrenchment of New Criticism. With New Criticism comes close textual study and even more rigid standards of "correct" reading, including a new vocabulary to help articulate that reading. While New Criticism may appear constricting to current undergraduates, it inspires some insightful and enlightening studies of *As You Like It*; the approach's fixation on form and pattern coaxes out many of the play's nuances and complexities. New Criticism's attempt to negate subjective impressions of a character or a work also opens the door to studies of relationships between works, including their influences upon each other.

Beginning with Chapter 3, this guide is organized around dominant theoretical approaches to *As You Like It*. Chapter subheadings occasionally are provided in this and subsequent chapters to highlight the critics who initiate the theoretical approaches or who contribute the most influential statements within them.

Covering the years 1948–83, Chapter 4 overlaps much of Chapter 3 chronologically, but in this chapter those texts which resist or pursue matters left behind by New Criticism receive attention. Eventually, New Criticism's linking of structure and pattern to older works countermands its tendency to perceive the text as a world unto itself, and this development ultimately produces the first forays into Cultural Studies, whose proponents see the text as inseparably intertwined with its era's politics, social customs, and economic systems. These studies begin to infuse, if not yet rely upon, ideology in their arguments, and discussions of *As You Like It* expand into issues of patriarchy, social class, and politics.

Chapter 5 focuses on Cultural Studies critics writing from 1978 until the present. Beginning in the 1960s, many politicized, even activist, theories arise and eventually supplant New Criticism as the predominant critical theory; today, few scholarly enquiries into any early modern text fail to employ at least some aspect of culture or history in their assessments of the work. These politicized theories and praxes often inspire examinations of issues such as the colonial experiment, subjectivity, and domesticity, among others.

Chapter 6, which features those critics who identify as New Historicists, covers the years 1980 to the present. New Historicism rose out of the studies of hierarchy, governance, and order pursued by, among others, Michel Foucault (1926–84), Roland Barthes (1915–80), and Clifford Geertz (1926–2006). These studies led to *Renaissance Self-Fashioning* (1980) by Stephen Greenblatt (b. 1943), a work that changed the way we read early modern literature. Through a New Historicist lens, critics examine *As You Like It*, for example, in relation to issues such as patriarchy, economics, family, race, and ethnicity, among others.

Chapter 7 involves itself with the feminist critics writing from roughly 1965 until today, although, as many of these essays make clear, we should not relegate feminism and gender identity to any particular period. No study of *As You Like It* is complete without a discussion of gender, for, starting in the 1960s, scholars notice Shakespeare's manipulations of gender and identity through several of the play's characters as well as the play's unique employment of cross-dressing, even in light of Shakespeare's frequent use of the practice in comedies from *Two Gentlemen of Verona* to *The Winter's Tale*. Rosalind's adoption of masculine dress, behaviour, and language have generated reactions concerning gender, identity formation, and male–female relations in *As You Like It*.

The critics included in Chapter 8, who write between 1981 and the present day, all have been influenced by Gender Studies and Queer Theory. As Gender Studies expands to include examinations of masculinity and male and female desire, Queer Theory emerges from these discussions and complicates the accepted bifurcations of male and female. Practitioners of these theories find much to debate in the jumbled love relations that take place in *As You Like It*'s Arden. For a while, Phebe obsesses romantically over Ganymede-Rosalind, while Orlando kisses Ganymede-Rosalind as a substitute for the "real" Rosalind. These queerings of desire open the door to numerous interpretations of Shakespeare's rehearsals of love and sexual attraction.

This guide's conclusion briefly reminds us of the obvious: scholarly studies of *As You Like It* continue to enrich our understanding of this complex and popular play. While discussions that focus on the play's negotiations of gender, male–female relationships, love and loyalty, property rights, and family will continue to fill the pages of monographs and journals, other matters embedded in the play may occupy future scholars' attention, as witnessed in recent essays on teaching *As You Like It* and on the play's relationship to the colonial experiment.

CHAPTER ONE

1709–1800: "To Breed Me Well": Determinations of Genre and Character

The eighteenth century

During the eighteenth century, a far-reaching and totalizing "Shakespeare apparatus" came into being. Scholarly editions of the playwright's works, biographical accounts, and "expert" explanations of Shakespeare's drama proliferated. In short, an industry intent upon immersing the English middle classes in the reading and attending of Shakespeare's plays commenced. These eighteenth-century evangelists formed many of our "conceptions" of the man, according to Michael Dobson, and included testaments from esteemed men and women who established his importance for all.[1]

Much of the early praise for Shakespeare's achievements centred around his trueness to "nature", his realistic portrayals, that is, of the world and its beauties, pitfalls and disappointments, and, most importantly, its inhabitants. Writing in "An Essay on the Art, Rise and Progress of the Stage in *Greece, Rome* and *England*", Charles Gildon exemplifies his age's devotion to nature as a guide:

■ For the Business of Poetry is to copy Nature truely, and observe *Probability* and *Verisimilitude* justly; and the Rules of Art are to shew us what Nature is, and how to distinguish its Lineaments from the unruly and preposterous Sallies and Flights of an irregular and uninstructed Fancy. [Gildon's italics][2] □

Any variance from a diligent copying of nature, Gildon admonishes, "can never be *Beautiful*, but *Abominable*".[3]

Some overly exuberant critics granted Shakespeare special powers as concerns his representations of nature: though he possessed no formal training in Greek or Latin poetic and dramatic styles, for instance, Shakespeare employed them effortlessly in his writings, as if by "nature", many observers believed. John Dryden set the tone for this exuberance in his 1668 essay, *Of Dramatic Poesy*: Shakespeare:

■ was the man who of all Modern, and perhaps Ancient Poets, had the largest and most comprehensive soul. All the Images of Nature were still present to him, and he drew them not laboriously, but luckily: when he describes any thing, you more than see it, you feel it too. Those who accuse him to have wanted learning, give him the greater commendation: he was naturally learn'd; he needed not the spectacles of Books to read Nature; he look'd inwards, and found her there.[4] □

On numerous occasions, moreover, critics paralleled Shakespeare's affinities with nature with a moral correctness, one they urged his readers to follow.

As witnessed in Dryden's comments, early commentators also admired Shakespeare's seemingly instinctive adherence to classical traditions, particularly to those established by Aristotle and then embraced by the French, whose commentaries on dramatic style influenced eighteenth-century British opinions. Brian Vickers notes that Shakespeare's early readers, including Dryden, Thomas Rymer and Charlotte Lennox, "still expected justice to be enforced, still believed that the three unities were essential".[5] In Dryden's Preface to *All for Love* (1678), an alteration of Shakespeare's *Antony and Cleopatra* but also informed by *As You Like It*, especially in Antony's parallels with Jacques in his melancholy and self-indulgent flights of fancy, Dryden draws attention to Shakespeare's fidelity to the unities, particularly of time. Shakespeare's plays, he claims, are unique: "without Episode, or Underplot; every scene in the Tragedy conducing to the main design, and every Act concluding with a turn of it."[6] Neoclassical critics also judged plays, Vickers summarizes, "in terms of function and economy",[7] and they felt Shakespeare's dramatic structure leant itself to the consistency implicit in neoclassical expectations.

It has become commonplace in our time to see in Shakespeare's works explorations of issues and ideas relevant to our own: "He was not of an age, but for all time!" Ben Jonson (1572–1637) proclaims in his commendatory poem included in the 1623 First Folio of Shakespeare's works, and this belief in the playwright's universality takes hold in the mid-eighteenth century when, in Dobson's words, his works were "appropriated to fit what became the dominant, nationalist ideology" of England.[8] During this century Shakespeare became known as the man who dramatized a "virtuous family life, vigorous trade, and British glory" all in one, Dobson continues.[9] Readers of eighteenth-century criticism of Shakespeare, moreover, as Hugh Grady adds, "can scarcely be surprised at a connection between the praise of Shakespeare and the nationalistic celebration of his native land".[10]

Nicholas Rowe

Critical appraisal of *As You Like It* starts at a trickle, and typically involves only passing glances at a particular character or the play's generic inclinations. Nicholas Rowe (1674–1718), for example, whose 1709 *The Works of Mr. William Shakespear* enjoys distinction as the first "scholarly" edition of the playwright's works – with editorial emendations and notes, as well as Shakespeare's first comprehensive biography – remarks only briefly that Rosalind's "conversation" is full of "wit and sprightliness all along".[11]

Rowe stands, however, among the first critics to note and to view in a positive light Jacques' melancholic disposition: "'twill be a hard task for any one to go beyond him in the description of the several degrees and ages of man's life, though the Thought be old, and common enough".[12] Rowe also initiates what will become an ongoing debate as concerns the generic categorization of Shakespeare's plays, as he identifies only *The Merry Wives of Windsor*, *The Comedy of Errors*, and *The Taming of the Shrew* as "pure Comedy; the rest, however they are call'd have something of both" comedy and tragedy.[13]

Charles Gildon

Included as part of Nicholas Rowe's 1710 *The Works of Mr. William Shakespear*, "Remarks on the Plays of Shakespear", including those on *As You Like It*, by Charles Gildon (1665–1724), rarely extends beyond plot summaries, "occasional remarks on sources, and the quotation of select 'beauties'", Jonathan Bate (1958–) observes.[14] For example, Gildon calls Jacques' commentary on the seven ages of man "fine", and describes Rosalind's account of a man in love as "very pretty".[15] Gildon also claims that Shakespeare "has succeeded by the Force of Nature",[16] a sentiment reflecting his age's belief that Shakespeare innately understood the patterns, rhythms, and workings of the natural world: "*Oliver's* Management of the provoking *Charles* the wrestler against *Orlando*", for example, "is artful and natural". Gildon also observes, perhaps for the first time, that *As You Like It* "has nothing Dramatic in it",[17] a comment that several later New Critics as well as practitioners of Cultural Studies will repeat frequently.

William Warburton

Fiery Bishop of Gloucester William Warburton (1698–1779) published *The Works of Shakespeare* in 1747. While this edition strays not far from his friend Alexander Pope's 1723 edition of Shakespeare (on which Warburton worked), it includes a note on 5.4.90–103 of *As You Like It*, where Touchstone discusses lying and duelling. Warburton comments that in the clown's monologue Shakespeare

> ■ rallied the mode of formal dueling then so prevalent with the highest humor and address; nor could he have treated it with a happier contempt than by making his *Clown* so knowing in the forms and preliminaries of it. [Warburton's italics][18] □

Warburton then conducts one of the earliest source studies of a Shakespeare text, as he attributes the passage to the "ridiculous" *Of Honour and Honourable Quarrels*, written by the Italian swordsman Vincentio Saviolo, who by 1589 was living in London and in 1591 licensed his book to Richard Jones (the book appeared in English translation in 1594). Saviolo's book, Warburton observes, contains a chapter on maintaining one's honour, and of *"giving and receiving the lye"*. Warburton then summarizes the subsequent chapters, and notes Saviolo's discussion of the "particle IF" in a chapter on *"conditional lies"*. Warburton explains that no combatant can cut another's throat when *"no sure conclusion can arise"* as concerns what the fight entails [Warburton's italics and capitalization].[19]

Samuel Johnson

Except for some notes he included with the play, Samuel Johnson (1709–84) never discussed *As You Like It* at length. His reputation as Shakespeare's most perceptive and influential eighteenth-century critic, though, earned largely through his 1765 Preface to *The Plays of William Shakespeare*, compels readers to pay attention to his insights.

Johnson praises Shakespeare for the "progress" of *As You Like It*'s "fable" as well as "the tenor" of his "dialogue".[20] According to Johnson, each character speaks and acts in the same fashion that any given reader "should himself have spoken or acted on the same occasion".[21] He also notes that these verbal interactions between characters seem "determined by the incident which produces" them, and are "pursued with so much ease and simplicity, that it seems scarcely to claim the merit of fiction, but to have been gleaned by diligent selection out of common conversation, and common occurrences".[22] He notes Jacques' "natural and well preserved"[23] character, for example, and at 3.4 of the play, when Rosalind and Celia discuss Orlando's hair, Johnson finds "much of nature" in Rosalind's "pretty perverseness", she:

> ■ finds fault in her lover, in hope to be contradicted, and when Celia in sportive malice too readily seconds her accusations, she contradicts herself, rather than suffer her favorite to want a vindication.[24] □

On occasion, though, Johnson believes some characters exceed the bounds of nature: he doubts that women readers "will approve the facility with which both Rosalind and Celia give away their hearts" to Orlando and Oliver, for instance, and he notes Celia's perverse "heroism" in her friendship with Rosalind. He also questions Shakespeare's judgement in not allowing a "dialogue" between Frederick and the "hermit" who converts him near the play's end: such an interchange would provide "an opportunity of exhibiting a moral lesson in which he might have found matter worthy of his highest powers".[25]

Johnson comments as well on Shakespeare's breaking of the traditional boundaries of genre:

■ Shakespeare's plays are not in the rigorous and critical sense either tragedies or comedies, but compositions of a distinct kind; exhibiting the real state of sublunary nature, which partakes of good and evil, joy and sorrow, mingled with endless variety of proportion and innumerable modes of combination; and expressing the course of the world, in which the loss of one is the gain of another.[26] □

Richard Hurd

Among the first source studies of *As You Like It, Epistula ad Pisones* (1766), by Bishop of Worcester Richard Hurd (1720–1808), traces pastoral drama to the sixteenth-century Italian poet Torquato Tasso, who engrafted elements of the pastoral with drama. While Hurd praises Tasso's hybrid form, he hails "our own poets", John Fletcher and William Shakespeare in particular, as "by far, the best". Hurd claims that Shakespeare's most significant alteration of Tasso's form involves his truncation of all tragic elements: seeing that "pastoral subjects were unfit to bear a tragic distress"[27] and understanding that comedy "admits" only of "humbler distresses",[28] Shakespeare focused exclusively on the comic opportunities that pastoral provided him.

In an attempt to "make up in *surprize* what was wanting in *passion*", Shakespeare also, "with great judgement", incorporated the "popular system of Faeries", which in *As You Like It* "supplies the place of the old sylvan theology [and] gives a wildness to this this sort of pastoral which is perfectly inimitable". While Tasso deserves credit for developing pastoral drama, Hurd observes, Shakespeare added to it "pastoral poetry", which enhanced "the display of characters and the conduct of the poet's plot [Hurd's italics]".[29]

Francis Gentleman

Irish actor, playwright, and critic Francis Gentleman (1728–84) published the first volume of *The Dramatic Censor; Or, Critical Companion* in 1770. Throughout his text, Gentleman emphasizes the moral values *As You Like It* provides; he also identifies the play as a pastoral comedy, and believes it "will afford" not only "considerable instruction" but also "pleasure".[30]

Much of Gentleman's attention centres on individual characters, and nearly all of those from the ruling class exemplify the charm and integrity expected of gentle-born citizens. Rosalind and Celia's "favour" towards Orlando, just before he wrestles with Charles, for example, strikes Gentleman as a "genteel compliment to female generosity".[31] And even though he faults both women for their long-windedness, when they "propose" fortune "as a subject of their mockery" in Act 1, "we cannot help transcribing [it], on account of the truth and pleasantry of those ideas they create".[32]

An "amiable character", Duke Senior receives even higher praise, largely because of his status as the play's righteous but wronged duke: Gentleman construes his representation as "sustained with philosophical dignity, turning the frowns of fortune, as every man should do, into the means and motives of instruction".[33] Gentleman even suggests that Shakespeare should have included "an interview between" Duke Senior and his reformed brother Frederick: such a conversation "would have afforded an opportunity for genius and judgment to exert themselves commendably".[34] Despite his "cynical, speculatist" inclinations, Jacques, too, exudes "much good sense with great oddity", Gentleman attests.[35] His recalling of the stag, which satirises "that most abominable perversion of nature, ingratitude", Gentleman finds "pathetically pleasing",[36] while Jacques' declamation on man's seven ages portrays a "masterly picture of human life".[37]

Non-aristocratic characters, in contrast, rarely receive praise. Touchstone, "in sentiment and expression, is made up of whim, a character quite outré; therefore" his actions "cannot be tied to any exact line of nature".[38] When he bandies words with Corin, "delicacy is much offended",[39] and his humiliation of William in 5.1 "consists more of mere whim than good sense or useful satire".[40] Among the labouring classes, only Adam receives Gentleman's praise; his "distinction" between "temperate and licentious youth" appears to Gentleman "admirably instructive".[41]

Gentleman finds fault with the "hurried" plotline's "imperfect catastrophe". He also observes how "the unities suffer severe invasion" and "several scenes are very trifling",[42] while Oliver's conversion in the forest approaches "absurdity". How could all that Oliver "mentions have happened during the short interval of Orlando's absence; particularly, how has he had time to change from the wretched state of being ragged and overgrown with hair, in which he lay under the oak, to his present appearance"?[43]

(Mrs) Elizabeth Griffith

Marianne Novy argues that Elizabeth Griffith (1727–93), who published "from the start, under her own name" as Mrs Griffith, "provides the first example of explicit concern with Shakespeare's image of power relations in marriage".[44]

As the title of her 1775 book, *The Morality of Shakespeare's Drama Illustrated*, denotes, Griffith concerns herself with eighteenth-century codes of morality, particularly those inculcated in Britain's aspirant classes.

In her Preface, Griffith explains Shakespeare's significance to England's reputation and prosperity, and repeats several commonplaces of eighteenth-century Shakespeare criticism. In Griffith's eyes, for example, Shakespeare stands as "a Classic, and contemporary of all ages";[45] a reader should emulate him as "a *model*, not a *copy*", for "he looked into nature, not into books [Griffith's italics]".[46] Griffith's emphasis on practical values within Shakespeare's works underpins much of her desire to situate Shakespeare's ethical "merits in a more conspicuous point of view, than they have ever hitherto been presented to the Public".[47] She believes, in essence, that Shakespeare's "moral and instruction" in his plays extends beyond the "moral purely ethic" to include:

■ the general economy of life and manners, respecting prudence, polity, decency, and decorum; or relative to the tender affections and fond endearments of human nature; and more especially regarding those moral duties which are the truest source of mortal bliss—domestic ties, offices, and obligations.[48] □

In Griffith's eyes, Shakespeare's "whole Dramatis Personae seem to be *our acquaintances and countrymen*", and his figures set examples for one's contented domestic life [Griffith's italics].[49]

Griffith's discussion of *As You Like It* focuses on particular scenes' thematic or moral emphasis. The play's opening, for example, when Orlando laments his neglected state, foregrounds "the education of children", in Griffith's eyes. Men often prove "more sedulous in training the brutes of their kennels, their mews and their stables, than they seem to be about the heirs of their blood, their fortunes, or their honors".[50] One's education, in fact, becomes the focus of several scenes Griffith discusses, and its importance to one's personal and social improvement is tantamount. Love, moreover, and one's transformation because of it, often prove the best teachers:

■ There is no passion which Shakespeare more frequently, or so poetically describes, as that of love; and as it is the one which, by its despotism in our youthful years, often forms the destiny of our future life, and holds so immediate a relation to morals, we should suffer no occasion to pass unnoticed, however humorously or ludicrously expressed, which either defines its nature, or remarks upon its effects.[51] □

Moments of strife between lovers, as when Orlando fails to meet Rosalind on time, also bring with them instructive opportunities: "Resentments may interrupt affection; but they must rise to something more."[52] And instructions on a woman's proper behaviour pervade the play, including the scene where Rosalind describes her misery and, with Celia, devises a means of lessening it (1.3): "There is a very proper hint given here to women", Griffith maintains, "not to deviate from the prescribed rules and decorums of their sex. Whenever they venture to step the least out of *their walk*, in life, they are too generally apt to *wander astray* [Griffith's italics]."[53]

Love manifests itself in myriad forms, Griffith avers, and can include same-sex friendship, exemplified in Celia's condolence of Rosalind as she frets over Orlando, or in a peasant's loyalty to his master, represented in Adam's warning to Orlando to flee Oliver in 2.3. Griffith also discusses the value of "retired contemplation" in life, as witnessed in Duke Senior's praise of Arden in 2.1,[54] and praises Jacques for his "*charming*" "*melancholy*" and "*sullen fits*" throughout several scenes [Griffith's italics]:[55] while Rosalind rightly "condemns his extremes" of emotion in 4.1, Jacques nonetheless should elicit from readers "a favorable impression".[56] Corin and Touchstone's interaction over the merits of court and country in 3.2, in Griffith's view, brings home to readers the reality that "this world was never designed as our place of rest".[57]

William Richardson

By the close of the eighteenth century, Brian Vickers observes, entire books began to appear which devote themselves "to individual characters", and some of these books contain "the best critical work" on Shakespeare the period offers.[58] These character studies, prominent among them *A Philosophical Analysis and Illustration of Some of Shakespeare's Remarkable Characters* (1780), by William Richardson (1743–1814), also reveal what Vickers calls a "new interest in character psychology", an attempt to understand what compels characters to act the way they do, including their past histories and current states of mental health. Two other important "theoretical expectations common to nearly all" these character studies, Vickers adds, include a "concern that characters should be consistent" and they "should fulfill some moral purpose: they should seek virtue, avoid or condemn vice, and be rewarded or punished accordingly".[59] Richardson devotes attention to all these concerns.

Throughout his book, Richardson encourages the study of Shakespeare's characters as an essential aid to one's personal and social betterment. Through the study of human nature that Shakespeare's dramas provide, as well as through mingling "in society",[60] Richardson assures readers, "we become desirous of higher improvement", and we "purify and refine" our desires.[61]

Richardson's text includes an examination of *As You Like It*'s Jacques, who at this time emerges as one of Shakespeare's most popular figures. Richardson identifies Jacques' "most striking" quality as his "extreme sensibility". His "heart" is:

■ strongly disposed to compassion, and susceptible to the most tender impressions of friendship: for he who can so feelingly deplore the absence of kindness and humanity, must be capable of relishing the delight annexed to their exercise.[62] □

While "sensibility begets affection", and "affection begets the love of society", Jacques remains "unsocial".[63] Displaying the psychologist's desire to explain his anomalous behaviour, Richardson conjectures that Jacques' kindness may be "blighted by unkindness or ingratitude" wrought upon him in his past, which incites in him "bitter drops of misanthropy".[64] Where Orlando expresses "sorrow", intensified by "repulsed and languishing affection, with that arising from the disappointment of selfish appetites", Jacques suffers from sorrow *and* melancholy, which causes him to "complain" and to "inveigh". He is at once "amiable and benevolent" and unsocial, misanthropic.[65]

Richardson ends his discussion by paralleling Jacques' predicament with his readers' own situations. Every person possesses a "passion" that, "either by original and superior vigor, or by reiterated indulgence, gains an ascendant in the soul, and subdues every opposing principle".[66] Jacques obviously suffers from some disappointment or improper deployment of his passion, and now presents himself as one of the "most eloquent teachers of abstinency and self-denial".[67] Readers learn from Jacques that it "is always to obtain some enjoyment, or to avoid some pain or uneasiness, that we indulge the violence of desire, and enter eagerly into the hurry of thoughts and of action". With the advent of melancholy, however, "we no longer cherish the gay illusions of hope; no pleasure seems worthy of our attention; we reject consolation, and brood over the images of our distress".[68]

Walter Whiter

In one important respect, Walter Whiter (1758–1832) anticipates many critics who follow him, at least until the advent of postmodernism: Whiter writes in *A Specimen of a Commentary on Shakespeare* (1794) that a critic's task involves the discovery and establishment of the author's "original language".[69] Since Lewis Theobold's edition of Shakespeare in 1733, scholars and editors sought to provide a play text that matched as closely as possible that which Shakespeare intended, and Whiter offered a coherent and scholarly means of doing so.

To recover Shakespeare's true text, Whiter developed and advocated a method of scholarship he called "Association of Ideas". Because combinations of words, expressions, sentiments, circumstances, or metaphors are "not formed by the invention, but forced on the fancy of the poet, he is totally unconscious of the effect and principle of their union",[70] Whiter explains. The reason they return to the poet when they do, moreover, never reveals itself, so their appearance lacks any "intentional allusion to the source from whence they are derived"; and because they impose themselves "on the recollection of the writer by some accidental concurrence" they "have no necessary resemblance in the secondary application to that train of ideas, in which they originally existed":[71]

■ Certain terms containing an equivocal meaning, or sounds suggesting such a meaning, will often serve to introduce other words and expressions of a similar nature: This similarity is formed by having in some cases a coincidence in sense, or an affinity arising from sound; though the signification, in which they are really applied, has never any reference and often no similitude to that, which caused their association."[72] ☐

Whiter believes that we often "doubt" Shakespeare's "meaning" largely "because we do not understand the succession of his ideas".[73] He argues that one can identify this succession by tracing the author's memory. When an author remembers "a familiar phraseology, of a known metaphor, or of a circumstance, *not* apparent in the text", this remembrance can "lead" the author into "language or imagery derived from these sources; though the application may be sometimes totally different from the meaning and spirit of the original".[74] The critic, therefore, must "illustrate passages which are dictated by a train of thoughts abounding with these materials", and "exert the same knowledge in the phraseology and customs belonging to the age of his author, which he employed in the explanation of *direct* and *intentional* allusions".[75]

Primarily an editing device, Whiter's Association of Ideas coaxes forth, he believes, as accurate a text as possible from earlier compositor's errors and editorial emendations, and provides readers a product more grounded in Shakespeare's own imagination. In the words of Alan Over and Mary Bell, Whiter claims one can ascertain "the peculiar individuality" of the playwright's "style and expression", what we might refer to today as the "ideal of organic unity",[76] all lodged in Shakespeare's frequent employments of figurative language, puns, and imagery.

In his discussion of *As You Like It*, Whiter argues that Shakespeare draws upon his past observations of certain prints, statues, tapestries, and paintings in his portrayal of Rosalind, both "the coarse hangings of the poor and the magnificent arras of the rich":[77] in creating parallels between Rosalind's attractiveness and the "prominent perfections"[78] of Helen, Cleopatra, Atalanta, and Lucretia, Shakespeare creates in his heroine a "model of female excellence".[79] In 1.3, for example, when Rosalind considers what she should wear in Arden, Whiter states:

■ The Poet therefore might very properly invest her with the majestic air of Cleopatra; and that figure, which was so well adapted to become the curtle-ax and the boar-spear, would naturally suggest to his recollection the manly though elegant appearance of Atalanta attired for the exercise of the course, or furnished with the dress and implements of the chase.[80] ☐

Allusions to these representations, Whiter continues, "which are on all hands acknowledged to be *derived from Painting*", may be found as well in 3.2, when Celia and Rosalind discuss the verses Orlando has hung in the trees.

Whiter also describes Duke Senior's preference for the forest in 2.1 as a "reflection" upon his conviction that his and his men's banishment affords them a "philosophical retirement of ease and independence", one that provides "for the promotion of their good, and the improvement of their virtue".[81]

CHAPTER TWO

1800–1900: "Dancing Measures": Arriving at Critical Consensus

The nineteenth century

While eighteenth-century scholars recreated Shakespeare as England's national poet, nineteenth-century critics ushered him into the British educational system, including English colonial schools. These critics increasingly regarded Shakespeare's oeuvre, in Hugh Grady's words, as a "secular Bible, a revered body of thought, values, characters, words, and forms held to be the common property of culture".[1] According to Grady, these sentiments reveal a commitment "to preserve a sense of cultural unity in the face of the fragmentation and differentiations brought on by modernization".[2] They also mark the passage of Shakespeare studies "out of the sphere of public discourse" and into "new bureaucratic institutions", including the universities.[3]

In literary circles, Grady observes, concerns surrounding the concept of unity began with Samuel Taylor Coleridge and the Romantics, who sought a "fusion of reason and emotion" in literature,[4] a wholeness and integration that replaced eighteenth-century neoclassical bifurcations of "art" and "nature". Preferring a more "organic form", Romantic writers looked to Shakespeare as this form's "great exemplar".[5] Augustus William Schlegel's praise of Shakespeare's integrative propensities demonstrates what this century held dear in both a poet and a poetic work: Shakespeare "unites in his soul the utmost elevation and the utmost depth; and the most opposite and even apparently irreconcilable properties subsist in him peaceably together".[6] Charles Cowden Clarke's adoring ruminations over Shakespeare's method of composition, moreover, illustrate this century's fixation on Shakespeare's wholeness and integrity: "whenever Shakespeare adopted any distinctive class of character, his 'mind's eye' took in at a glance all the concomitant minutiae of features requisite to complete its characteristic identity" and, almost as if "'from a watch-tower,' he comprehended the whole course of human action".[7]

Shakespeare's frequent "deviations from the learned practice of art" also became "in part a function of the movement from neoclassicism to romanticism", Marianne Novy asserts. Nineteenth-century critics "valued academic rules less" than their predecessors, Novy continues, and "the outsider" became a "more common image of the writer".[8] Despite efforts to free themselves from convention, however, many Romantic writers and critics – Coleridge, Charles Lamb, and William Hazlitt among them – professed the tenet of "ruling character", particularly in their writings on Shakespeare, according to Uttara Natarajan. Proponents of the "ruling character" tenet assert "an inner principle of unity, the unity of character, which supersedes and negates the neoclassical unities, dismissed by the romantics as artificial and externally exposed", Natarajan explains.[9]

Many later nineteenth-century critics embraced Romantic beliefs in literature's value as a counter to industrialization and in Shakespeare as a model of the artist. Coleridge's fantasy of a "clerisy, a secular caste" who would advance literature in the face of a capitalist world, for example, was adopted by Matthew Arnold, who "saw that the recently instituted national public educational apparatus could in fact, with the right curriculum, undertake" the same task, Grady observes.[10] Although he perceived literature as removed from politics, Arnold nonetheless saw it as a civilizing force, one inherently political. Despite these shifts in focus and increased attention to informed readings of a text, many nineteenth-century critics remain overly concerned with "character", "story", and "moral quality", C.L. Barber claims.[11]

Samuel Taylor Coleridge

Samuel Taylor Coleridge (1772–1834) comments on *As You Like It* infrequently, only in the marginalia (c. 1808–18) he scribbled into his copies of Lewis Theobold's 1773 *The Works of Shakespeare* and of Samuel Ayscough's 1807 *The Dramatic Works of William Shakespeare*. In these marginalia we catch a glimpse of Coleridge's fascination with Shakespeare's characters and the consequences of primogeniture. In one note on Orlando's compromised circumstances, Coleridge acknowledges the "mournful alienation of brotherly Love occasioned by Primogeniture in noble families, or rather by the unnecessary distinctions engrafted thereon, and this in Children of the same Stock".[12]

Coleridge seems fascinated with Oliver's demeaning reference to his brother as "boy" in 1.1, and how the designation "naturally provokes and awakens in Orlando the sense of his manly powers". Orlando initially responds verbally, with "elder brother", Coleridge observes, but then "grasps [Oliver] with firm hands, & makes him feel tha[t] he is no *Boy* [Coleridge's italics]". There "is a Beauty here", Coleridge asserts.[13] Coleridge also ponders Oliver's vaguely explained hatred for his brother: Oliver's rumination:

■ *expresses* truths which it almost seems impossible that any mind should so distinctly and so livelily have voluntarily presented to itself in connection with feelings and intentions so malignant and so contrary to those which the qualities expressed would naturally have called forth.—But I dare not say, that this *unnaturalness* is not in the nature of an abused *Wilfulness* when united with a strong intellect. In such Characters there is sometimes a gloomy self-gratification in making the *absoluteness* of the Will (sit pro ratione Voluntas! [let will stand for reason]) evident to themselves by setting the Reason & Conscience in full array against it. [Coleridge's italics][14] □

Coleridge describes Oliver's hatred as "one of the most unshakespearian Speeches in all (the genuine works of) Shakespear", but he trusts that, with further contemplation of this particular scene, he "should be nothing surprised, & greatly pleased, to find it hereafter a fresh Beauty as has so often happened with me".[15] Coleridge faults Shakespeare's seeming discontinuities between character, situation, and speech, though; at 1.3.11, when Rosalind jokes with Celia about her "child's father", Coleridge complains, "This is putting a very indelicate anticipation in the mouth of Rosalind, without reason: not to speak of the strangeness of the Phrase".[16]

Augustus William Schlegel

German poet and critic Augustus William Schlegel (1767–1845) produced, in *A Course of Lectures*, the first comprehensive critical introduction to Shakespeare's plays, and in Lecture XXIII (c. 1811) Schlegel writes briefly on *As You Like It*. Throughout *A Course of Lectures* Schlegel's comments exemplify the Romantic conception of Shakespeare as "the master of the human heart"[17] – but they also anticipate later nineteenth-century critics' placement of Shakespeare in the rarified atmosphere of the university. To Schlegel, Shakespeare stands as "a nice observer of nature", a skilled copyist of the "technical language of mechanics and artisans", and a student of both his own country and of those regions far beyond it.[18] Perhaps more significantly, Shakespeare merits study because his plays reveal the mind of an intellectual:

■ That notion of poetical inspiration, which many lyrical poets have brought into circulation, as if they were not in their senses, and like Pythia, when possessed by the divinity, delivered oracles unintelligible to themselves—this notion, (a mere lyrical invention,) is least of all applicable to dramatic composition, one of the most thoughtful productions of the human mind. It is admitted that Shakespeare has reflected, and deeply reflected, on character and passion, on the progress of events and human destinies, on the human constitution, on all things and relations of the world.[19] □

Such ascriptions of drama and Shakespeare contribute to the playwright's partial displacement from popular culture.

Only in the haphazard "structure" of Shakespeare's plays does the playwright grant leave "to the dominion of chance", Schlegel goes so far as to say, and thereby allow "the atom's [sic] of Epicurus" free rein. Knowing that he must "please the unlettered crowd" and achieve "theatrical effect", Shakespeare allows elements of the chaotic or perverse into his plays.[20] In *As You Like It*, for example, Schlegel notes that it:

■ would be difficult to bring the contents within the compass of an ordinary narrative; nothing takes place, or rather what is done is not so essential as what is said; even what may be called the *denouement* is brought about pretty arbitrarily.[21] □

Shakespeare's purpose in *As You Like It* imparts more than a tenable plot, Schlegel suggests, and corroborates the Romantic belief that art and nature remain essential components of human contentment and growth:

■ Throughout the whole picture, it seems to be the poet's design to show that to call forth the poetry which has its indwelling in nature and the human mind, nothing is wanted but to throw off all artificial constraint, and restore both to mind and nature their original liberty.[22] □

In order to do so, each character must find an environment that allows this freedom. When the characters enter Arden, they leave behind all "[s]elfishness, envy, and ambition", and they meet characters who likewise have freed themselves of these maladies. Of "all the human passions, love alone has found an entrance into this wilderness, where it dictates the same language alike to the simple shepherd and the chivalrous youth".[23]

William Hazlitt

Characters of Shakespear's Plays & Lectures on the The English Poets (1817), by William Hazlitt (1778–1830), is largely a character study, but it takes this genre in directions heretofore untraversed. In the words of Jonathan Bate, Hazlitt stretched the boundaries of character study by illustrating "how similarities and antitheses between characters are a formative structural principle" of Shakespeare's drama;[24] as such, characters' relationships to each other determine a play's "wholeness".[25] In "On Shakespeare and Milton", included in his *Lectures on the English Poets*, Hazlitt explains Shakespeare's achievement in characterization: "Each of his characters is as much itself, and as absolutely independent of the rest, as well as of the author, as if they were living persons, not fictions of the mind."[26]

Hazlitt considers *As You Like It* the "most ideal" of Shakespeare's plays. He categorizes the drama as a pastoral because "the interest arises more out of the sentiments and characters than out of the actions or situations". The play's significance lies not in "what is done", Hazlitt explains, but in "what is said". Although Hazlitt comments only briefly on the play, he clearly trains his attention on the relationships between characters, and considers their implications. After distinguishing Jacques as "the only purely contemplative character in Shakespeare" because he "thinks, and does nothing",[27] for instance, Hazlitt determines that he "resents Orlando's passion for Rosalind as some disparagement of his own passion for abstract truth".[28]

Rosalind, on the other hand, comports "sportive gaiety and natural tenderness: her tongue runs the faster to conceal the pressure of her heart", while Celia's "silent and retired character" serves as a "necessary relief to the provoking loquacity" of her cousin.[29] Silvius' unrequited love for Phebe illustrates the "perversity of this passion in the commonest scenes of life", Hazlitt asserts, "and the rubs and stops which nature throws in its way, where torture has placed none".[30] Hazlitt appears most interested in the clown Touchstone, whom he describes as a "a mixture of the ancient cynic philosopher with the modern buffoon". Touchstone "turns folly into wit, and wit into folly, just as the fit takes him". His wooing and winning of Audrey, furthermore, "not only throws a degree of ridicule on the state of wedlock itself, but he is equally an enemy to the prejudices of opinion in other respects".[31]

Anna Brownell Jameson

Shakespeare's Heroines. Characteristics of Women Moral, Poetical, and Historical (first published in 1832) by Dublin-born Anna Brownell Jameson (1794–1860), went through five English editions in her lifetime as well as several American editions and German translations. Fully knowledgeable of Shakespeare's sources as well as the nineteenth-century critical tradition, Jameson stands as the first critic to examine Shakespeare's female characters with the same seriousness "accorded to his male ones", according to Jonathan Bate.[32] Jameson practised "social criticism" and drew her readers' attention to "gendered inequalities", Cheri Lin Larsen Hoeckley (b. 1961) argues, and she maintained a "dual interest in considering female exemplars and in demonstrating female intellectual ability"[33] throughout her criticism. Her aim in presenting Shakespeare's female exemplars consisted not only in providing a study of her "sex's psychology", as Russell Jackson (b. 1949) suggests,[34] but in presenting in a more positive light "female behaviors that would be seen as problematic in traditional nineteenth-century gender ideology".[35]

Jameson chooses Rosalind as one of her subjects of study, and offers a view contrary to nearly every critic of her time. While Jameson sees in Rosalind a "greater degree of her sex's softness and sensibility, united with equal wit and intellect" when compared to Beatrice from *Much Ado about Nothing*, she nonetheless remains "inferior in force" as a "dramatic character".[36] In Jameson's view, Rosalind "was not made to bandy with lords, and tread courtly measures with plumed and warlike cavaliers, like Beatrice; but to dance on the greensward".[37] Rosalind:

> ■ says some of the most charming things in the world, and some of the most humorous: but we apply them as phrases rather than as maxims, and remember them rather for their pointed felicity of expression and fanciful application than for their general truth and depth of meaning.[38] □

Rosalind lacks not only the "impressive eloquence of Portia" from *The Merchant of Venice*, Jameson concludes, but also the "sweet wisdom of Isabella" from *Measure for Measure*.[39]

Celia, on the other hand, strikes Jameson as "full of sweetness, kindness, and intelligence, quite as susceptible, and almost as witty [as Rosalind], though she makes less display of it". Shakespeare gives Celia "some of the most striking and animated parts of the dialogue", moreover, and she speaks as "one who has made herself worthy of our love, and her silence expresses more than eloquence".[40] Phebe, too, receives from Jameson a response that slights Rosalind somewhat, albeit for a different reason: she "is quite an Arcadian coquette; she is a piece of pastoral poetry" in whose speeches Shakespeare "has anticipated all the beauties of the Italian pastoral".[41]

William Maginn

Journalist, editor, and occasional fiction writer William Maginn (1794–1842) wrote and published "The Shakespeare Papers" serially in *Bentley's Miscellany*. Many of Maginn's character studies are remembered today for their nonconventional and, occasionally, outlandish views. He views Jacques, for example, as not melancholy: he possesses "no secret anguish to torment" him, "no real cares to disturb the even current of" his temper, and he remains throughout the play "not soul-stricken in any material degree".[42] His abandonment of social station exemplifies instead a "noble and an honorable" commitment to duty and responsibility, Maginn argues:[43]

> ■ He is nothing more than an idle gentleman given to musing, and making invectives against the affairs of the world, which are more remarkable for the poetry of their style and expression than the pungency of their satire.[44] □

Maginn's explanation of Jacques' character at times smacks of sexism and lacks grounding in textual evidence: in creating Jacques' character, Shakespeare "passes by all allusion to women; a fact which of itself is sufficient to prove that his melancholy was but in play". The playwright, Maginn continues, "well knew that there is no true pathetic, nothing that can permanently lacerate the heart, and embitter the speech, unless a woman be concerned. It is the legacy left us by Eve".[45]

Jacques' monologue on the seven ages of man, moreover, serves only as a set piece in contrast to Duke Senior's "consideration that more woful and practical calamities exist" than the "exile of princes and the downfall of lords".[46] His description of life's progress, in Maginn's view, suggests how, at each stage, all matters "are well taken care of"; the baby is "nursed", the boy "educated", the youth worries over nothing more than "a lady", and so on, even into the last stage, where Jacques never tells the reader that the feckless man "is left unprotected in his helplessness".[47] And in his discourse over the fallen stag, Jacques "complains of the injustice and cruelty of killing deer, but unscrupulously sits down to dine upon venison", and labours only in constructing rhetorical flourishes drawn from his ruminations on the pain he observes.[48]

Hermann Ulrici

German philosopher Hermann Ulrici (1806–84) wrote *Shakespeare's Dramatic Art: And His Relation to Calderon and Goethe* (1839; translated into English in 1846) soon after he rejected Hegelian materialism and pursued instead the proof of God's existence through scientific means. Like his English contemporaries, Ulrici saw in Shakespeare and his works models for the integration of art and nature, reason and intuition. In anticipation of many critics who followed him, though, Ulrici often took these sentiments to new extremes as regards Shakespeare and his abilities as an artist. He claimed, for example, that Shakespeare and his theatre company sought not merely fame and riches but "the real improvement of dramatic art",[49] and that Shakespeare's poetry was "animated by the lofty inspiration" and "kindled by the sense of his own power and greatness".[50] Shakespeare was a "great and noble man", one who sought to illustrate God's presence in "nature and history" as well as the "purely human".[51] In Ulrici's view, Shakespeare embodied the nineteenth-century ideal of an individual, an outsider, whose "moral tone", unflagging "pursuit of *truth* [Ulrici's italics]",[52] and desire for "genuine piety"[53] warranted his abandonment of Aristotle's rules.

Ulrici also noted Shakespeare's elision of all traces of himself from his characters, much like T.S. Eliot (1888–1965) described in "Tradition and the Individual Talent". Shakespeare's "descriptions, figures, and similes, exhibit the most intimate affinity between his creative poetic mind and the great eternal artist who planned the universe".[54]

Ulrici splits Shakespeare's comedies into two categories, "fancy" and "intrigue",[55] and he assigns *As You Like It* to the "fancy" group – although he makes clear that in the play Shakespeare draws his shepherds and shepherdesses "to the truth of nature" and only "the presence of lions and serpents in an European forest" reminds us that "we are standing within the intellectual domain of poetical fancy".[56] The play's title leads the reader towards its "life-giving and animating ground-idea", Ulrici contends:

> ■ life itself is contemplated in the light it would appear, if it were presented to a man, as it were, on a salver, with the courteous invitation to take it as he likes it. Throughout the whole piece, every one does just as he likes; every one with unrestrained willfulness and caprice, gives himself up either to evil or to good as the fit strikes him; every one looks upon, turns, and shapes—life as he fancies.[57] □

Shakespeare's purpose here involves a "fanciful reflection" upon the human experience, whereby "the true director of human life, which is nothing less than the eternal order of things, is brought to light".[58] Its message consists of two truths; first, Shakespeare dramatizes the "profound truth" that "the mind of man, by its free-will and faculty of self-determination, can really shape, turn, and direct his own life as he likes". The second, and in Ulrici's mind the more overlooked truth, involves "eternal harmony and law – the everlasting counsels of God, ruling and superintending the history of the world". This reality is often "turned away from our regard in darkness and obscurity".[59]

Ulrici sees throughout *As You Like It* a consistent sense of "irony", manifested in nearly every character's "one-sided" view of life, each of which "becomes its direct opposite". "This dialectic of irony", Ulrici continues, "and therein the fundamental meaning" of the play, "appears at its greatest height in the two fools".[60] Jacques in his "profound superficiality" and "merry sadness" reveals a "folly and perversity" which contrasts with others' merriment and joy. Touchstone proves Ulrici's case even more certainly, for in his remarks and behaviours lie all ironies, "perversities and contradictions"[61] of human existence:

> ■ While the other lovers are in chase of some fancied ideal of beauty, amiability, and virtue, and yet, after all, run into the arms of very ordinary and every-day sort of beings, he takes for himself an ill-favored piece of flesh of a country girl – he loves her because he chooses her – and he chooses her because he loves her. This is, indeed, the willfulness of love, as it is depicted by Shakespeare in his comedies, in its full force. But it is even this very unreasonableness that renders it the wonderful and fatal power which seizes upon the heart and life of man without his knowledge or consent; while at the same time it represents that higher power,

which, uninfluenced by human caprice and subjectivity, guides the life and history of mankind with unseen hand.[62] □

For Ulrici, Touchstone alone enters the forest with no purpose or cause; therefore, he stands as the one character who "evinces a truly noble disinterestedness and fidelity" in what he says and does, and thus holds the "first necessary element of true intellectual freedom – the mastery over himself". Shakespeare provides as contrast Sir Oliver Martext, the embodiment of the "common prose of life" who "ever mars the profound, eternal meaning of the book of life".[63]

G.G. Gervinus

A German scholar of Shakespeare, G.G. Gervinus (1805–71) practised what Hugh Grady calls a "systematizing criticism", one designed for "discovering Hegelian patterns of growth and development into a logically complete philosophical system". Gervinus stands among the vanguard of later nineteenth-century scholars who use "versification tests" to determine the chronological order of Shakespeare's plays. He also took a positivist approach to Shakespeare's works, Grady continues, which typically involves an "emphasis on historical continuity and growth and a concomitant valorization of logic, character, and responsibility".[64] While Gervinus' advocacy of systematizing criticism and of versification tests situates him among those critics influenced by Charles Darwin and more scientifically informed methods of study, he still embraced earlier critics' convictions that, by the "healthfulness" of his "own mind", Shakespeare influences "the healthfulness of others", and through "abstract representations" he provides a "preparation for life *as it is*; for *that* life which forms the exclusive subject of all political action [Gervinus' italics]".[65]

In *Shakespeare Commentaries* (1849–50), Gervinus employs his systematizing method on *As You Like It* to challenge the belief that the play's plotline succumbs too frivolously to whimsy or the fantastic: a scrutinizing look at Frederick's, Oliver's, and others' character traits, or at Frederick's usurpation of Duke Senior, uncovers no hint of "whimsically capricious" behaviour, nor can one call Oliver's stalking of Orlando or Orlando's choice to wrestle Charles "accidental".[66] Instead, readers should:

■ consider this piece as probably intended for a masque, a style of drama in which the poet, whether by the introduction of wonderful machinery or by the display of all kinds of pageantry, permitted himself somewhat more license than elsewhere.[67] □

While Gervinus acknowledges that some characters are "sketched in general outline", he declares that Shakespeare nonetheless has "involuntarily improved and elevated every new material and style which he touched", including the elimination of "pastoral mannerism", simplification of the "motives of the actions", and ennoblement of the "actions themselves".[68]

Gervinus isolates "patience" as the defining moral in the play: we, as well as nearly all of *As You Like It*'s characters, "must brave misfortune with equanimity and meet our destiny with resignation".[69] Each character encounters love as a "new evil", and each learns to employ "control and moderation" in dealing with it, "not too much evading it, nor too much desiring it, paying more regard to virtue and nature than to riches and rank". Phebe and Silvius serve as a "contrast in this respect": Silvius "loves too ardently, whilst Phoebe despises love too coldly", and "the intention of the narrative is to extol self-mastery, equanimity, and self-command in outward suffering and inward passion".[70]

Gervinus fills the remainder of his appraisal with descriptions of the characters. About Oliver and Frederick, Gervinus reminds readers that they "are only sketches of characters, not intended to play conspicuous parts". He sees in both men the "same vein of avarice and envy", and that through avarice and envy both of them "equally forfeit the happiness which they seek".[71]

About Jacques, Gervinus again parts from consensus; where most critics view his melancholy as "mild, human, and attractive", Gervinus situates its roots in "bitterness and ill-humor which render the witty and sententious worldling far rather a rude fault-finder than a contented sufferer like the rest".[72] Jacques:

■ blames the whole world, finds matter for censure in the great system of the world, and stumbles over every grain of dust in his path. Long experienced in sin, he has learned to find out the shadow side of every age of man; he has satiated himself with the world, and has not entered upon this life of retirement furnished with the patience and contentment of the others, but from a natural passion for the contrary.[73] □

While Jacques and Duke Senior draw "wisdom and philosophy" from their observations of the world, Jacques' "reflections" all "have assumed a touch of despondency". And in the contrast between Jacques' despondency and Duke Senior's resilience, Shakespeare demonstrates a conviction that "those who would desire enjoyment and advantage from this life must in themselves have a natural disposition for moderation and self-mastery; they must be able to disarm misfortune and to do without happiness". Such a contrast reaches far beyond the "trivial tradition of the pastoral poets", where "praise of the quiet life of nature" trumps the intrigue of court.[74]

In Rosalind, Celia, and Orlando, Gervinus urges readers not to "overlook the predisposition to a natural power of resistance against the overwhelming force of outward evil and of inward emotion". Blessed with this endowment, they "bear about with them a spring of happiness".[75] In Rosalind, readers "recognize plainly" her "disposition to command herself and to deprive misfortune of its sting":[76]

■ She feels deeply that fortune has punished her with disfavor; and when in the person of Orlando she meets one equally struck by fate, her heart, taken unawares, betrays how accessible she is to the most lively feelings.[77] ☐

Despite her ill-treatment, Rosalind never allows vengeance to influence her actions, and her example aids the "naturally excitable" yet emotionally "uninjured"[78] Orlando in mastering his desire to even the score with Oliver. Celia, too, "exhorts herself to love with patience, not to be too timid nor too bold; she only yields when Oliver speaks of marriage; modesty is here also the guide of action".[79]

Gervinus stands among the first to recognize in Touchstone a "fool of a somewhat more elevated nature". He registers Touchstone's amorality and freedom to "speak the truth, to rend asunder, as often as" he wishes "the veil of mere propriety and hypocrisy, and wittily to unmask the folly of others under cover of their own".[80] Touchstone serves as a "useful test of head and heart" and "the comic chorus in the comedy".[81]

Charles and Mary Cowden Clarke

Author and editor Charles Cowden Clarke (1787–1877) married Mary Victoria Novello (1809–98) in 1828, and the two collaborated on various studies of and guides to Shakespeare until his death. Beginning in the late twentieth century, scholars and critics began to pay more attention to Mary Cowden Clarke, largely because she is the first female editor of Shakespeare, the first Shakespeare Concordance compiler (in 1844–45), and the first woman to make her living writing about Shakespeare. While the 1863 *Shakespeare-Characters; Chiefly Those Subordinate* is attributed to her husband Charles alone, Mary no doubt participated in its composition. Her consistent "attention to the positive images of women" occurring throughout Shakespeare's plays, as well as her "respect for 'married lovers'", in Ann Thompson's and Sasha Roberts' words, pervade *Shakespeare-Characters*.[82]

Cowden Clarke praises the playwright's utility for his and future generations in his Preface: he hopes his essays:

■ will aid in directing attention to the ethical scope and design of the several dramas, and to the sustained harmony with which the Poet has delineated his characters throughout: accordingly, I may express my trust that the Essays will prove acceptable to all who are interested in the due appreciation of our great Moral Teacher.[83] ☐

While much of his sentiments bear the telltale marks of a mid-nineteenth-century student of Shakespeare, the fact that he collaborated with his wife so closely and over such an extended period of time "represents a striking alternative to the Romantic paradigm of the author as 'solitary genius', working in isolation and solitude", argue Thompson and Roberts.[84]

Cowden Clarke praises *As You Like It* as "altogether so perfect a piece of homage to the happy state of a rural, unartificial life", delivered in variations by Duke Senior, Touchstone, Corin, Adam, and Jacques.[85] He also observes how in the play Shakespeare manifests a "habit of drawing conclusions as to his characters from *acts*, and not from *descriptions* [Cowden Clarke's italics]".[86] To Cowden Clarke, for instance, the Duke stands as the:

■ perfect exemplar of what should comprise a Christian's course – a cheerful gratitude for the benefits that have been showered upon him; a calm, yet firm endurance of adversity; a tolerance of unkindness; and a promptitude to forgive injuries.[87] □

Cowden Clarke doubts that Duke Senior "could have so perfected his native character had he never known the reverse of fortune" and experienced exile as well as the coldness and isolation of Arden.[88] Of all characters who "has most cause to complain" of his circumstances, he remains the "most hopeful and cheerful".[89]

Although he offers descriptions of Orlando's kindness, gentleness, and mercy that diverge hardly at all from those of many contemporary critics, Cowden Clarke divulges an interesting obsession with this young man's physique: in the scene with Charles the wrestler, Cowden Clarke notes, Shakespeare "has markedly and vividly kept before us" evidence of Orlando's "personal strength as a counterbalance to the extreme mildness of his disposition". When Orlando comforts the exhausted, starving Adam, moreover, the playwright "takes distinct care all the time to maintain in us the recollection of the young fellow's massive proportions, by making him bear the aged serving-man in his arms".[90] And once again, when Orlando rescues Oliver from the lioness, he "uses his strength of body, instructed by his strength of bland spirit, to protect, not to injure his enemies". Orlando's physical strength, Cowden Clarke suggests, reflects upon his spiritual perfection, for in each instance where Orlando employs his body to inflict destruction on others, he "destroys their enmity instead of themselves".[91]

As concerns the "sedate and most loving of all cousins, the devoted, the cordial, the confiding Celia",[92] Cowden Clarke takes note of her exceptionally close relationship to Rosalind: she serves as an "unfailing resource" when Rosalind "needs assistance or advice – domestic or mental", and "can only dwell contented herself so long as she knows Rosalind to enjoy content".[93] As illustrated in her influence on Oliver, she "is hardly inferior to Rosalind in witty accomplishment", but Celia's aptitude in this regard only appears when it helps Rosalind's to "shine forth uninterruptedly";[94] otherwise, Cowden Clarke avers, Celia "seems not only content, but best pleased, to listen while Rosalind gives free scope to her gay-souled sallies".[95] After listing her "womanly" proclivities, Cowden Clarke concludes that Celia's "ideal of excellence – morally, intellectually, and personally" – lies in Rosalind, and she "unwittingly allows her heart, mind, and frame to become as much *one* as possible with those of this cherished being [Cowden Clarke's italics]". Cowden Clarke resists calling Celia's behaviour towards Rosalind "copying"; instead, he sees it as "just the similarity, the accordance, that naturally grows out of a strong and enduring attachment".[96]

Somewhat like Celia, Touchstone strikes Cowden Clarke as "a fellow possessing genuine qualities of attachment and affection"; the court "becomes a second object in his choice when his young mistress is to leave it". He also "determines to act honorably by the trusting and doating Audrey".[97] Of all the play's subsidiary characters, only Jacques is "not an especial favorite with us", for he:

> ■ is the model of a man addicted to self-contemplation; he always appears to be before his own mental looking-glass. He has inherited or acquired the tact to discern the worthlessness of artificial society, but he has not carried that tact into the wisdom of turning his philosophy the sunny side outwards.[98] □

In Cowden Clarke's view, Jacques appears "either not a sincere man to himself, (and consequently is not true to others), or he is really a man without affection or attachment".[99] Shakespeare includes him here as "a satire upon your pretenders to wisdom",[100] for the truly wise person – as witnessed in the Duke, Celia, Rosalind, and Orlando – recognizes the "superior qualifications of cheerfulness and good-humor" in the face of adversity.[101]

Hippolyte A. Taine

"Shakespeare paints us as we are",[102] claims French critic and historian Hippolyte A. Taine (1828–93) in *History of English Literature* (1863; translated into English in 1873). Taine in no way means that Shakespeare practises a realist style, however; instead, the playwright's "all-powerful" and "excessive" mind frequently breaks "loose from the laws of the world of reality", largely through his employment of the "fantastical", which constitutes "the highest grade of unreasoning and creative imagination. Despite ordinary logic, it creates another; it unites facts and ideas in a new order, apparently absurd, in reality regular; it lays open the land of dreams, and its dreams seem to us the truth".[103]

The highly influential Taine – a proponent of sociological positivism and, some would argue, the first historicist critic – discusses *As You Like It* only briefly, but his emphasis on the play's fantastic elements anticipates C.L. Barber's later investigation of the play's festive qualities, as well as the many Bakhtinian readings that follow Barber. In *As You Like It*, Taine observes, there is no "action" or likelihood of behaviour or outcome:

> ■ [T]he absence of the serious is refreshing. There are no events, and there is no plot. We gently follow the easy current of graceful or melancholy emotions, which takes us away and moves us about without wearying. The place adds to the illusion and charm.[104] □

Taine also notes the "necessity of singing" that pervades the play: nearly all "prose" and "conversation end in lyric poetry". As the play builds, moreover, readers "feel the emotion and foolish gayety as if it were a holiday", and "[u]nlikelihood grows natural", so much so that no astonishment accompanies Hymen's leading of Rosalind and Celia "by the hand to give them to their husbands".[105] Shakespeare's reliance on improbability "deprives emotions of their sting": the play's succession of events and collisions of characters "interest or touch us without making us suffer".[106]

Rev. H[enry].N. Hudson

Shakespeare: Life, Art, and Characters (1872), by the Reverend Henry N. Hudson (1809–77), expresses many of the sentiments and attitudes towards Shakespeare that, by the mid-nineteenth century, had become commonplace. Hudson offers, however, some intriguing insights that enliven his rather pedestrian generalities about Shakespeare's ethical or intellectual merits. Hudson believed, for example, that nearly every character in the play becomes "purified by suffering" at the play's completion. The "discipline" that each character learns through "social restraint" helps him or her eventually to "go right without such constraint" once the play reaches its end.[107]

Orlando, who is "good without effort" and who "has no special occasion for heroism", exemplifies a "natural harmony of character wherein virtue is free and spontaneous, like the breathing of perfect health". His goodness inspires "others to forget" their maladies while it instinctually incites him to assist his brother Oliver in his time of need. Orlando never "thinks upon his high birth" to avoid his situation and represents the man whom "all true men would choose for their best friend".[108] Duke Senior, as well, is "thoroughly informed and built up with Christian discipline and religious efficacy; so that the asperities of life do but make his thoughts run the smoother".[109]

Much like Orlando's, Rosalind's "charms" stem from her "health of mind and symmetry of character". Her insightfulness as concerns other characters "neither stings nor burns", and anyone who comes "in her presence" experiences "the head and the heart draw[ing] together perfectly".[110] The "effect" of Rosalind's "humor", Hudson avers, is:

> ■ to *lubricate* all her faculties, and make her thoughts run brisk and glib even when grief has possession of her heart. Through this interfusive power, her organs of play are held in perfect concert with her springs of serious thought. Hence she is outwardly merry and inwardly sad at the same time. We may justly say that she laughs out her sadness, or plays out her seriousness: the sorrow that is swelling her breast puts her wits and spirits into a frolic. [Hudson's italics][111] □

Everything Rosalind does, furthermore, illustrates a "feminine modesty".[112]

While Jacques represents an "utterly useless yet perfectly harmless man", one who seeks wisdom "by abjuring its first principle", he nonetheless seeks the company of those who, "though deserving the best, still have the worst". He does so "because such moral discrepancies offer the most salient points to his cherished meditations".[113] Hudson considers Touchstone the "most entertaining" among Shakespeare's courtly characters, partially because he maintains "some precious sentiments" among his otherwise clownish "affections".[114]

Denton J. Snider

Dogmatically Christian and often ferocious in defending these convictions, Denton J. Snider (1841–1925) self-published the bulk of his numerous works under his own Sigma Publishing Company. In *The Shakespearian Drama* (1887), Denton explains his belief that the "common principle" pervading all Shakespeare's comedies is "Mediation":[115] Shakespeare's comic heroes all fall victim to "deception", and either contend with "a shadow" of their own minds or chase after "external" appearances.[116] In the end, and through the mediation of either the "real" or "ideal" world,[117] the hero always finds "outward harmony, as well as inward", in relation to "institutions, or with the whole Ethical World".[118]

Snider divides Shakespeare's comedies into two "large classes", the "real" and the "ideal", and the type of mediation the hero receives depends upon the type of comedy s/he occupies.[119] Snider defines *As You Like It* as an ideal comedy, where:

> ■ the individual and society are in a condition of strife and wrong, which has to be healed. But now there is a flight from this actual world of conflict, to an ideal realm

where the conflict does not exist. In the present instance, therefore, the Mediation does not take place in the sphere where the difficulty arose, and amid the institutional forms which are themselves in collision, but in a domain from which they are essentially eliminated – in some sylvan, pastoral, idyllic, or ideal world. Here the colliding individual must remain till, on the one hand, he is prepared for a return to society, and till society, on the other hand, has freed itself from the wrong or strife which compelled him to flee in the first place.[120] □

Snider further classifies Shakespeare's comedies into "Pure Comedies" and "Tragi-Comedies", and categorizes *As You Like It* as a pure comedy:

■ In the Pure Comedies the individual is given over to outer Accident or Chance, and to inner Accident or Caprice. He follows his whim or his senses without the corrective of reason, and so gets entangled in a conflict with the rational order of the world, which at last disciplines him out of his folly and ignorance, and thus restores him in a light-hearted, humorous way.[121] □

Whether of the ideal or real, pure or tragi-comic classes, Snider believes all Shakespeare's comedies contain three movements: "Separation, Mediation, Return".[122]

Having laid out this rather convoluted comic taxonomy, Snider then discusses Shakespeare's women and his habit of assigning to them the "mediatorial element", which provides women the "essential germ of their character, and calls forth the most brilliant galaxy of sisters that were ever limned".[123] Rosalind, for example, first must "test" the "worth and fidelity of her lover. She must find out the man whom she loves; it is her right, nay, her duty".[124]

But Rosalind must complete a more important task for the play to conclude harmoniously: "what she has done for herself she must do for others, thus she makes her own life truly universal".[125] In *As You Like It*, the "world is truly in a state of wrong and dissolution" and both Rosalind and Orlando suffer as its victims. Simultaneously, however, an "opposite force is … in the act of being born". Snider identifies this force as "Love, the grand social organizer, and primal founder of all institutions".[126] Rosalind will introduce, mediate, and prove to all others that love is the "bed-rock of social organization".[127]

Helena Faucit Martin (or, Helen Faucit, Lady Martin)

In 1881 actress Helena Faucit Martin (or, Helen Faucit, Lady Martin, 1817–98) began publishing her "Letters on Some of Shakespeare's Heroines" in *Blackwood's Magazine*, which in 1893 were collected and published as *On Some of Shakespeare's Female Characters*. These essays comprise the first commentaries on Shakespeare's female characters written by an actress. In her passages on *As You Like It*, Faucit Martin emphasizes Rosalind's power and autonomy: no one but Shakespeare could have:

> ■ carried out this daring design, that the woman thus rarely placed for gratifying the impulses of her own heart, and testing the sincerity of her lover's, should come triumphantly out of the ordeal, charming us ... by her wit, her fancy, by her pretty womanly waywardness.[128] □

Rosalind's emotional and intellectual dominance leads the reader to conclude that, "through the guise of the brilliant-witted boy, Shakespeare meant the charm of the high-hearted woman, strong, tender, delicate, to make itself felt".[129]

Faucit Martin often bolsters her high regard for Rosalind by diminishing the lustre typically accorded to other characters. Orlando, for instance, suffers the "saddest of all plights" because "chance" offers him no opportunity to prove he is above "the common herd",[130] while Duke Senior exudes none of Rosalind's "vivacity or force", even though he possesses "something of her sweetness of disposition".[131] Even Celia wilts in comparison to Rosalind, for she "is by no means of a highly imaginative nature".[132] Jacques also falters: because "he has squandered his means and used up his finest sensations" he "sees only the dark side of human nature and of the world".[133]

Faucit Martin may push Rosalind's autonomy and influence beyond their established bounds, but she maintains both the nationalist and positivist approaches long held by earlier critics. Rosalind's abilities bear a "certain native distinction",[134] and when Faucit Martin considers Shakespeare's development as a dramatist, she believes that, by the time he writes *As You Like It*, his "mind had assuredly worked its way through the conflicts and perplexities of life, within as well as without, and had settled into harmony with itself".[135]

Frederick S. Boas

Shakespeare and His Predecessors (1896), by Frederick S. Boas (1862–1957), represents an increasing number of late nineteenth- and early twentieth-century studies in which critical interest shifts towards more textual and historical matters. One of Boas' prime concerns with *As You Like It*, for example, lies in the play's form, especially as regards its complicated relationship to the pastoral tradition. Boas interrogates Shakespeare's negotiation of his own culture's pastoral conventions and the medieval folk poetry that preceded them.

Boas understands the early modern pastoral tradition as an "outcome of a superfine and 'decadent' culture", one where its "sophisticated" practitioners interpreted and exploited pastoral shepherds as "the most piquant of contrasts to the problems of their own existence".[136] Given pastoral's ubiquity, Boas finds it interesting that Shakespeare employs it in only a "single episode", that involving Silvius and Phebe, and for an entirely different purpose: the scene:

> ■ is worked up into an exaggerated form of the conventional pastoral method, so that the contrast between it and the natural charm of the simple woodland life is the most effective satire upon this growth of the literary forcing-house.[137] □

In essence, Shakespeare "transposes" Silvius and Phebe "into the region of caricature". In contrast to Celia and Oliver or – especially – Orlando and Rosalind, they "speak uniformly in verse instead of prose, and this in itself gives a distinctively idealistic flavor to their sentiments". Silvius parodies Orlando's "true loyalty of heart", and Phebe's quintessentially pastoral "inky brows, black silk hair, bugle eyeballs, and cheeks of cream" become a "burlesque" as Shakespeare festoons her with a "leathern hand, a free-stone colored hand".[138]

Shakespeare's manipulations elide the "sentimentality" that once informed pastoral. In its place, "we have the ruddy vigor, the leaping pulse and play of the open-air life",[139] which include Audrey and Corin, "drawn probably" from Shakespeare's "personal observation" of Warwickshire's denizens and from "old English popular poetry".[140] It also includes Touchstone, whose caustic wit "tempers the lusciousness of the conventional pastoral", as well as Jacques, through whom Shakespeare challenges "the idea that in an idyllic life every nature will find an anodyne for its peculiar malady". In the Forest of Arden as in life, Shakespeare suggests, "real sorrow and real evil imply stability of character, and a recognition of the facts and laws of life".[141] Rosalind understands this reality more concretely than any character: knowing she cannot escape the coldness of her world, she instead feels passionately. The "pictures that she draws for Orlando's benefit of the changeable humors of a coquette and of a wife's wayward moods" stand in "ironical antithesis" to the "passionate devotion with which her own heart swells almost to bursting".[142] □

George Bernard Shaw

Playwright and critic George Bernard Shaw (1856–1950) saw *As You Like It* on stage several times throughout the 1890s, and found very little to commend. His comments illustrate a departure from the typical appraisals of Shakespeare's unity of plot and character, his ties to nature, and his ethical value to England's populace. Having seen George Alexander's production at the Lyric

Theatre on 16 November 1896, for instance, Shaw attributes Rosalind's growing popularity "to three causes" (review published as "Toujours Shakespeare!" in *The Saturday Review*, 5 December 1896):

> ■ First, she only speaks blank verse for a few minutes. Second, she only wears a skirt for a few minutes (and the dismal effect of the change at the end to the wedding dress ought to convert the stupidest champion of petticoats to rational dress). Third, she makes love to a man instead of waiting for the man to make love to her: a piece of natural history which has kept Shakespeare's heroines alive, whilst generations of properly governessed young ladies, taught to say "No" three times at least, have miserably perished.[143] □

And after he saw Augustin Daly's production of the play at the Fifth Avenue Theatre on 2 October 1897 (his review appeared in *The Saturday Review* on 9 October), Shaw described the major characters as such:

> ■ Rosalind is not a complete human being: she is simply an extension into five acts of the most affectionate, fortunate, delightful five minutes in the life of a charming woman. And all the other figures in the play are cognate impostures. Orlando, Adam, Jacques, Touchstone, the banished Duke, and the rest each play the same tune all through. This is not human nature or dramatic character; it is juvenile lead, first old man, heavy lead, heavy father, principal comedian, and leading lady, transfigured by magical word-music.[144] □

Shaw calls Orlando "an amiable, strong, manly, handsome, shrewd-enough-to-take-care-of-himself, but safely stupid and totally unobservant young man"[145] (*The Saturday Review*, 2 May 1896). Focusing on his attachment of verse to the trees in Arden, Shaw declaims:

> ■ Why cannot all this putrescence be cut out of the play, and only the vital parts: the genuine storytelling, the fun, the poetry, the drama, be retained? Simply because, if nothing were left of Shakespeare but his genius our Shakespearolaters would miss all that they admire in him. (*The Saturday Review*, 5 December 1896)[146] □

Duke Senior and Jacques fare no better. Shaw describes the Duke as an "unvenerable imposter, expanding on his mixed diet of pious twaddle and venison",[147] while Jacques' seven ages monologue arouses in him the comment: "How anybody over the age of seven can take interest in a literary toy so silly in its conceit and common in its ideas ... passes my understanding" (*The Saturday Review*, 5 December 1896).[148]

The increased attention to form and context that we witness in Taine, Boas, and Shaw – including Shaw's comments on theatre audiences – eventually took precedence, and commentators on Shakespeare increasingly hailed from academic institutions. The next chapter, which introduces and covers the New Critics, illustrates the near totality of belief that an understanding of Shakespeare comes only from a systematic training in his verse and form. Later, of course, this education expanded to include an understanding of culture, history, and politics.

CHAPTER THREE

1906–72: "A Great Reckoning": New Criticism

With *New Criticism*, which began in the American South soon after the conclusion of World War I and dominated critical praxis into the 1970s, came close textual study and even more rigid standards of "correct" reading, including a new vocabulary (theme, image, symbol, juxtaposition, and irony, to name only a few) to help scholars articulate the discoveries that close reading afforded. Its goals included a separation of the literary text from other forms of writing, largely because New Critics believed literature should be considered art and not merely an expression of ideas or emotions. As such, the study of literature demanded a more systematized, some would say scientific, method of making sense of a text, one that sought, first, the discovery and then the articulation of a text's unity. While New Criticism may appear constricting to twenty-first-century undergraduates, graduate students, and scholars, it inspired some of the most insightful and enlightening studies of *As You Like It* to date; the approach's fixations on form, pattern, and structure coaxed out many of the play's nuances and complexities.

The first New Critics – Cleanth Brooks, John Crowe Ransom, Allen Tate, and Robert Penn Warren, all American southerners – lamented the decline of Christian faith and orthodoxy and the "universal truths" they communicated to the culture, largely the result of industrialization, capitalism, and World War I. Like Samuel Taylor Coleridge and Matthew Arnold before them, the New Critics sought through the educational system to preserve – or to re-establish – a pre-industrial cultural tradition, one through which critics could instil ethics, emotional connections, and truth by means of reading and literary study. To the New Critics, literature could and should fill the emotional and spiritual void left by Christianity's retreat.

New Criticism claims to remove the literary text from history, politics, and the author's biography (although in actuality it always reflects upon, and even frequently engages, all three), and its adherents insist that a text's meaning resides solely in the text. As if a god, the author intends and establishes a unity in the text, and imparts a purpose unto every word, phrase, and even punctuation mark contained within the text; there exists in the text, then, a coherent, self-contained world. It remains the reader's task to read attentively, and to gather from this close reading of a text's constituent parts (its images, symbols, repetitions, form, and even seeming contradictions) the meaning implicit within, free from distortion. The themes, or general ideas, conveyed through the text, always loom larger, and more significant, than the text's parts, and herein lies the text's power, New Critics argue. The best texts, those containing within them the most comprehensive representations of the human experience, reward the careful reader with insights into the human condition, universal truths regarding our world, and transcendence into a higher understanding of the self.

New Criticism contributed very much to the institutionalization of literature in colleges and universities, largely by offering an almost spiritual alternative to the alienation wrought by postwar consumerist society. It offered to readers timeless and permanent truths where capitalism encouraged trendiness and impermanence. New Criticism's cohesion countered anarchy and dehumanization, and one's mastery of close reading skills provided refinement, discernment, self-assurance, and even potential advancement.

Because of New Criticism's attention to a text's form and themes, many of the essays discussed here concern themselves with possible relationships or oppositions between *As You Like It* and the comic, pastoral, or romance traditions that influenced Shakespeare. The tensions Shakespeare creates by contrasting the Forest of Arden and Duke Frederick's court – city with country, simplicity with complexity, comfort with stress, work with play, envy with nurture, male with female, etc. – represent for many critics Shakespeare's consciousness of a genre's utility in signalling his preference for one mode of life over another.

Early gleanings: J.B. Priestley, Elmer Edgar Stoll, and P.V. Kreider

Beginning with scholars such as Frederick S. Boas (see Chapter 2) and through the early decades of the twentieth century, various tenets of New Criticism informed scholars' appraisals, but they came slowly and tentatively.

Despite New Criticism's increased attention to the play's form and structure, character study still occupied scholars' studies, even those of influential critics such as J.B. Priestley (1894–1984), whose book, *The English Comic Characters* (1925), included a chapter on Touchstone and provided a lengthy discussion of Jacques as well. Despite his coverage of already traversed ground, Priestley does register, especially in his considerations of Touchstone, some elements that the New Critics later explore in depth. First, Touchstone's dismissive account of country life exposes "the defects" inherent in the pastoral tradition and, in anticipation of such critics as C.L. Barber and Harold Jenkins, "those human limitations that prevent our declaring, with any sincerity, that any way of life is perfect". As concerns the play's form, furthermore, Priestley touches upon, ever so briefly, the idea that Touchstone's articulations also serve as a "distorted reflection of what passes elsewhere in the drama".[1]

One of the twentieth century's more interesting students of Shakespeare, Elmer Edgar Stoll (1874–1959), is, in Hugh Grady's words, "remembered for his contributions to an evolving professional methodology in literary academics".[2] Stoll also demands attention, albeit of a less fond feather, for his insistence upon the "production of a single correct interpretation" of a literary work.[3] His wresting away of Shakespeare from the common reader partly involved his condemnation of notions such as J.B. Priestley's, in which he sees Touchstone as "universal": Shakespeare's characters do not roam our streets and cities, Stoll believes, but instead occupy the rarified environs of art and text.

In one of his early essays, "Shakespeare, Marston, and the Malcontent Type" (1906), Stoll's research on malcontents in Elizabethan times exemplifies the professionalization of Shakespeare studies that would reach even greater heights with the New Criticism and beyond. Through diligent research into contemporary documents, he connects the term "malcontent" to Elizabethan conceptions of "melancholy" and determines that it meant to Elizabethans what "cynicism" means to us today.[4] For Stoll, Jacques' identity in *As You Like It* is that of a "professional fantastic mediator, a professional cynic and censor", and his purpose involves the exposure of "follies and abuses of society" and the "world in general", and then the "contemplation – in picturesque fashion – of the vanity and transitoriness of human pretensions, distinctions, and existence itself".[5]

In a later book, *Shakespeare's Young Lovers* (1937), Stoll returns to *As You Like It*, but this time concentrates on Rosalind, whom he understands as "ideal", almost "to the point of being idyllic; witty and humorous or innocent and naïve, and often all at once and together, without much in the way of individual opinions concerning life or love in general".[6] Stoll concludes his examination of Rosalind, and of all women in Shakespeare, by stating that they "are not emotionally sophisticated or intellectually exalted".[7] Obviously, Stoll's legacy does not lie in any influence he may have exerted on feminist scholars.

Stoll's attention to Shakespeare's satiric bent, however, as well as the playwright's implicit restlessness as concerns generic conventions, strikes a chord with several subsequent critics, including P.V. Kreider. In his "Genial Literary Satire in the Forest of Arden" (1935), Kreider argues that in no other play does Shakespeare include "so much criticism of the literary genre represented by the piece itself". Kreider divides the characters inhabiting *As You Like It* into three groups, and assigns each group to a generic tradition. While Phebe, Corin, and Silvius belong to the pastoral tradition originating in Theocritus, Ganymede and Aliena "typify" the tradition's "social aspects" only, and embody "the romantic enthusiasm which induces people who know nothing about country life to indulge in a synthetic pastoralism". The third group, comprising William and Audrey, represents "the contemporary English countryside"; their presence not only countermands "the claims of both the social and the literary bucolic conventions", but also defames "traditional, artificial pastoralism". Furthermore, they "represent the state of society to which courtly ladies and gentlemen, in their ignorance, believe they would like to revert".[8]

In taking none of the characters' "stereotyped, perfunctory business seriously",[9] then, Shakespeare simultaneously exposes the limits of the pastoral tradition and satirizes those who buy into it as a restorative or honest alternative to the real world. Touchstone, who belongs to no group, reflects most tellingly Shakespeare's chilliness towards "the literary and social trumpery which surrounds the pastoral life", yet the playwright delimits even his value as objective observer because he never discounts the "genuine feelings" Rosalind, Orlando, and others express.[10]

E.K. Chambers

While by no means the first to discuss the play's generic inheritances, E.K. Chambers' (1866–1954) study of *As You Like It*, part of his *Shakespeare: A Survey* (1925), provides a comprehensive assessment of its romance, pastoral, and comic roots. While he acknowledges that the play embodies the pastoral "temper of urban disillusion, the instinctive craving of the man who has been long in cities pent for green fields and quiet nights",[11] Chambers defines *As You Like It* as "romance incarnate":

> ■ All the wonderful elements of the secular tradition are gathered together there in its light-hearted compass. There is the romance of friendship in Rosalind and Celia, "like Juno's swans, still coupled and inseparable"; the romance of Adam's loyalty, "the constant service of the antique world"; the romance of love at first sight, acknowledged in words by the smitten Phebe's quotation of a dead Marlowe's saw, and acknowledged as the mainspring of the whole plot when young Orlando wrestled and overthrew more than his enemies, and witty Rosalind, for all her cousin's warning, fell deeper in love than with safety of a pure blush she might in honor come off again.[12] □

Orlando, of course, serves as "the typical lover of romance, the love-shaked sonneteer".[13]

In addition, many of the "conventional issues of romance" dominate the play, Chambers notes: "the sudden changes of fortune which betray" the "beneficent" Duke Senior, "the repentance of Oliver and the conversion of Frederick to a religious life", and "the romantic spirit of adventure with which the play is filled".[14] Finally, the forest itself emerges as "the essential forest of romance", a "spiritual force" which offers "medicine to the hurt souls of men".[15]

At his most insightful moment, however, Chambers also identifies *As You Like It* as a comedy, and notes that, because of its comic tendency towards characters' psychological and material transformations, the play challenges the same "romantic ideals" it "sets out to expound". Despite her pastoral upbringing and demeanour, for example, the "vain and disdainful and wanton" Phebe must "learn her lesson" every bit as much as Oliver or Frederick.[16] Chambers also categorizes Touchstone as the first in a line of "that dramatic type" which includes Feste in *Twelfth Night*, Lavache in *All's Well That Ends Well*, and the Fool in *King Lear*. Anticipating Elmer Edgar Stoll's remark that Touchstone and others of his type serve a "choric function", and moving towards the New Critics' conviction that Shakespeare's characters do not always voice the playwright's views, Chambers sees in Touchstone's caustic analyses an alternative, satiric view of the romance or pastoral conception of things.[17]

H.B. Charlton

Chapter 9 of H.B. Charlton's *Shakespearean Comedy* (1938), "The Consummation", offers one of the most thoroughly articulated New Critical appraisals of Shakespeare's *Much Ado About Nothing*, *Twelfth Night*, and *As You Like It*. In these plays, Charlton claims:

■ Shakespearean comedy realizes its most perfect form, and therefore in them Shakespeare's comic idea, his vision of the reach of human happiness in this world of men and women, is richer, deeper, more sustained, and more satisfying than in any other of his plays.[18] □

In these comedies, Charlton continues, Shakespeare "fully satisfies the curiously Elizabethan aesthetic demand for a drama which would gratify both the romantic and the comic instincts of its audience".[19] Charlton defines Elizabethan comedy as a genre in which the playwright "seeks to envisage the way to happiness in a material world", and he believes Rosalind's "experience" in Arden "is worth infinitely more"[20] than that of any other comic heroine: while she falls in love, she remains "unswervingly conscious of the obligations of common sense"[21] and "aware of the follies into which love may delude its victims".[22] Despite her "modesty",[23] moreover, Rosalind stands as "Shakespeare's representation of the office of love to lift mankind to a richer life".[24]

While Charlton blazons *As You Like It*'s shortcomings of form – its barely moving plot, its introduction of lions into Arden, and its hasty and not always "suitable" marriages – he emphasizes the play's:

■ unified shape of an embodied idea, the representation of a created world which has become an organic universe because its every operation manifests the universality of its own proper laws.[25] □

This unifying idea involves a radical departure from "traditional classical comedy". At no point does *As You Like It* "assume that the conditions and the requisites of man's welfare have been certainly established, and are therefore a sanctity only to be safeguarded". Instead, Shakespeare "speculates imaginatively" on the means through which both the characters and we can enlarge and extend "the possibilities" of goodness. Because of this quality, Shakespeare's mature comedies become far more "poetic" than "satiric".[26]

As You Like It revels in humanity's irrationality: characters' "moods" emerge as being as significant as their "reason" and "common sense", and we all begin to understand the "validity" of "intuitions" and "emotions" as we recognize "the fuller capacities of the spirit". Because of Shakespeare's expanded consideration of the human condition, Charlton concludes, the theme of love assumes "its place in Elizabethan comedy as the recognized presiding genius".[27]

C.L. Barber

In "The Use of Comedy in *As You Like It*" (1942), by C.L. Barber (1927–81), we see a pronounced leap into the type of critical enquiry practised today. Barber's approach simultaneously exemplifies the contributions New Criticism brought to Shakespeare studies and implicitly challenges the strict boundaries that New Critics placed around their scholarly concerns. Barber examines the play's comic form and purpose, its manipulations of the pastoral tradition, and its surprisingly "serious" themes, and his insistence that Shakespeare shows readers how life is and not what it should be throws open doors to critical inquiry through which later generations would enter and establish entirely new approaches to *As You Like It*.

In the missionary spirit of many New Critics, Barber asserts that prior criticism of Shakespeare's comedy is more "impressionistic and appreciative" than "analytical". He then proposes that in his comedies Shakespeare employs a "method" that does not avert "serious themes", but provides "an alternative mode of developing them".[28] Ultimately, both tragedy and comedy:

■ express the difference between what life might be and what it is, and both function to adjust our feelings to the difference, the one by laughter, the other by purgative pity and fear. The final effect of both is reconciliation to reality without sentimentality or cynicism.[29] □

While not altogether "comic", *As You Like It* establishes a pattern whereby the "practice of making fun of something which is presented seriously a moment before or a moment after is standard throughout the play".[30] Jacques and Touchstone, for instance, poke fun at the "pastoral innocence and romantic love" expressed by the foresters Silvius, Phebe, Audrey, and Corin.[31] What seems Shakespeare's point in all this ridicule lies in one's understanding that the ideals fuelling the pastoral convention, as well as romance and marriage, never enter the real world: Shakespeare "represents or evokes ideal life, and then makes fun of it because it does not square with life as it ordinarily is".[32]

Hearkening back to medieval fool humour, Barber notes how Shakespeare's comedies give "form to ideal life, whether romantic or heroic", but resist "this artistic idealization", in much the same fashion that "medieval burlesque was a response to the ingrained idealism of the culture". For the first time, Shakespeare employs in *As You Like It* his fool figures (both Jacques and Touchstone) to provide "commentary and burlesque", and while he concerns himself "with man's possible perfection", he now more insistently makes "explicit the comedy's purpose of maintaining objectivity".[33]

Throughout *As You Like It* Shakespeare devotes attention to the romantic, and, through Rosalind's interactions with Orlando, we experience in the final scene a bond "independent of illusions".[34] As she observes around her the excesses of adoration and devotion as exemplified by Silvius and then Phebe, as well as the burlesque of romantic love as practised by Touchstone upon Audrey, Rosalind eventually can describe "with delight, almost in triumph, not the virtues of marriage, but its fallibility". And because she recognizes love's and marriage's limitations and shortcomings, she can express a love for Orlando which never becomes "less intense".[35]

"Romantic participation in love", then, and "humorous detachment from its follies, the two polar attitudes which are balanced against each other in the action as a whole, meet and are reconciled in Rosalind's personality", and herein lies the play's "value".[36] Humour elicits a "wider awareness" of love, one where proportion emerges as essential. Any "less disciplined and coherent art falsifies" this reality "by presenting a part as though it were the whole".[37]

Harold Jenkins

As do several critics before him, Harold Jenkins (1909–2000) explains in *"As You Like It"* (1955) how Shakespeare "presents the conventional pastoral, and duly burlesques it". The playwright does so, however, "with a surer knowledge of life" than other poets, and as an example of his surer knowledge he "seems to suspect that the burlesque" of the pastoral tradition, as well as the "convention" itself, "may also miss the truth". In Jenkins' eyes, the play instead proves that, in "city or country, *all* ways of life are at bottom the same [Jenkins' italics]".[38]

Shakespeare's style in *As You Like It* distinguishes the play from his other comedies: in it he nearly abandons the "more robust and boisterous elements" usually found in comedy, including "big theatrical scenes" and "events linked together by the logical intricacies of cause and effect". The play's "defectiveness of its action" forces readers to consider more carefully its "very elaborate structure",[39] and to accept that its general "pattern" involves "constant little shifts and changes".[40] Situated just as much in "fairy tale and folklore roots"[41] as in pastoral tradition, *As You Like It* depicts "numerous shifts of angle, alternating valuations, and variations of mood".[42]

One common attribute of his comedy that Shakespeare retains involves his setting together of "contrasting elements in human nature" and then leaving them "by their juxtaposition or interaction to comment on one another":[43] Oliver's furious violence and Orlando's humble forgiveness, Jacques' passionate melancholy and Duke Senior's serene optimism, Corin's country manners and Touchstone's doubting urbanity. Silvius and Phebe, moreover, represent the "familiar literary norm" of the "pure pastoral world", and, through interactions and juxtapositions with them, Rosalind and Orlando become "freer to act like human beings". First, Silvius' pining for Phebe lifts the "burden" of assuming the role of pastoral lover from Orlando's shoulders so he can perform "the traditional hero's fabulous feats", and act as a "common man like ourselves". Likewise, Rosalind's admonishment of Silvius allows her to examine "his wounds" and to find and heal her own.[44]

Out of all this juxtaposition and contrast comes a more comprehensive and inclusive picture of humanity:

> ■ Shakespeare, then, builds up his ideal world and lets his idealists scorn the real one. But into their midst he introduces people who mock their ideals and others who mock *them*. One must not say that Shakespeare never judges, but one judgement is always being modified by another. Opposite views may contradict one another, but of course they do not cancel out. Instead they add up to an all-embracing view far larger and more satisfying than any one of them in itself. [Jenkins' italics][45] □

While he satisfies the pastoral tradition's requirement that a contrast between the ideal and real takes place, Shakespeare deflates any assumption that a better world exists anywhere else than the here and now. In order for the characters, as well as for us, to understand this truth, we need a "readjustment of view", which Shakespeare provides at the necessary moments.[46]

Marco Mincoff

As You Like It succeeds, Marco Mincoff (1909–87) claims in "What Shakespeare Did to Rosalynde" (1960), because the dramatist attains a "complete and harmonious fusion of his two comic themes, love's foolishness and the clash between appearance and reality".[47] In typically New Critical fashion, Mincoff first interrogates the play's pastoral frame and Shakespeare's departures from the pastoral features found in his source, Thomas Lodge's *Rosalynde*. He then concludes that, while Shakespeare may "poke some gentle fun" at this tradition, particularly its "imagery", he neither condemns nor fully abandons it.[48]

Shakespeare instead takes aim at "the follies and affectations of Petrarchism", as illustrated in Silvius and Phebe especially, but also in Rosalind's and Orlando's initial appearances. Lovers "may behave foolishly", but the play encourages their movement "down to earth" from "Petrarchistic heights". Phebe's desire for Ganymede, arising "out of sheer perversity", renders her "a figure of fun", and Silvius transforms from a "selfless martyr of love" into a "silly dupe".[49]

Mincoff locates Shakespeare's soft rebuttal of pastoral, as well as his more concentrated attack on Petrarchism, in the playwright's treatments of William, Audrey, and Corin, and in the "ironic commentators Jacques and Touchstone".[50] In particular, Touchstone and "all his sophisticated contempt for the rustic life" provides "the most flagrant example of love's blindness and waywardness".[51] Touchstone's "sham wooing" of Audrey, furthermore, exposes the excesses of Petrarchan devotion, and mirrors Rosalind's correction of her own and then Orlando's romantic imbalances through their own sham wooing. Shakespeare's "alterations" of Lodge, Mincoff concludes, provide a "balance" between love and impulsive desire.[52]

Jay L. Halio

According to Jay L. Halio (b. 1928) in "'No Clock in the Forest': Time in *As You Like It*" (1962), Shakespeare may challenge several pastoral conventions throughout his play, but he treats time and timelessness less satirically. Shakespeare connects the timelessness found in Arden to "an older, more gracious way of life that helps regenerate a corrupt present"[53] and establishes a "dialectic" between court and forest.[54] In Arden, therefore, where "past and present merge",[55] Shakespeare provides a "temper, or balance" to the ruthlessness of Frederick's court and Oliver's estate.[56]

Frederick and Oliver force the past's "gracious ideal" into Arden, but they never extinguish it: it resonates in the loyal Adam, in Duke Senior and his retainers, in Rosalind and Orlando, and in Orlando's memory of his father. Halio observes how parallel conflicts, between Frederick and Duke Senior and between Oliver and Orlando, "suggest an alignment" between Senior and the deceased Sir Rowland, as well as between the "golden world" and the "antique world" of Robin Hood, "now led by the banished Duke".[57] Despite these parallels, Shakespeare's Arden includes certain "other, qualifying elements" – cold winter winds, greasy sheep and greasier denizens, and the dubious Sir Oliver Martext, to name a few. In Halio's estimation, the forest "takes account of both the ideal" and "the actual", and offers Rosalind and Orlando a more realistic counterview to the restrictive court.[58]

Recollections of his father's goodness and the "adversity" Orlando experiences in Arden both mature him: his interactions with Duke Senior elicit his recognition of a "code" of virtue, and through him "gentleness joins with gentleness" and the "golden world merges with the antique world". His newfound benevolence "reminds us of what civilization *might* be like, or once was [Halio's italics]".[59] Rosalind, too, changes because of the forest. She moves towards a "realistic" view of time while she also moves Orlando towards a more "unharried awareness" of his desire for her.[60] As both lovers come together in their mutual acknowledgement of the "good life", they unite in marriage and then re-enter the court as leaders of a fuller, more cognizant regime.[61]

Madeleine Doran

In "Yet am I Inland Bred" (1964), one of the most insightful essays of the New Critical era, Madeleine Doran (1905–96) focuses on the theme of civilized man, a theme to which she believes Shakespeare returns repeatedly throughout his career. Doran exemplifies the rewards that close textual reading yields, while she simultaneously limns and exceeds this approach's boundaries.

In 2.7 of *As You Like It*, after Orlando violently interrupts Duke Senior's dinner feast, the Duke asks him why he "seem'st so empty" of "civility". While Orlando confesses his lack of "smooth civility", he also explains, "yet am I inland bred,/And know some nurture" (93, 96–97). Doran seeks to know "what bearing this unusual but precisely placed epithet may have on" the play's "central theme", and examines the words and phrases Shakespeare employs in this passage to determine the epithet's significance. Aware that the

Duke's "reproach of rudeness and incivility carries a deeper social implication than just bad manners",[62] Doran accesses lexicons and dictionaries contemporary to the play, including those written by Thomas Elyot (c. 1490–1546), Thomas Cooper (c. 1517–94), Thomas Thomas (1553–88), John Florio (1553–1625), and others.

Before Doran commits herself to what "inland" or "inland bred" may denote, she interrogates the terms "nurture" and "civil" and registers the relationship between them. "Civil" meant for Shakespeare not only "self-control and the respect for others that life in society demands and that may be expected of rational men"[63] – qualities expected in "inland" men – but it also carried a hint of humaneness, "to be human in the best sense, for only a human being is capable of kindness, of putting the welfare of others before his own selfish impulses, hence capable of civility".[64] The opposite of "civil", according to Doran, is "rude", which in Shakespeare's time could mean "ignorant", "unlearned", "untaught", "rustical" – deprived of nurture, essentially. To be rude or uncivil, in other words, not only classified one as "unfit for ordered society" but identified one's lack of "instruction" as the cause of his "unfitness", and "a man untaught is like a beast".[65]

Before his escape into Arden, Orlando bemoans his brother's refusal to provide him nurture, largely through education, which has resulted in his "removedness" from the attitudes and behaviours associated with civility. While Shakespeare relies on the belief that "birth will tell, that the gently born, with or without nurture, are naturally gentle in behavior",[66] he simultaneously challenges this belief by creating in Oliver and Frederick characters "morally declined from an earlier stage of innocence and honest simplicity", despite their breeding. Doran then takes a direction which anticipates the New Historicists: she focuses upon how these conflicting ideas "may be philosophically accommodated to each other",[67] not only in the play but in Shakespeare's culture.

Doran connects Orlando's rudeness to myths of the Golden Age, where "primitivism" was explored and explained through two variant lenses. From Ovidian and Virgilian conceptions of primitivism, Shakespeare inherited a view of humanity that emerges from a world free of want and labour, until the god Jupiter imposes a change in seasons and thus drives humans "to seek shelter against the weather and to begin tillage" and, ultimately, to develop "competitive trade, the enclosure of property, mining, and warfare".[68] Conceptions derived from myths involving Prometheus, Amphion, and Orpheus, on the other hand, may have influenced Shakespeare's view of humans as in need of gifts beyond technological advancement, gifts "of reverence and justice in order to govern themselves in the cities they had built". In these myths the gods bestowed on man three means of assistance: "reason to invent, speech to communicate, and hands to accomplish whatever he has invented or learned".[69]

Never questioning "the fundamental assumption" in both myths that "'civil' man, living in an orderly society with its amenities, is superior to 'rude' man, Shakespeare creates in *As You Like It*" his own world, where "the possibility of innocence and happiness" exists because the inhabitants of both the court and forest express the qualities inherent in being "inland bred",[70] albeit in manifestations appropriate to their respective locales. Allowed time for reflection in Arden, the Duke, Orlando, Rosalind – even Frederick and Oliver – learn to choose goodness and forgiveness, while the forest denizens find peace and harmony by observing and learning from nature.

Sylvan Barnet

Shakespeare "goes out of his way to heighten the improbabilities in *As You Like It*",[71] Sylvan Barnet (1926–2016) argues in "Strange Events: Improbability in *As You Like It*" (1968), largely because "suddenness and improbability are part of the meaning of the play".[72] Barnet compares Shakespeare's play to its source, Thomas Lodge's *Rosalynde* (1590), and determines that Shakespeare purposefully created a storyline less plausible than Lodge's. Barnet lists and describes several matters that he identifies as improbable: once the courtly characters arrive in Arden, for instance, they reside in an "Eden-like world", one where they do little else but remark on the improbability of their circumstances.[73] In addition, Oliver acknowledges he has no reason to hate Orlando; Frederick provides no reason to hold a wrestling tournament, offers the weakest of excuses for Rosalind's banishment, and then voices no justification for sending Oliver in pursuit of Orlando; and the "magnitude" of devotion Celia shows Rosalind really has no basis.

The most glaringly implausible actions in the play involve the swiftness and thoroughness with which characters such as Celia and Oliver fall in love, as well as the even more abrupt conversions to goodness and love that Oliver and Frederick undergo in the forest. Barnet suggests that such transformations of character find their roots in Judeo-Christian influences. With Oliver, for example, Orlando "requites evil with good" when he finds Oliver in danger. As the apostle Paul submits absolutely to Christ after his experience on the road to Damascus, Oliver submits absolutely to Orlando. Oliver's transformation parallels the Prodigal Son story, moreover, since he stands as the son who inherits everything, loses it (to Frederick), and nevertheless finds welcome and reintegration into his family. Like Oliver's, Frederick's personality initially shows signs of "unpredictability" and instability; he, too, stands "open to sudden re-information, or reformation",[74] and his instantaneous conversion signals the "existence of a benevolent Providence".[75]

David Young

Shakespeare writes *As You Like It*, David Young (b. 1936) suggests in *The Heart's Forest: A Study of Shakespeare's Pastoral Plays* (1972), to "explore more fully" the pastoral form. Pastoral allows him "a more searching look at the ideal through an intensive examination of its distance from the real".[76]

Young notes the "deliberate self-consciousness" that pervades the play: Shakespeare emphasizes the more "artificial aspects" of the romance and pastoral forms, which directs attention to the "theoretical and fictive" components of his text. Nowhere is this more apparent than in the depiction of Arden, where the forest's "natural details" receive such a "stylized and mannered" portrayal that even Shakespeare's original audience would have felt distanced from them.[77]

Shakespeare's stress on artifice involves several allusions to "feigning and counterfeiting", including Rosalind's disguise as Ganymede and Shakespeare's "remarkably extensive use of 'if'", which foregrounds Arden's "conditional" nature.[78] Shakespeare combines this stress on pastoral's artificiality with the "relativity and subjectivity of the experience of sojourn" to illustrate "the fundamental relativity of human experience". For all visitors, then, and much like the theatre experience, Arden becomes a "special sort of mirror that reflects the subject under the guise of objects",[79] as it consistently "gives back to its inhabitants and visitors images of their own selves and preoccupations". Via their interactions, characters reflect each other, too, and Touchstone emerges as the "deftest reflector".[80]

According to Young, mirroring in Shakespeare's comedies also reveals "limitations of awareness", and in *As You Like It* Shakespeare links mirroring to a "sense of relativity":

■ As the play progresses it becomes clear that blanket judgements and rigid categories will not suffice in this world; they must be adapted to the characters and situation in question.[81] □

Shakespeare's focus on relativity also informs the play's distinctions between nature and art, as well as characterization and time, Young notes. Rosalind's seemingly contradictory behaviours, for example, allow her the widest possible "means of revelation".[82] Shakespeare "welcomed the opportunities for ambiguity and contradiction" that Rosalind and others express, and found them "consistent with his comic aims".[83]

Young also considers Shakespeare's employments of paradox, juxtaposition, and "reversals of attitude" in the play, and determines that they "join to produce the play's movement toward a comic reconciliation of opposites".[84] For instance, Shakespeare uses chance encounters between characters to highlight "thematic juxtapositions which are the stuff of pastoral": Touchstone's encounter with Audrey contrasts worldliness and innocence, while Corin's time with the clown distinguishes country from court. In his registering of these juxtapositions, Young isolates an "interesting" effect: nearly every encounter reveals a character's initial "tendency to grow equivocal".[85]

With the exception of Jacques, Young surmises, all characters adjust their points of view, and shift away from "oversimplifications" and "conventional attitudes". Throughout the comedy, moreover, characters engage in a process of "reduction" (*encomium*), or narrowing of character or idea to one restrictive feature, and "expansion" (*meiosis*), or inflating the significance of something beyond its actual dimensions or impact. This "continual readjustment of attitudes by inflation and deflation" creates a more effective "synthesis" between "idealism and satire" that constitutes the pastoral tradition.[86]

Young concludes by examining the pastoral tradition's – and *As You Like It*'s – "generalizing tendency", its propensity towards the creation of "microcosms and to explore, by setting up of a hypothetical alternative, the deficiencies and advantages of life as it is". Rosalind "excels" in her generalizing tendencies and in making it clear that the world she inhabits serves "as a means of examining and criticizing the life that has been abandoned".[87]

CHAPTER FOUR

1948–83: "Not for All Markets": Movements Away from New Criticism and the Authority of the Text

Even while New Criticism dominated scholarly and pedagogical practice well into the 1980s, departures from it always existed and allowed critics alternate approaches to a text. These disparate voices set the stage for subsequent critical practices which, borrowing from disciplines such as Freudian psychoanalysis, myth studies, Marxist economic and political thought, sociology, anthropology, and linguistics, developed new lines of argument and eventually became known as *Cultural Studies*, *feminism*, and *New Historicism*, among other terms. Practitioners of these methods regarded the text as inseparably intertwined with its era's politics, social customs, gender relations, and faith and economic systems, yet these critics still considered close reading essential.

Northrop Frye, myths, and archetypal criticism

"The Argument of Comedy" (1948–49), by Northrop Frye (1912–91), stands as a major early alternative to New Criticism. Although Frye adheres to the New Critical principles of attention to form, pattern, and theme, he situates Shakespeare's comedies in a more culturally significant context: that of "social reconciliation". To Frye, literature exists as an outgrowth, an evolved product, of what he classifies as the pre-literary modes of ritual, myth, and folk tale. In Frye's vision, any culture's literature stems from these pre-literary articulations, and the culture inherits and espouses ideologies inherent in them through exposure to its literature.

The critic's task lies in attending to the archetypes – the remaining traces of myth, ritual, and folk tale – that constitute and inform the ideologies within texts and which influence a reader's response to the texts. In order to perform her or his task adequately, the critic must develop an awareness of the archetypes as they recur in a text's conventions, symbols, and other features, and explain how an author blends these components to create and impart meaning. In essence, the critic explains an archetype's impact upon a culture's ideological leanings, and also relates the work to other works claimed by the culture, especially as concerns their ideological commonalities. Because archetypes consist of a distinct ordering of words – a code, of sorts – Frye believes the critic can identify a text's archetypes by recognizing and understanding their codes.

In "The Argument of Comedy", Frye links Shakespeare's comedies to the traditions found in Greek drama, pagan and Christian death-and-resurrection myths, and traditions that centre on "heroic triumph".[1] Frye groups *As You Like It* among Shakespeare's comedies which feature "the same rhythmic movement from normal world to green world and back again".[2] As the play follows this pattern to its comic conclusion (typically the union of a young male with a young female), the society around the couple – or, at least, "all the right-thinking" ones among them – "come over to" the young male's "side" and form with him and his mate a "new social unit". This more harmonious reintegration of the society (some characters, however, such as Jacques, remain outside) then celebrates its reunion in the same manner as in life: through "festival" which marks a "social reconciliation" of "as many as possible".[3]

Several of the patterns that Shakespeare adopts find their roots in Greek Old and New Comedy – exemplified, respectively, in the works of Aristophanes and Menander: the youth's outwitting of the older *senex* (a figure, typically an old man, which blocks, temporarily, the progress of the young male towards the female), for example, or the "theme of the withdrawal and return of the heroine" (which Shakespeare adapts from death-and-resurrection myths and enhances by placing the heroine in male disguise).[4] Other patterns, however, stem from "the drama of folk ritual" as well as dramas "that punctuated the Christian calendar" with "rituals" rooted in pre-Christian theology.[5] The green world and its theme of life's triumph over death dominates these rituals in Shakespearean comedy, and Shakespeare, who recognizes a "profounder pattern" in comedy than any playwright before him, recalibrates the theme of life over death to one of "deliverance",[6] a transformation of oneself into "self-knowledge".[7]

Frye focuses more exclusively on *As You Like It* in portions of his *A Natural Perspective* (1965). Here, he enlarges upon his conception of the green world by linking it to another myth, that of a "lost paradisal garden".[8] In the play, the forest of Arden symbolizes "natural society", or "the original human society which is the proper home of man, not the physical world he now lives in but the 'golden world' he is trying to regain".[9] Erotic love drives much of the movement towards this proper home of man, as it "individualizes" the people engaged in it.[10]

The world Arden represents initially strikes readers as "unnatural", though, because it depicts "attributes of nature" as "miraculous" and as possessing "irresistible reviving power", either through "dream, magic and chastity or spiritual energy as well as fertility and renewed natural energies".[11] As the play develops, however, Duke Senior's world reveals itself as ideal but also achievable: Arden is the "upper or purely human world toward which the comic action moves" and "begins to take shape, and around which the world crystallizes".[12] In the "action" that leads the characters to Arden and to a natural society, moreover, the "kind of force associated with 'wish fulfillment'" is not helpless or purely a matter of dreams. Instead, it is "a power as deeply rooted in nature and reality as its opponent"; it also constitutes "a power that we see, as the comedy proceeds, taking over and informing the predictable world".[13] As such, all the magical, restorative forces that constitute Duke Senior's adopted home contrast with the divisive and life-threatening forces associated with Frederick's court.

According to Frye, *As You Like It* – as well as much of Shakespeare's comedy – closes with a newly formed society "remarkably catholic in its tolerance". However, one or more of the characters involved in the play – and, perhaps more importantly, we the readers – remain "spectator[s], detached and observant, aware of other nuances and values" that deny us full participation in the comic resolution.[14] Frye classifies this outlying character as the *idiotes* and identifies Jacques as his representative in *As You Like It*. At times this isolated figure holds his feelings of separation inside, but more often he discusses them, and through his utterances "something external to us is suddenly internalized, so that we are forced to participate in what we have been conditioned to think of as removed from us and our sympathies".[15]

Structuralism, signs, and semiotics

Frye's critical approach marks a moment in which scholarly attention shifts, somewhat, from the rigorous examinations of a text's form and structure to analysis of how the text reflects or responds to forms and structures inherent within the culture itself. While Frye never associated himself with the critical practice we now call *structuralism*, his contention that literature manifests itself in a recurrent series of archetypes, or patterns of words and images, and that these archetypes reflect and represent larger patterns in a culture, parallels some tenets of structuralist theory as set forth by Ferdinand de Saussure (1857–1913) and later adapted by Roman Jakobson (1896–1982), Claude Lévi-Strauss (1908–2009), and Roland Barthes (1915–80).

Structuralists argue that all components of a culture (its language, laws, rituals, social customs, belief systems, etc.) can be studied and understood as systems of signs, which operate much like language in forming and relaying meaning from one person, or subject, to the next. Each sign possesses and transfers meaning from one subject to another because of this sign's differences from other signs: a "dog" is a "dog" because it is not a "cat", for instance. Because each sign is arbitrary – no explanation exists as to why we would call a dog a dog – understanding what a sign signifies comes through the subject's reference to the culture's convention, or code, which determines a sign's fixed meaning. For example, the white line painted in the middle of an asphalt road is a sign that delineates the side of the road on which we should drive, and, depending upon whether the line is continuous or broken, also determines for us whether we should pass a slower vehicle or remain behind it. The sign itself always is arbitrary – no quality of white paint signifies one's position or safety – but the meaning we assign to it matters in terms of how a highway functions.

In much the same fashion as Northrop Frye, structuralists developed a semiotics, or science of signs, whereby they could explain a culture by examining its myths (as did Lévi-Strauss in his "The Structural Study of Myth", (1955) or Barthes in his *Mythologies* (1957)), its uses of humour (as did Mikhail Bakhtin in his *Rabelais and His World* (1965)), or its mundane nature (as did Michel de Certeau in his *The Practice of Everyday Life* (1980)). As structuralists began to understand and articulate societies' various unified systems of signification, or its "grammar", scholars such as Frye, who concerned themselves more exclusively with literary texts, likewise perceived literature as reliant upon a set of codes, the same codes with which readers interact and determine their reality. The author, structuralists posit, also operates from an internalized assortment of codes and conventions. And while they recognize the world an author creates because of the myriad mutually shared codes, structuralist critics resist defining literature as an exercise in realism. Instead, reading a text enables one's understanding of how codes and conventions assist in our conveyance of meaning.

C.L. Barber, Saturnalian ritual, and social contexts

C.L. Barber's monumental *Shakespeare's Festive Comedy* (1959) links *As You Like It* to Saturnalian rituals that, in turn, tie the play to social contexts involving class and power. As Barber's and subsequent studies begin to infuse, if not yet rely upon, ideological viewpoints in their arguments, their discussions of *As You Like It* expand into issues of patriarchy, social class, and contemporary politics. In the words of Peter Erickson, Barber's method of "structuring the social tensions as represented in Shakespeare's theater" helped to "provide a critical discourse" for subsequent generations.[16] Among the first to recognize how theatre "subjects popular forms" such as the festive Saturnalian ritual "to self-conscious exploration and testing",[17] Barber anticipates the New Historicist contention that hegemonic structures often create social space wherein political or social challenges may be voiced, but only temporarily and in order to procure their containment within the dominant discourse.

In Chapter 1, "Introduction: The Saturnalian Pattern", Barber argues that "festive" describes not simply the "atmosphere" that pervades Shakespeare's comedies from *Love's Labour's Lost* to *Twelfth Night*, but also defines these plays' "structure". According to Barber, the "saturnalian pattern" of "inversion, statement and counterstatement" appears in each play's "basic movement" from "release to clarification".[18] Barber equates the "whole experience" of these festive comedies with that of a holiday revel: each play situates its characters "in the position of festive celebrants"[19] and, because festive comedy comprises "a version of pastoral",[20] in locales where "Nature reigns", characters' immersion in the natural world instils in them a sense of liberty, which then stimulates "mirth, an accession of wanton vitality".[21]

Clarification ensues from the characters' liberation and mirth, and involves their recognition and mockery of all that is unnatural: inhibition, pride, greed, or the folly and "highflown idealism" that accompanies romantic love. Those who fixate on impossible ideals such as "love's finality", in other words, find themselves as equally outside the community of revellers as those who cannot let go of their grief, avarice, or negativity.[22] Once characters learn to recognize and laugh at their own and others' unnaturalness, they then form communities where the pleasure and solidarity of holiday obtains.

In Chapter 9, "The Alliance of Seriousness and Levity in *As You Like It*", Barber illustrates the pattern of release and clarification as it develops in this play. The play's first half moves characters from a corrupt court into the Forest of Arden, an action that provides them with a "sense of freedom" and a "release from the tension"[23] of the court, and also creates a contrast between their everyday worlds and that of holiday. Each character's release stems from his or her realization that Fortune holds sway over nothing; instead, life consists of the "natural and seasonal and physical",[24] which includes unpleasantness and folly.

Each lover in the play manifests a type of folly, a "different version of the incongruity between reality and the illusions" that romantic love "generates and by which it is expressed". Most firmly rooted in the pastoral tradition, Silvius and Phebe exhibit a "formal spectacle" or a "pageant" of romantic love, one where Silvius suffers from unrequited love and seeks pity from his lover, and Phebe "refuses to believe in love's invisible wound" – even though Silvius serves as living proof of it. Rosalind's mockery of their relationship "humorously underscores the exaggeration of conventional sentiment" that they exemplify.[25]

Rosalind's ability to participate in romantic love and to remain detached from the follies that accompany it becomes an example for all characters to follow. At the end of the play, she and Orlando demonstrate a love "independent of illusions, whose incongruity with life is recognized and laughed off".[26] She helps them (and her audience) to understand that believing in love as "an ultimate and final experience, a matter of life and death" actually is a submission to a "master illusion". Barber notes that Rosalind's insistence in this clarified view of love comes with a hint of sorrow, that "love is not so final as romance would have it".[27] Her clearer perspective on love, shared by the other pairs of lovers in varying degrees of cognition, becomes what T.S. Eliot describes as an "alliance of levity and seriousness" that characterizes this play.[28]

Back in the first chapter, Barber comments on Shakespeare's employment of clowns: "clowning could provide both release for impulses which run counter to decency and decorum, and the clarification about limits which comes from going beyond the limit".[29] While in *As You Like It* nearly every character acts clownishly, each one either exhausts his or her indecent or indecorous impulses and then comes to understand and correct his or her erroneous behaviours (Oliver and Frederick in particular), or learns his or her limits after exceeding them (Rosalind and Orlando). Then, of course, these characters enter into bonds and communities that illustrate the benefits of release and clarification each has experienced. As actual clowns, however, Jacques (an "amateur" clown) and Touchstone (a "professional" one) stand outside the pattern – especially that of romantic folly. They still make fun of it, though, and, through their mockery of "pastoral innocence and romantic love"[30] serve several functions: both clown's reluctance to become part of the community in Arden assists others in achieving more realistic understandings of life and love. Also, Touchstone's often callous commentary on others' sentiments "forestalls the cynicism with which the audience might greet a play" so rife with lovelorn characters; Touchstone simultaneously "embodies the part of ourselves which resists the play's reigning idealism".[31] Ultimately, and along with Rosalind, these clown figures clarify Shakespeare's "affirmation" of humanity's "certain imperfection".[32]

Jan Kott and real world politics

Jan Kott (1914–2001) infuses his criticism with autobiography: born in Poland and until Stalin's death a fiercely loyal Stalinist, Kott witnessed the horrors of World War II by serving in the Soviet People's Army. Several years after he renounced all ties to communism, Kott defected to the United States and held teaching positions at Stony Brook University, Yale, and the University of California.

As he avers in *Shakespeare Our Contemporary* (1966), Kott perceives in Shakespeare's oeuvre representations of Western culture as well as the playwright's, particularly as concerns social and political matters. Throughout his text, Kott takes issue with critics who "try to detect" in the playwright a "calm and light-heartedness",[33] a connectedness to the harmony that supposedly pervades the natural world. Instead, what we see in Shakespeare involves a more "real world, always the same, bitter, cruel, and fascinating; the world that one cannot accept, but from which there is no escape; a world for which there is no justification except that it is the only one that exists".[34]

Even the Forest of Arden depicts this world:

■ In Shakespeare's forest, life is speeded up, becomes more intense, violent, and at the same time, as it were, clearer. Everything acquires a double significance: the literal and the metaphorical. Everything exists for itself and is also its own reflection, generalization, archetype.[35] □

At first, Arden seems to promise escape for Rosalind, Celia, and Orlando; refuge from Duke Frederick's life-threatening court; and denials or usurpations of birthright. Once in the forest, however, we see that nature acts as ruthlessly as the court, and its denizens behave as self-servingly as the courtiers: Audrey is "plain and stupid", while Phebe possesses the "red hands of a swineherd".[36] In essence, there "is no return to primeval harmony" when one retreats into nature.[37]

Instead, Shakespeare's "mixture of techniques and styles" in his Arden matches it to his "confused image of the world".[38] While Shakespeare "makes mockery" of Arcadian myths involving a lost paradise in his portraiture of the forest, he simultaneously imbues his portrait with the classical myths of androgyny, myths which "had wide and active circulation" during the years encompassing Shakespeare's professional career.[39] As did the myths of Arcadia, androgyny myths often focus upon a lost paradise, while they also traditionally evoke the "archetype of unity of male and female elements" and serve as "the sign of reconciliation of all contradictions".[40] As "an almost perfect" manifestation of androgyny, one who "personifies" our "longing for the lost Paradise where there had as yet been no division into male and female elements",[41] Rosalind embodies the play's movement towards reconciliation and fulfilment. The reconciliation and reunion she brings to the play's close, however, diminishes in scope when we realize that they stem from "falseness – original falseness, rather like original sin".[42]

In order to comprehend fully Kott's somewhat startling perspective on Rosalind and the play, we first must understand that Kott relies heavily on performative representations of Shakespeare, and insists on their reinstitution into studies of the playwright. One of the first in what would become a steady stream of critics to insist on considerations of staging alongside readings of the text, Kott anticipates a tenet of Cultural Studies, and does so to make history more relevant to the present – to make Shakespeare "our contemporary" – and to challenge the text's authority and provide a voice to the marginalized.

As Kott considers Shakespeare's theatre, then, he posits that, because boys played the women's parts, the "borderlines between illusion and reality, between an object and its reflection, are gradually lost". While the theatre "represents in itself all human relationships", in other words, the representation consistently reveals human falsity because an actor always "plays a character he is not. He is who he is not. He is not who he is". The significance lies in the fact that to "be oneself means only to play one's own reflection in the eyes of strangers". With its complicated juggling of gender and identity, especially as concerns Rosalind, *As You Like It* reminds readers and auditors that everything "is real and unreal, false and genuine at the same time".[43]

Rather than replicating a mythology increasingly challenged by his culture, Shakespeare "creates his own myths" and "constitutes" in his Arden a "new Arcadia", one where longing for an edenic fulfilment remains, but also is tempered with a "system of mirrors that enables" the playwright to "discredit and ridicule courtly refinement with its code of honor, all the charms of the 'natural state,' and the conventions of pastoral romance".[44]

Anne Barton

As do many New Critics, Anne Barton (1933–2013) writes, in *"As You Like It and Twelfth Night*: Shakespeare's Sense of an Ending" (1972), that the plot of *As You Like It* "barely exists". Forward movement occurs instead exclusively through Shakespeare's "shifts in the grouping of characters", and his rearrangements of characters among each other encourage a "concentration upon attitudes rather than action" throughout the play. The end result is "the fullest and most stable realization of Shakespearean comic form".[45]

While Barton focuses her study on the play's "form", she also acknowledges how Frye's and Barber's expansions of the New Critical purview coax forth "a subtler and more consequential achievement" embedded in Shakespeare's comedies,[46] especially as concerns assuring a theatre audience that "the facts of the world as it is have not been forgotten".[47] She hints at the social and class issues into which Barber delves, but examines more diligently elements in concert with Frye's conception of a "natural society", an environment ideal for all humanity. Even here, though, as Barton registers the numerous manifestations of idealization and even fantasy that abound in *As You Like It*, she emphasizes the play's inclination towards the inescapable realities of life.

Barton notes, for example, how in *As You Like It* "[r]eminders of mortality flicker everywhere",[48] and that Shakespeare never represents Arden "as magical". Rather, the forest serves both denizens and visitors as a locale where "people are free to be themselves as they are not in the court of Duke Frederick":

> ■ At the end of the comedy as at the beginning, William will be a clod and Audrey awkward and ill-favored. Frogs remain frogs and ugly ducklings stay ugly; they do not change into princes or into swans.[49] □

Barton cites Shakespeare's "masterful" integration of romance and realism, and draws attention to the playwright's insistence that any changes the characters undergo "are really self-discoveries, a deepening and development of personality" whereby "these people earn their own happy endings".[50]

Even though several "implausible" and "fairy-tale elements" imbue the play's conclusion, "an image of reality" nonetheless dominates, particularly in the "flexibility of the new social order" that will return to court, as well as in this order's "ability to accommodate deviation", or most of it, from here on in. One exception lies in Jacques, whose self-imposed exclusion from the play's unifications and reconciliations suggests "there are certain kinds of experience after all, certain questions, which lie outside the scope of the happy ending".[51]

Peter Erickson

Peter Erickson (b. 1945) devotes Chapter 1 of his *Patriarchal Structures in Shakespeare's Drama* (1985) to *As You Like It* (as well as *Love's Labour's Lost*), and observes that, because Rosalind's "androgynous allure" and "linguistic virtuosity" captivate us so thoroughly, we frequently ignore the play's other, more structurally and socially significant, features.[52] According to Erickson, the male friendship that Orlando establishes between himself and Duke Senior leads to a "transmission of patriarchal heritage", from the elder Senior to the younger de Boys. This transmission serves as the "framework that diminishes and contains Rosalind's apparent power" over the other characters and the play's forward movement.[53] By the time her wedding day arrives, Rosalind has submitted herself "not only to two individual men but also to the patriarchal society that they embody". Patriarchy, furthermore, informs the play as "an exact term for the social structure that close reading reveals", Erickson asserts.[54]

As You Like It may end "smoothly", Erickson contends, because "male control is affirmed and women are rendered nonthreatening", but before this happens, the love Orlando and Rosalind feel for each other "brings out a disparity between male and female intelligence and power". Orlando experiences love "as incapacitation": it initially renders him "humorously but embarrassingly naïve and helpless".[55] Rosalind, on the other hand, initially finds freedom in her disguise, but, in order to create a loving bond with Orlando, eventually must step away from this artificial empowerment and "reveal herself directly" to him, which makes her more "vulnerable".[56] Her "voluntary"[57] yet resistant opening up to Orlando also will extend to her "co-option and assimilation by a society ruled by men".[58]

For all the gender-specific disruption that *As You Like It* foregrounds, Erickson argues that the play never "questions the conventional categories of masculine and feminine". Despite her disguise, for example, Rosalind "does not reconcile gender definitions in the sense of integrating or synthesizing them",[59] and Orlando re-establishes "patriarchal normalcy" by marrying Rosalind and inheriting a dukedom.[60] In order to unite with Rosalind and assume his political station, however, Orlando must "give up violence" and shift, emotionally, from "toughness to tenderness".[61] Through his repeated examples of benevolence and tolerance, Duke Senior teaches Orlando how to enact these transitions. Duke Senior's actions also illustrate the extreme degree to which *As You Like It* leans in terms of its advocacy of patriarchy: men commandeer even "the traditional female prerogative of maternal nurturance".[62]

Erickson registers a distinction between the temporary nature of Rosalind's disguise and Orlando's more permanent transformations from naïve bumbler to steady lover and from angry younger brother to benevolent future duke. Orlando's "access" to the "traditional female attributes of compassion and nurturance" bestows an "emotional enlargement" upon him. Erickson then explains how most discussions of androgyny in the play "focus on Rosalind whereas in fact it is the men rather than the women who are the lasting beneficiaries of androgyny". In this distinction Erickson challenges C.L. Barber's contention (as well as that of several New Historicists) that the licensed misrule characteristic of festive comedy lasts only in limited intervals: "the conservatism of comic form does not affect all characters equally".[63]

As he continues his analysis of patriarchy in *As You Like It*, Erickson also reimagines an aspect of Northrop Frye's green world: that which involves the freedom it offers to visitors. Instead of unbounded freedom, Erickson observes in the green world a "strong paternal presence", as well as a "clear political structure", both of which insist upon orderly patriarchy: "A benevolent patriarchy still requires women to be subordinate",[64] and Arden is not a "space apart where a youthful rebellion finds a refuge from the older generation".[65]

Erickson anticipates some of the directions many later Cultural Studies and Gender Theory critics take in their considerations of Shakespeare's plays in performance. The early modern English stage's practice of assigning the female roles to young males provides men an "opportunity to imagine sex-role fluidity and flexibility", Erickson avers. The "potential for male acknowledgement of a 'feminine self' and thus for male transcendence of a narrow masculinity", a "discovery", in other words, of "those qualities suppressed by a masculinity strictly defined as aggressiveness"[66] becomes possible in any performance, and herein emerges the "efficaciousness of art".[67]

Later incarnations of close reading: structuralism into deconstruction

Our earlier example of white paint on asphalt proves instructive in yet another fashion, for it invites considerations of the values a culture imposes on signs and the effects such values have on the culture's subjects. As they developed a semiotics, or scientific study of signs, structuralists discovered that some signifieds – those things a sign represents in language or writing – at times assumed a dominant position over related signifieds: white over black, for instance, or man over woman. As already discussed, the words "white" or "man" contain within them no inherent meanings or values. When applied to subjects within a culture whose gender is male or whose skin tone matches, roughly, the determinate, or fixed, signification of "white", though, other significations frequently appear, and with them certain values.

In essence, proponents of *deconstruction* employ close reading to illustrate how a text contains within it any number of contrary readings. Instead of arriving at a universally logical and acceptable meaning within the text, the deconstructionist critic proves that a work contains within it several opposing discourses, or strains of narrative, all of which contradict and often confound one another. Because all language, written or spoken, encompasses many competing narratives, no one narrative or "meaning" can arise as the precise or correct one.

Created, named, and explained by philosopher Jacques Derrida (1930–2004), deconstruction exposes the limits of the Western European tendency to conceive of the world in terms of binary oppositions (masculine/feminine, white/black, light/dark, etc.), oppositions which in Derrida's view produce hierarchies (linguistic, of course, but ultimately social and political) where the language's users privilege one term as better (i.e., superior or more good) than the other. Derrida encouraged a blurring of the boundaries between the terms, one where the privileged term becomes challenged or undermined and, thus, its hegemony negated. Building on the studies of structuralist theorist Ferdinand de Saussure, Derrida focused on Saussure's premise that a word, as does any sign, exists only as a "deferred presence": any word, that is, stands as a mere representation of the thing itself and, as such, possesses no absolute validity as the thing itself. The word "chair", then, is only a five-letter, voiced (or written) stand-in for an object on which one would sit; the word in no way is the thing itself (think of how we just as easily use the word "chair" to identify the leader of a committee or other group of people), so it should never be trusted as absolutely defined in any particular usage. Instead, any given word always suggests multiple connotations, each one open to individual preference or interpretations and, therefore, impossible to reduce to one concrete meaning.

While deconstruction rose in prominence (and as a potential threat) during the 1970s and 1980s, the theory and practice impacted Shakespeare criticism only slightly, especially when compared with those studies of the playwright that hailed from feminist and New Historicist approaches. Perhaps Shakespeare's critics' longstanding awareness, and requisite explorations, of the playfulness and indeterminacy that informs his drama neutralizes much of the effect that a deconstructive analysis can deliver. Contrasting – and, frequently, contested – explanations of such passages as Jacques' "Ducdame, ducdame, ducdame" (2.5.46) or Rosalind's-Ganymede's "If I were a woman" (Epilogue 12), for example, passages once referred to as "cruces" because of the seemingly unsolvable indeterminacies of meaning they harboured, have held Shakespeare's readers' attention since the beginning of Shakespeare studies. Because Shakespeare's critics already acknowledge these textual indeterminacies, deconstruction largely has failed to disturb Shakespeare criticism as uproariously as the critical traditions that surround other authors or periods.

Terry Eagleton and the emergence of deconstruction in Shakespeare criticism

With that said, however, a few deconstructionist readings of Shakespeare and of *As You Like It* warrant attention. Arguing in Chapter 6 of *William Shakespeare* (1986) that *As You Like It* distinguishes itself as Shakespeare's first play wherein the playwright "deconstructs" the binary opposition between nature and culture and consequently resolves several "problems" that inhabit this as well as other plays, Terry Eagleton (b. 1943) explores how "every self-presentation" in *As You Like It* becomes a "kind of play-acting", where Shakespeare presents "every process of natural development" in "theatrical terms".[68] Shakespeare infuses *As You Like It*, in other words, with an ideology that performs the naturalness of hierarchy and private ownership.

Eagleton urges us to see nature and culture as simultaneously transforming and transformative:

> ■ Nature itself produces the means of its own transformation, contains that which goes beyond it. What goes beyond it – art, civilization, culture, language, love – is thus no mere external "supplement" to it, but is internal to its very design. If nature is always cultural, then a particular culture can always be seen as natural.

Those forms of surplus are legitimate which have their roots in the very natural order they transcend, and which provides the source of that transcendence.[69] ☐

Eagleton posits, then, that the nobility, although equal in every respect to the lower classes, over time have "refined" themselves "by civilized breeding" and thus have created substantial "hierarchical differences" between themselves and others. At once the same and different, and inherently so, all humans follow the natural dictates to practise justice and mercy upon each other while simultaneously respecting and even promoting "distinctions of class and rank".[70]

As concerns the issue of common versus private property ownership, which so inflects the discourses within Shakespeare's culture and *As You Like It*, Eagleton sees a similar process: private property is "naturalized" in the play through a "logical slide" in the meaning of the word "nature": just because "everything in the world springs from the stuff of the world", Eagleton points out, we should not perceive everything, including class stratification and enclosure, as "morally desired as conducive to human welfare". In *As You Like It*, language emerges as Shakespeare's "primary symbol of the culture which surpasses and transforms its limits".[71]

Brian Gibbons

Brian Gibbons' (b. 1938) "Amorous Fictions and *As You Like It*" (1987) stands among the earliest essays to link Shakespeare's adoption of the pastoral in *As You Like It* to the possibilities as well as the limitations of theatre. Gibbons focuses upon the degree to which an audience's tastes and expectations, in concert with pastoral's often constrictive "system of construction",[72] influence a playwright's "translation" of the text and its contexts, as well as the genre itself.[73]

By comparing *As You Like It* to Thomas Lodge's *Rosalynde* and Philip Sidney's *Arcadia* (the text to which Shakespeare's play "owes more", Gibbons argues), Gibbons isolates Shakespeare's "particular use of pastoral" and describes the "ways" Shakespeare "found to translate into the language of theatre" those "effects achieved" in pastoral.[74] Throughout his essay, Gibbons assumes structuralist postures; yet, when he discusses pastoral's tendency to "lament the gap between representation and its imagined subject", he engages in a deconstruction of Shakespeare's supposed commitment to the pastoral tradition, although he rarely employs the terms associated with deconstruction.

Gibbons notes that *As You Like It* and *Henry V* continually foreground "questions of narrative technique and dramatic and literary form", while they simultaneously examine "theatre's unique expressive resources" as well as its "stark limits". He then identifies the pastoral genre as the ideal environment wherein Shakespeare can entertain his recurrent fascinations with literary form and theatre. It:

■ is entirely appropriate that he should decide to turn to pastoral, given that mode's particular reputation and particular traditions, its oblique treatment of its narrative subject, its invitation to the artist to reflect upon his art, its prompting an audience to recognize his artistry.[75] □

Because the pastoral always involves an "awareness of the absent imagined subject", moreover, its subject often "is this gap".[76]

As do *Rosalynde* and *Arcadia*, *As You Like It* highlights its "status" as an "imitation" of the pastoral, which exposes a gap between the play and the romance tradition from which pastoral derives. According to Gibbons, romances consist of "configurations" that:

■ correspond to deep emotional patterns and whose process irresistibly absorbs the solitary reader, who finds his secret hopes, desires, and dreams represented there in forms his conscious mind permits him to feed on uninhibitedly.[77] □

Gibbons reminds readers that Shakespeare, too, depicts in his romantic comedies multiple examples of protagonists who overcome obstacles through "major personal development", a process pioneered by Sidney.[78]

According to Gibbons, Sidney employs throughout his *Arcadia* a narrative practice that "continuously alters the degree" of the "sympathy with which the narrative engages the reader" and "the angle of vision from which it is recorded". In Gibbons' view, Sidney's technique "enacts rather than simply conveys this incessantly dialectical record".[79] Gibbons' thrust here involves Shakespeare's similar adoption of Sidney's style in *As You Like It*, in order to "set the written in contrast to the spoken word". Shakespeare juxtaposes throughout the play episodes delivered in verse with those in prose, and the "revelation of character through realistic conversation is contrasted to formal emblematic descriptions of people".[80] In tandem with these contrasts, Shakespeare describes key elements of the plot instead of providing them for the audience's view (Orlando's confrontations with the lioness and serpent, for example). In doing so, Shakespeare:

■ not only reproduces the ingredients of non-dramatic pastoral as readers like it, he ensures also that the variety of ways of representing experience, which the contrasting styles afford, will constitute an implicit critical debate, to which nonsense and parody make telling contributions.[81] □

Shakespeare's preference for representing a variety of experience and of inviting critical debate – both encouraged by his juxtapositions of characters and situations – contrasts with romance's "tendency to randomness of real life".[82]

Despite its seeming rejection of romance, however, *As You Like It* reveals several "affinities with the technique of Shakespeare's last romances", especially in Shakespeare's tendency towards "sudden changes in style and even mode as part of an overall dramatic strategy, awakening surprise, shock and wonder in the audience". While the play repeatedly relies on replications of "lifelike spontaneous conversation", these moments "are embedded in a plot whose overall shape is determined by the inexplicable and astonishing".[83] Hymen's and Jacques de Boys' sudden appearances illustrate Gibbons' point. Such moments, such "archetypes", ensure "a deep structure in fable and keep the audience subliminally in touch with the primitive sources of the narrative's power".[84] Shakespeare finds a way, in other words, of creating a play that emphasizes transformation, particularly through love, while he remains true to the pastoral tradition's structure, which the audience expects. The "equal status of thing signified and sign", a mainstay of the pastoral tradition, remains, while Shakespeare maintains playfulness and "stylistic subversion".[85]

Martha Ronk

In her "Locating the Visual in *As You Like It*" (2001), Martha Ronk (b. 1940) evokes the predominant tenet of deconstruction, that language falls short in its conveyance of meaning, but she also convincingly relocates this destabilization of meaning from the play's text to its theatrical representation. What *As You Like It* "enacts explicitly", and all of "Shakespeare's theater" demonstrates, "is how different sets of signs undercut one another and purposely problematize theatrical representation itself".[86] That "which seems theatrically most obvious" in the play – that is, "what one sees" onstage – actually reveals and foregrounds its "unrepresentable nature", its "impossibility" in terms of delineation, because "what is obviously set forth is simultaneously erased and refigured".[87] In *As You Like It*, Shakespeare introduces a "theory of theatrical production" wherein we witness, through a series of disruptions – in voiced self-descriptions, staging, writing, and even in generic expectations – "the various ways in which any character, scene, or abstract idea might be represented".[88] In doing so, Shakespeare informs his play's structure with references that "call attention to its construction" as well as to its ultimate "failure".[89]

Throughout the play, Shakespeare employs *ekphrasis* (a Greek term that denotes a description of a scene or work of art) as a means of slowing the "forward movement of the plot in order to allow contemplation, spatial exploration of a specific character or moment".[90] More than any other play, *As You Like It* "creates seeing" through figurative language and "the overtly emblematic language of ekphrasis". This technique enables viewers and readers to "see" his characters "more fully and completely", and at times his technique even casts the characters into an allegorical significance.[91]

Theatrical representation, however, also relies on visual portrayal, and visual representations in *As You Like It* – of Rosalind in particular – fall short of the ones Shakespeare creates through his words. This "tension" between visual and verbal representation "enacts a semiotics of theater: the relation of emblem to word or page to stage". All too often, Shakespeare's "clarity of representation in an ekphrastic moment" undermines its theatrical representation.[92]

Ronk also explores how this tension between verbal and visual in Shakespeare's theatre parallels certain "cultural anxieties concerning the value or danger of the visual". Debates over whether truth "resides in image or in word" occupied Reformation discourse, and many Protestants held a "general distrust of images", especially those associated with Catholicism.[93] Simultaneously, however, both Protestant and Catholic monarchs flooded their realms with visual images depicting their potency, "to dazzle the populace" and enhance their power.[94]

More than any other character, Rosalind repeatedly "provokes" among readers and auditors a "strong mental image" as she becomes "differently gendered and differently erotic at different moments in the play", all of which she achieves "in an exclusively linguistic form".[95] And when one adds Orlando's verbal and poetic representations of Rosalind to her own, such "vivid and disjunct" representations create "gaps" between "what we believe we are seeing and what we name it":[96]

> ■ Rosalind is not only *not* the picture hanging from the trees and *not* the figure in the Epilogue, she is also *not* (or, again, not exactly) the picture she creates of herself within this framed inner world of the play. [Ronk's italics][97] □

The "problematics of representation" thus become the play's focus.

As the play concludes, the "patently and conventionally" artificial nature of the world it represents emerges, and one becomes aware of the "discrepancies and fissures in representation" that it foregrounds.[98] To Ronk, these matters stand as the central focus of *As You Like It*; Ronk explains how Shakespeare employs the pastoral tradition, a genre "designed to deceive", only in order to reveal it as "an outmoded literary form".[99] Shakespeare sends Rosalind and her companions into Arden, but his employment of ekphrastic and emblematic speech in the forest dwellers results in a "fracturing of character into highly visual and highly verbal" components, and, thus, in a "disruption" in what his stage can and does represent.[100]

Robert N. Watson

As deconstruction approached the apex of its influence in the mid and late 1970s, its practitioners encountered challenges from readers who, among other concerns, believed that deconstructionists' almost obsessive attention to the free play of language, as well as their conviction that language could disseminate meaning almost limitlessly, robbed literature of its connections to the material, political, and social worlds in which it took part. An advocate of literature's cultural significance, and concerned that readers misunderstood deconstruction, Derrida re-focused his later writings and drew more concrete connections between the text and culture. While Derrida's efforts could not curtail the reaction against deconstructionist readings of texts, he began to emphasize how a deconstructionist approach assists in revealing how the indeterminacy of language reflects and responds to historical and cultural circumstances.

In Robert N. Watson's "As You Liken It: Simile in the Wilderness" (2003), Watson concentrates on how in *As You Like It* Shakespeare fixates simultaneously on "imperfect identity" and "the way that 'liking', even in apparently benign forms, necessarily imposes on its objects", particularly women.[101]

As regards issues of identity, Watson believes the play reflects an anxiety in Shakespeare's culture, one stemming from "urbanization, capitalism, and the Protestant Reformation", as well as from "humanism and colonialism". These socially transformative phenomena initiated a "recognition that the world is less observed than constructed", and that, because the world is "less an accessible reality than a manufactured contingency" we understand it only through likening its qualities and phenomena to other things. The revival of the pastoral tradition, of which *As You Like It* is part, furthermore, signalled for Shakespeare's culture a "desire to recover some original and authentic reality",[102] but instead of allaying this anxiety through his pastoral drama, Shakespeare reflected upon "the irreversible human fall into the mediations of self-consciousness and language".[103]

Arden, for instance, only vaguely reflects Eden, and Duke Senior's and Jacques' desires to identify with the forest's wildlife – as well as their feeble attempts to express concern for the deer's well-being – only reveal a "presumption of the human mind",[104] one sullied by a narcissistic "suggestion that these invaders are so absorbed in Self that they can receive no true impression of the Other". Ultimately the play indicates that, to "perceive ultimate reality", we must abandon "this earthly life".[105]

Orlando's desire for Rosalind reveals people's inability to know the Other, as well as their impulse to impose themselves upon, and thus to dominate, it. His "fantasies about the disguised Rosalind link two archetypal modes of male aggression, two meanings of 'venery': hunting and lusting". In addition, Orlando's love language eventually renders him and all:

■ masculine aggressors self-conscious, turning the linguistic tools by which we conquer reality against us, letting slip the dogs of word, sending into a wilderness.[106] □

In the same fashion as Senior's and Jacques' sentiments regarding the forest's deer, Orlando's poorly conceived Petrarchan lines distort the reality that is Rosalind, as well as reveal his desire to possess her. His poetry also illuminates:

■ the way the otherness of a woman in a man's hetero-eroticism resembles and perhaps reflects an unconquerable otherness already present in nature, present in material reality itself.[107] □

Perhaps more so than any other character, Touchstone exposes "the alienation of the prejudicial mind from any absolute, pre-existing reality":[108] through the clown's interactions with Corin and Audrey, we see how we all fail to understand another's perspective, and our language reveals how distant one perception can be from another.

In Rosalind's blurring of gender, Watson continues, we witness Shakespeare's "test" of the "membrane separating the biological world from human artifice and illusion".[109] Her assuming the role of Ganymede, as well as the reader's/auditor's knowledge that she is a female character played by a young man who intermittently adopts both feminine and masculine identities, "shows how difficult it is either to discover or to erase the facts of biology, to end the dialogue of artificial and natural". The play:

■ is ostentatiously concerned with the temporary obliteration of opposition, the narrowly failed effort to crush together polarities such as female and male, rich and poor, civilization and savagery.[110] □

It also acknowledges our "desire to connect", as well as our inability to do so.[111] The "irreducible distances between likeness and identity, and between the human and the natural" hold us in a perpetual state of anxiety.[112]

Wolfgang Iser and Reader Response criticism

Along with Hans Robert Jauss (1921–97), Wolfgang Iser (1926–2007) established in the late 1960s what came to be known as *Reader Response* criticism, a theory in which its practitioners concentrate upon the "dialogue" that emerges between a reader and a text once the reader becomes immersed in it. In many ways Reader Response criticism opposes New Criticism, for a Reader Response critic believes that any meaning derived by reading comes not from the text but in the interaction that occurs between reader and text during reading.

Influenced by linguistic-anthropologist Mikhail Bakhtin (1895–1975), Iser employs the term "dialogue" in the sense that, when one reads, s/he brings certain expectations to the text, and also allows the text to create certain expectations, nearly all of which the text dashes by veering off in different, unexpected directions. The reader, then, must fill in the gaps between these expectations and the text by repeated consultations with the text, paying attention to its structure, relying on the individual's own experiences – both with a text and with one's perception of reality – and recognizing and then re-considering the text's contents as other features come to light. While the reader brings a "horizon of expectations" (Jauss' phrase) to any given text, the text simultaneously anticipates an ideal reader – not an actual person, but rather an entity who participates in the creation of meaning by considering a text's structure and filling in the gaps that the dashed expectations expose. To a Reader Response critic, these gaps signify that all texts consist of written and unwritten portions, and the gaps invite the reader to participate in the production of meaning.

In "The Dramatization of Double Meaning in Shakespeare's *As You Like It*" (1983), Iser contends that the play "is based on the principle of doubling". First of all, pastoral romance, *As You Like It* being an example, always represents two worlds, the "political world" and a confrontation of it. The political world of *As You Like It*'s court, too, doubles itself repeatedly: Oliver has a double in Orlando and Duke Frederick in Duke Senior; additionally, most characters who enter Arden as exiles (excepting Touchstone) become "split into two persons, and by doubling themselves" act out the difference "between what they have been and what they have now become".[113]

■ Playing a double role reflects the duality of the worlds represented by the characters themselves, and in speaking with two voices, they are able to exceed the limitations of each of those worlds.[114] □

While this doubleness – that which is written or spoken and that which is not – exists in all language, it appears in various forms in *As You Like It*.

Oliver's speech, Iser observes by quoting Bakhtin, reveals a "fusion of *two* utterances into one [Iser's italics]": Orlando speaks to Oliver in a dialogic way, one that reveals – without Orlando ever saying it – Oliver's "unsuspected implications".[115] There emerges everywhere in Orlando's speech habits a doubleness, consisting of what he says and then what negates what he says, "as alien meanings insinuate themselves" into his speech. Like all tyrants, Oliver, on the other hand, demonstrates a more "deliberately monologic" employment of words, and therefore speaks in an "illusory" manner that "eradicates the interconnection between what is said and what is implied".[116] However, because "the unspoken is always present alongside the spoken" or, to put it differently, the "latent" always emerges with the "manifest", Oliver never can "suppress" the "true intention" behind what he says. Viewed on a larger scale,

Oliver's limitations illustrate how in this play the "dialogue" of the "political world" always must contend with "the unspoken" all around it. No one escapes the "doubleness of language".[117]

The pastoral world to which the political exiles flee mirrors "what is concealed in" the political world, Iser argues. Arden "is a place of freedom", a "counter-image" of the court, and whatever "may be the realities" of the court's political world "in the pastoral they take on the character of a game":

> ■ Whatever the actual events, life in the Forest of Arden is put in brackets, thus providing an opportunity for the characters to bring out in the open what the code of the political world had denied them. The substance of the ensuing game is a repeat of the lives of the characters who, being released from the encroachments of reality, indulge in playing themselves. Turning themselves into actors allows them to stage their own other selves.[118] □

The characters also "rehearse their actions" in the forest as a test of reality in order to "revolutionize the political world to which they will eventually return". And because the game reveals what the political world conceals, it also suggests that "no single possibility can ever be equated with the world", as well as "represent[ing] the very conditions according to which a world may be assembled".[119]

Assuming "roles opposite to themselves", Celia and Rosalind enter the pastoral world. Rosalind, especially, "will not only speak with two voices" while there, but "will also use both registers of this double-voiced language simultaneously":[120]

> ■ Rosalind always speaks through Ganymede as if she were someone else, and Ganymede, when she speaks, can only elucidate what Rosalind is. If Rosalind is the hidden reality behind Ganymede, Ganymede is a sort of guinea-pig through whom Rosalind can adapt to reality.[121] □

When Ganymede challenges Orlando's claim that he loves Rosalind, for example, he expresses Rosalind's desire to "hear more about his love", while simultaneously he challenges "a love that clearly regards the Petrarchan code as an adequate means of describing itself". The double meaning informing all Rosalind's/Ganymede's words differs from that Orlando practised with Oliver at court, where Orlando's exposure of Oliver's intent always remained "hidden"; Rosalind's violation of Orlando's Petrarchan "code" illustrates instead that in Arden "the hidden may be expressed".[122]

Rosalind seeks to change in Orlando that which she already has changed in herself, to "bring forth" a "truer level" of devotion than Petrarchan cant and posturing.[123] Orlando slowly catches on, and "enacts the fulfilment of his passion" by leaving behind the Petrarchan codes of love. All this is accomplished by "dialogue":

■ This seems only natural as dialogue is *the* medium of drama, and is moreover governed by the basic rule of linguistic interaction: the interplay between the overt and the covert. This rule enables language to function and appears to be a property of language existing independently of the context and code which further condition it. [Iser's italics][124] □

In contrast to Rosalind's success with Orlando (and Orlando's success with himself), the two usurpers Oliver and Frederick fail, perhaps because their "use of language prevents them from controlling the implications of their words"; they fail, in other words, to see how the "unspoken can rebound on the spoken".[125] On the other hand, Rosalind's "play within a play" – her assumption of the character Ganymede – becomes a "complete carnivalization of all utterances", and "so accelerates the toppling movement that double meaning appears as a process of transformation". "Performance", and not "mimesis", then, proves the best means of "bridging difference".[126]

Iser also discusses both Jacques and Touchstone. Concerning Jacques, Iser argues that to him "double meaning simply reflects concealment" and, because of this, his only motivation throughout the play involves bringing other speakers' "overt behaviour[s] crashing down".[127] He never discovers that "the code he keeps unmasking would also apply to himself", and "does not recognize that the melancholy by which he defines himself is as much a definition by convention as that which he applies" to others.[128] Touchstone comes from both the "political and pastoral worlds", though at the same time he remains an "outsider to both".[129] As a fool, he never has to disguise or double himself, and never adopts the monologic language of the usurpers or the dialogic language of Orlando, Celia, and Rosalind. At such a remove from everyone, he "is in a position to bring out the many potential meanings inherent in a situation", which he does repeatedly throughout the play, and "reveals the extent to which meaning fulfils its pragmatic function by consolidating itself to the exclusion of other meanings".[130]

As the texts discussed in this chapter make clear, Frye's, Barber's, and, to a somewhat lesser extent, Kott's and Iser's departures from close reading – particularly as regards these authors' placements of Shakespeare's texts more firmly into his own as well as our cultures – transformed our understanding not simply of Shakespeare, but of literature itself. Their influence on examinations of *As You Like It*, moreover, can be felt in nearly every work of criticism discussed in the following chapters, and helps to expand these discussions into areas such as subjectivity, privacy, male–female relations, property ownership, and power, to name only a few.

CHAPTER FIVE

1978–Present: "All the World's a Stage": Cultural Studies

In 1987, critic Walter Cohen (b. 1949) commented that a "comprehensive survey of recent Shakespearean scholarship would undoubtedly reveal that the majority of publications do not engage in ideological critique".[1] Now, no scholar worth his or her salt would venture such a statement. Beginning in the 1970s a generation of scholars, informed by the political and social unrest of the 1960s and engaged in political activism, emerged. Educated in their respective graduate programmes by C.L. Barber, Northrop Frye, Jan Kott, and Raymond Williams (1921–88), among others, and thoroughly versed in cultural, political, linguistic, and psychoanalytic theorists such as Louis Althusser (1918–90), Mikhail Bakhtin, Jacques Derrida, Michel Foucault (1926–84), Sigmund Freud (1856–1939), Clifford Geertz (1926–2006), Antonio Gramsci (1891–1937), Jacques Lacan (1901–81), and Karl Marx (1818–83), these younger critics freighted their investigations of Shakespeare's corpus with examinations of contemporary historical documents, analyses of social phenomena, and considerations of political influences, and changed radically the way we read and understand the playwright, his epoch, and his theatre.

Cultural Studies critics, as well as those critics who identify with the closely related *feminism*, *Marxism*, and *New Historicism*, still follow many tenets of close reading laid out in New Criticism. Instead of pretending that the literary text stands removed from the world around it, and that it speaks for itself and the critic merely repeats and explains what it says, however, Cultural Studies critics view literary analysis as part of a larger social construction, one to which the critic contributes. In Cultural Studies, the meaning of Shakespeare resides not in the text, nor can it escape or transcend ideology. Art never rises above history or politics, nor do critiques of it: all interpretation reveals the historical moment in which the critic wrote it, and reflects political and/or social investitures. In their interrogations, Cultural Studies critics also often consciously and conspicuously reflect upon their own culture's present state.

Much of a Cultural Studies critic's task involves reuniting the text with its culture by exposing and interrogating the agendas propagated in the text by a culture's various interwoven power structures. Through close textual analysis, the critic brings to light the discourses employed by institutions exerting power over others, discourses that seek to sustain a hegemony, or dominance, over those outside or subordinate to these institutions.

The earliest Cultural Studies practitioners' revelations of textually embedded agendas initiated two major shifts in emphasis as concerns literary study. First, critics focused on the text's subjectivity, and with the understanding that authors only can relate, and readers only discern, what they think they know or believe or see, and much, if not all, of what we perceive is informed by ideology. Definitions of ideology abound, but one useful definition, provided by Jean E. Howard and Marion F. O'Connor, serves our purpose: ideology consists of the "inescapable network of beliefs and practices by which variously positioned and historically constituted subjects imagine their relationship to the real world and through which they render intelligible the world around them".[2]

Second, Cultural Studies scholars broadened the term "political" to include matters of class, gender, and race. And while these critics also exposed the hegemonic infrastructures and discourses of those they recognized as dominant in Shakespeare's culture, most of them heeded Gramsci's and Williams' insistence that culture consists of a complex interplay between opposition and conformity within any given class or group: interpretations that merely bifurcate one class or group's discourse from the dominant one never paint a satisfactory picture of the culture.

Part of their goal as critics, particularly if they hailed from the British Isles, involved the splintering and disabling of monolithic myths surrounding Shakespeare's value as national poet or stature as dispenser of truth. Other Cultural Studies critics revealed the ways in which factors specific to a historical moment helped articulate a historically specific "Shakespeare", to be considered in an increasingly professionalized critical debate, taught in the classroom, and produced in theatres. In Jonathan Bate's words, Shakespeare stopped being a playwright who lived from 1564 to 1616, and instead became "a body of work that is refashioned by each subsequent age in the image of itself".[3]

Cultural Studies critics, also, are more open to performances of Shakespeare's texts, for herein lie further opportunities to subvert the text's authority, to give voice to the marginalized and to make history relevant by connecting it to the present. These types of studies perceive the text as a site of ideological struggle, conducted through discourse, and explore how Shakespeare's theatre mediated and rehearsed in its audience's presence these struggles. Seen through a Cultural Studies lens, literature becomes history, a place where competing perceptions of the real, often referred to as "representations", are voiced, tested, and evaluated by the populace. Assuming that all discourse attempts to further a particular point of view, Cultural Studies critics also note that every circumstance, every condition in which a culture finds itself, will result in an ideological reaction. Additionally, Cultural Studies critics often disclose the many different incarnations of a Shakespeare text throughout succeeding points in history: how the text is manipulated by various ideologies, to both produce and influence specific meanings.

Judy Z. Kronenfeld

In "Social Rank and the Pastoral Ideals of *As You Like It*" (1978), Judy Z. Kronenfeld resists some prevailing accounts of the pastoral tradition, largely informed by Marxist theory, which claim that pastoral distorts class relations in favour of the privileged segments of culture. Kronenfeld contends that pastoral authors registered "tensions" not only between the high and the low (a term employed to great effect by Mikhail Bakhtin), but also between the "values" held by the "lowly and plain Christian" and those of "rank and privilege"; the pastoral shepherd:

> ■ so rich in its connotations, was ideally suited to deal with such tensions, because it could contain opposed meanings. As a figure of leisure, the shepherd may indeed be a gentleman ... Or, the shepherd's idleness may be of quite a different sort.[4] □

While Shakespeare explores in *As You Like It* the tensions between "the high and the low, the Christian and the courtly", and frequently "calls the pastoral idealizations of these relationships into question", his representations ultimately "revitalize and reaffirm the pastoral vision of charitable relations among humans".[5] Duke Senior, for example, maintains an "equality and kinship" in his forest court that "springs from Christian fellowship and charity", even though he often performs as if in a "pastoral masquerade". Nearly all forest dwellers, furthermore, share with the Duke "the best of Nature" while they simultaneously escape all "corruptions of Nurture".[6]

Shakespeare "revitalizes" the pastoral by redefining both aristocrat and shepherd and modifying their relations to one another within the pastoral tradition: Rosalind and Celia never "count on the convention of pastoral hospitality" once they enter the forest; instead, they offer money for property and services rendered. Corin, on the other hand, represents a "day-laborer" more than an idealized, leisurely shepherd: he must work for his keep, and Rosalind and Celia provide him with meaningful employment. These and other modifications result in the depiction of a society that is "happy again" because representatives of patronage and service "are restored": patrons such as Rosalind and Celia now enjoy "a livelihood to dispense" and servants such as Corin find "an appropriate object" for their "service".[7]

As the example of Corin suggests, Shakespeare shows particular concern for the way dispossessed figures transcend "the mocking stereotypes of the country".[8] Shakespeare subjects court figures, however, to sharper scrutiny. While Duke Senior manifests kindness and charity, his performance of contentment may reveal a tendency to "celebrate a moral tonic somewhat more than he enjoys the tonic himself".[9] In addition, Touchstone's dismissive attitude towards Corin, Audrey, and William "implies that the claims of some 'nobles' to status are based merely upon such words of condescension".[10] Pastoral concerns itself with "reformation, not revolution", Kronenfeld concludes, and in *As You Like It* Shakespeare "reaffirms" the "virtues" the high-born should possess.[11]

Elliott Krieger

Elliott Krieger devotes Chapter 4 of *A Marxist Study of Shakespeare's Comedies* (1979) to *As You Like It*, and notes that neither Orlando nor Rosalind show any awareness of, let alone concern for, the fact that they share the same misfortunes as many of Arden's lower-class residents. Instead, they respond to their situations in manners that "contradict the material conditions in which other classes live".[12] Orlando and Rosalind believe their problems – including impoverishment, humiliation, and displacement – lie not in Fortune's mutability, but in an "opposition between Fortune and Nature", where the changeableness inherent in Fortune confronts Nature's permanency. More specifically, Orlando and Rosalind assume that "Nature itself, through its supposedly stable and hierarchic structure, justifies and secures aristocratic autonomy and social station". Therefore, both Rosalind and Orlando choose to "reconcile the opposition by retreat to the unchanging forest, the condition of Nature", where "the gap between internal and external, or self and other, closes and disappears". The protagonists' "subjectivity" then "merges" with what they perceive as the "objective conditions of the environment".[13]

The young lovers' actions mirror a "tendency" often found in pastoral, where aristocratic characters (and their authors) "subordinate the out-of-doors to human needs and conditions", just as Duke Senior, Rosalind and Orlando "stylize Nature", an action that, ultimately, "negates Fortune" by creating for the protagonists the illusion "that they control the external, objective forces" of Fortune and Nature.[14] Through "stylistic abstractions" they "protect themselves against cognizance of their disruptive position in Nature", and also "against cognizance of their conflicts with a culture".[15] Krieger provides several examples. First, the Duke's passivity when pondering his exile helps him create an impression whereby his loss stems "from something beyond direct human control".[16] And when, through disguise as a man, Rosalind "translates her exile into a life" that appears "determined solely by her own will", she fashions an environment wherein she acts "as if she controls her own emotions and the emotions of others".[17]

Krieger also suggests that Rosalind's homoerotic flirtations with Orlando, made possible by the freedom her disguise provides, "serves a psychodynamic function" as concerns her dealings with the usurper Frederick. By manipulating the fluidity of fatherhood, father figures, and gender encountered throughout *As You Like It*, Rosalind defrays the persecution she otherwise would feel as a result of Frederick's harsh treatment. Rosalind's success returns to her as other characters, first Orlando but then Silvius, Phebe, and, through Orlando, Frederick, give her back her own "conditions and prerogatives"; by the play's end, Rosalind has "negated the stubbornness of Fortune and reconciled her individual fortune with her own intrinsic nature". Somewhat spuriously, Krieger argues that Rosalind then "gives up her disguise to gain a wider and more profound control" through "projecting her style and control" onto Hymen, "presumably" a "figure in disguise" and not actually the god of marriage, and thus "creates the illusion" that the marriages and subsequent harmony come from "heavenly intervention".[18]

The matrimonial revelries at the play's conclusion "do not resolve the specific social tensions and oppositions" that inform *As You Like It*, however, largely because the less privileged forest dwellers lack "access to the strategy of stylistic abstraction".[19] Unlike Rosalind and Celia, who can manipulate to their advantage their "fortunes" through their wealth, Arden denizens such as Corin remain dependent on the actions of others. In other words, Corin's situation is "fixed" while the courtiers' is "variable", not because of any "natural hierarchy" but because of money.[20] Characters who rely upon others' labour "rather than on the objective conditions of their environment for their survival attain the independence of complete subjectivity".[21] Rosalind, Orlando, and even Touchstone never "perceive the actual country community", and the play likewise limits its view to the "privileged perceptions of one class".[22] This "willed misperception of environment" as portrayed in *As You Like It* "represents a creative social act, the formation of an ideology", one that "certifies" and "helps determine those who have 'superior natures' and who 'by nature' should rule".[23] Some social classes should work, the play suggests, while others should enjoy the fruits of the workers' efforts.

Martha Ronk Lifson

Sigmund Freud surmised that one's beliefs – "illusions", as he called them – stem from one's wishes and desires, Martha Ronk Lifson reminds us in "Learning by Talking: Conversation in *As You Like It*" (1988). Building on Freud's hypothesis, as well as on discussions of verbal facility found in various early modern rhetorical treatises, Lifson explores how "deceit" helps "to work out the complexities of conversation and sexuality" between Rosalind and Orlando.[24] Lifson sees both Rosalind and Orlando as teachers; they teach each other by engaging in "lying as a form of necessary and earned illusion", and, while they test and agree upon mutual illusions whereby they can live together contentedly, Touchstone teaches "the audience on stage with him and the one in the theatre about the value of lying", particularly through his Act 5 set piece on "If":

> ■ Touchstone's presence in the play signals the need for ways of shifting perspective and even "lying" a bit (so long as one avoids the "lie direct") for the sake of greater social and human value: peace – to which can also be added harmony, marriage and the relationship of both to the larger cosmos.[25] □

Lifson divides her essay into two sections: the first examines deceit, or "clever supposing", as a means of "demonstrating new habits of mind for Rosalind and Orlando, habits specifically dependent on rhetoric", while in the second section Lifson focuses upon deceit as a means of "disguising and revealing their sexual desire for one another".[26]

Both Orlando and Rosalind begin the play in relative reticence, Lifson observes, and, through their encounter during the wrestling match, realize the necessity of conversation. While Orlando's poems hung on trees push Rosalind towards using language, Rosalind ultimately must "create language, including the language of love, without adult help".[27] As her interactions with Orlando intensify, she "lets Orlando into the secrets of how to manipulate and quibble with language". While both revise their "self-image", their stronger, as well as more mutually achieved, focus lies in re-interpreting "Rosalind". Together, and with Touchstone's assistance, they "learn to see themselves more broadly, more loosely, and more foolishly", as well as more flexibly: both "come to learn that loving a human being is more complex than loving a picture".[28]

As Rosalind and Orlando come to "love and trust one another", Lifson suggests, their bond strengthens through "their mutual creation of and participation in a highly artificial and fragile world of language, constructed with vast amounts of energy, both mental and sexual". Their "witty talk keeps passion contained", while simultaneously it "serves as a kind of erotic foreplay".[29] Rosalind can maintain her virtue while she explores and voices her own desires, including sexual ones; Orlando, moreover, by learning through Ganymede of Rosalind's – and all women's – desires, can understand Rosalind and marriage more clearly. Both Rosalind and Orlando suffer from fears of deceit and disloyalty, and Rosalind's playful threats and jokes help prepare them for the "more serious relationship of marriage".[30] Hymen's appearance "marks the transition from playful lying" to "responsible illusion, recognized and sanctioned by a larger public world", for the god "seems to stand for the illusion and poetry necessary to bless, effect, contain, and represent a natural truth".[31]

Grace Tiffany

In "'That Reason Wonder May Diminish': *As You Like It*, Androgyny, and the Theater Wars" (1994), Grace Tiffany (b. 1958) argues that *As You Like It* mocks "the methods and aims of Jonsonian satire" and "attacks" the dehumanizing Petrarchan "idealization of women" prevalent in late-Elizabethan poetry.[32] By informing his play with these polemics, Shakespeare deepens his involvement in the theatre wars going on between playwrights Ben Jonson, Thomas Dekker (c. 1572–1632), and John Marston (1576–1634) during the late 1590s.

These theatre wars, or *poetomachia*, Tiffany believes, involved differing theories of comedy: satire, as advocated by Jonson and exemplified in his *Every Man Out of His Humour* (1599), and "mythic comedy", as endorsed by Shakespeare and represented in *As You Like It*. Tiffany describes Jonsonian satire as a splenetic, "scholarly" social criticism which leans towards misogyny in its "disdain for feminine charm".[33] This type of satire aims to educate audiences intellectually and morally, but also isolates the artist from his audience, both male and female, in its rationality and invective.

According to Tiffany, Jonsonian satire somewhat paradoxically finds its roots in the "frustrated erotic longing" frequently voiced by characters in Ovid's *Metamorphoses*. The satirist's "angry rhetoric", in other words, originates in the "romantic poet's self-obsessed, anti-relational", and often cynical "discourse".[34] Throughout *As You Like It*, Shakespeare voices not only his opposition to Jonson's brand of satire, but to Ovidean and Petrarchan expressions of desire.

Tiffany argues that, in *As You Like It*, Shakespeare instead encourages a "fundamentally *ir*rational erotic sensibility that connects audience members [and] should serve as a communal basis of judgment [Tiffany's italics]". Rosalind in particular invites other characters and her audience "to embrace erotic relationship as the antidote for human suffering". She "represents and validates the Shakespearean mythic comic method and specifically rejects the detached, misogynistic, and isolating satiric approach" underwritten by Jonson.[35] Rosalind resists "masculine attempts to define her or her gender". Doing so, she "undermines both the Ovidean/Petrarchan and satiric claims for the isolated male",[36] exemplified on occasion by Orlando but much more thoroughly and darkly by Jacques – a "Jonsonian character tellingly out of place in Arden".[37] In short, Rosalind:

■ vanquishes the satirical Jacques and repudiates the Ovidean/Petrarchan inclination that has frozen *As You Like It*'s lovers in postures of frustrated longing and replaces it with dialogic engagement.[38] □

Rosalind's efforts with all the play's lovers "allow sexual connection in marriage to occur". Posing as Ganymede, she assumes the role of "curative androgynous principle" and enacts the "symbolic joining of male and female opposites" in marriage, which eradicates "self-obsessed longing". In opposition to Jonson's "reformation of men and manners", then, Shakespeare through Rosalind transforms both "male and female psyches".[39] Through her interactions with Orlando, Silvius, and Phebe, Shakespeare also illustrates how a "ridiculous idealization of the beloved" only "marginalizes the lover" by trapping him/her "in a condition of separateness and discontent".[40]

Rosalind immerses Orlando, Tiffany observes, in a "witty dialogue that cynically recapitulates the tropes of Ovidean/Petrarchan convention in order to highlight their fictionality".[41] He is "saved" from Jacques' fate "through his willingness to be absorbed by a mythic paradox: to forsake his self-constructed 'Rosalinda' and engage with the real girl".[42] Tiffany concludes by paralleling Shakespeare's rejection of the Ovidean/Petrarchan idealization of women with Elizabeth I's appropriations of the same symbols and tropes.

Andrew Barnaby

Andrew Barnaby accomplishes something rather daring in "The Political Conscious of Shakespeare's *As You Like It*" (1996): as would most critics writing on Shakespeare in the mid-1990s, Barnaby notes *As You Like It*'s engagement in late-Elizabethan "crises points", such as:

> ■ the transformation of older patterns of communal organization under the pressures of new forms of social mobility, an emergent market economy, and the paradoxically concomitant stratification of class relations; the more specific problems of conflict over land-use rights, the enclosure of common land and its attendant violence, poverty and vagrancy.[43] □

He questions, however, New Historicism's "incoherent" and "reductive"[44] understandings of Shakespeare and his culture, as well as its inability "to register the possibility of the presence of dissenting voices within the dominant culture".[45]

Barnaby urges readers to see Shakespeare's treatment of the issues listed above (as well as others) as the playwright's own "interpretive response to the perceived nature of" these issues. Revisiting various tenets of close reading, including attention to an author's conscious creation of, as well as his intention as concerns, a text, Barnaby investigates how Shakespeare's play "at once signifies historical realities and constitutes its own reality, that it is both constantive [*sic* – this seems to be a misprint for "constative"] and performative".[46]

Barnaby outlines the play's exploration of issues involving social standing, "the vexed relation between aristocratic culture and the broader workings of political society", as well as the "representational and interpretive practices by which fictional accounts serve as mediatory sites of informed public concern over contemporary affairs".[47] He also explains how *As You Like It* situates these issues in the domestic sphere. These topics "are raised as part of an exploration of the customary bonds between the upper and lower orders", and the playwright "interlaces" an interrogation of "the nature and meaning of aristocratic conduct toward social inferiors" with this exploration. Orlando feels he has lost his status as an aristocrat, for example, because his brother Oliver, in a perversion of "the very link between nature and human social order – the family – " casts him aside to live as do the peasants on his inherited estate.[48]

In developing Orlando's relationship with Oliver, Shakespeare "transforms" the Prodigal Son story to focus on more "political" matters: primogeniture, familial obligation, and master–servant relationships.[49] He casts Oliver as the Prodigal Son, a man who inherits all wealth with no right to it other than his first-born status. Orlando represents the dutiful son, left to wonder why he suffers at the hands of his brother. Oliver's contempt for his younger brother serves as the means by which Shakespeare performs his culture's "political relations not just between elder and younger sons" but "between masters and servants, landed and landless, gentle and base". It quickly becomes obvious that Shakespeare implicates the aristocracy as the social segment that "fails to fulfill the obligations of status and custom, and especially to maintain cultural stability by sustaining the moral (and political) value that accrues to social place".[50]

Shakespeare expresses a "moral commentary", Barnaby asserts, throughout *As You Like It*, one that reminds the privileged classes of their origins and advocates an inclusiveness among all social classes:

> ■ if gentility is as much a social construct as it is a privileged condition of birth, its maintenance requires that it be continually reconstructed through meritorious signs, and these signs are to be made legible in the virtuous conduct shown toward those whose livelihood depends on how the "gentle" fulfill the obligations of their class.[51] □

Barnaby concludes with a discussion of how Shakespeare's particular iteration of the pastoral "is less concerned with celebrating nobles as virtuous than in reexamining the precise nature of aristocratic virtue".[52]

Louise Schleiner

The reader should take heed that Louise Schleiner (1943–2000), in "Voice, Ideology, and Gendered Subjects: The Case of *As You Like It* and *Two Gentlemen*" (1999), spends only a modicum of time in discussion of *As You Like It*; her essay nonetheless proves rewarding in that it examines the possibilities as to how "members of an Elizabethan audience, male and female" spoke of and perceived "themselves as subjects".[53] Schleiner focuses on Orlando's valorous conveyance of Adam into Duke Senior's forest court in 2.7, and determines that this scene illustrates "a fundamental ideological tension" occurring, throughout Shakespeare's era:

> ■ between the reconstruing of values by feminized, treacherous mercantilism and a narrative program of neo-feudal duty – a directive from what can be called the transcendent sender from within the social text, here the God of passionately faithful servants and masters.[54] □

In other words, the "duologues" between Adam and Orlando reveal not only Adam's loyal and humble service to Orlando and his family, but, more significantly, Orlando's valorized statuses as aristocrat and eligible husband.

Schleiner employs the example of Adam and Orlando in her mapping out of "our own century's development of a series of interlinked concepts about language, culture, psyche, and subjectivity". Engaging several sociolinguistic, political, and economic theorists, Schleiner argues that, on Shakespeare's stage, "ideological subject formation and functioning" frequently involved "servants performing the ways of their masters or mistresses".[55] In *As You Like It*, Shakespeare creates a "new ideologeme"[56] whereby Orlando's valour stems not so much from his "good qualities", but because "his good servant speaks" of his goodness.[57]

Peter Milward

In his "Religion in Arden" (2001), Peter Milward (1925–2017) encourages readers to view *As You Like It* as an anomaly among Shakespeare's dramas: in the playwright's choice of setting, as well as the fact that "in the religion of Arden we may discern something of Shakespeare's own allegiance among the three religions recognized in his own time", namely Catholicism, Protestantism, and Puritanism.[58] Milward suggests that Shakespeare's family, both father John Shakespeare (c. 1531–1601) and mother Mary Arden (c. 1537–1608), practised Catholicism with an increasing fervour as they grew older. Throughout *As You Like It*, readers should note Shakespeare's "loyalty" to his family and to several Warwickshire and Lancashire Catholics who knew and assisted him throughout his youth, as well as a palatable Catholic "resolve" and a "nostalgia for the good old days" before Henry VIII's Reformation.[59]

Milward creates several parallels between characters in the play and the Ardens, Shakespeares, and prominent figures associated with them. He begins with Edward Arden (c. 1542–83) of Park Hall, implicated in the Somerville Plot of 1583 and subsequently stripped of his property, and the exiled Duke Senior, who also suffers the loss of his land. Milward then connects the three clergymen in the play – the old uncle Rosalind describes to Orlando as her mentor, the religious recluse Jacques de Boys mentions as having converted the usurping Frederick (Milward also suggests that these two may be the same man), and Sir Oliver Martext – with John Frith, the parson who married Shakespeare and Anne Hathaway (1556–1623).

Later in the essay, Milward draws comparisons between Duke Senior and William Allen (1532–94), leader of the English College at Douai, who attracted many young Catholic men, including Shakespeare's neighbour Robert Debdale (1556–86), to him. While back in Lancashire, Allen received financial support from an associate of the Jesuit Edmund Campion (1540–81), Thomas Hoghton (1540–89), whose brother Alexander Hoghton (1519–81) may have accommodated the young Shakespeare as a schoolmaster in Lea Hall; Hoghton mentioned a "William Shakeshafte" in his will, and commended him to Sir Thomas Hesketh (1547/48–1605), a recusant neighbour of Hoghton's. Milward also conjectures that Shakespeare may have met Campion when he taught, and perhaps received dramatic training from him.

Nathaniel Strout

As do increasing numbers of Shakespeare critics, Nathaniel Strout makes clear in *"As You Like It, Rosalynde, and Mutuality"* (2001) that not all assessments of the "foundational conventions" of the playwright's work need to express a "deep skepticism about" these conventions' "status or value". Instead, "to note the conventional aspects of a human activity may merely be to record its very nature". Strout sees in an audience's approval of a company's theatrical performance the same acceptance of "conventions" and sharing of "experiences" as those that lead to lovers becoming mutually attracted and eventually marrying. *As You Like It*, as an example:

> ■ establishes connections between past mutual interactions and future mutual outcomes: Rosalind and Orlando's liking for each other leads to their becoming man and wife; our liking for the play and its players leads to our applause at the conclusion of the performance.[60] □

Strout notes the frequent use of narrative in *As You Like It*, and states that Shakespeare's employment of it involves connecting "the past to the future". Narrative helps "bring the past into the present so that characters (and audiences) can respond to it".[61] Throughout the play, characters continually tell stories, and this helps "establish and reinforce the importance of mutuality".[62]

Shakespeare distances his play from its source, Thomas Lodge's *Rosalynde*, in two significant fashions, Strout suggests, and relies on narrative to create the distance: Lodge's "understanding of social relations" and his "presentation of how people explain the ways they act". Throughout *Rosalynde*, Lodge privileges "male concerns" over female ones to the point where female concerns disappear. He also attributes nearly every relational development to certain "'infallible precepts' that are said to determine our actions".[63]

In Shakespeare's text, conversely, the love established "between men and women is grounded in mutual, not just masculine, behavior, and what has happened between people helps make possible what will happen". Strout contrasts the "rigidity of human behavior"[64] found throughout Lodge's work with the autonomy and freedom of movement of Shakespeare's characters. Shakespeare even provides Jacques as a contrast to the play's other characters: in much the same fashion as the characters and narrative in *Rosalynde*, Jacques speaks almost exclusively to – and about – the other male characters, particularly during the wedding ceremony. Silvius, too, seems stuck on the masculine, and his narrative of his predicament with Phebe "defines unreciprocated love, not a mutual relationship".[65] Shakespeare's "constant blurring of a single, masculine point of view"[66] also implicates Orlando, whose lines, in Strout's tally, contain the "highest frequency of the personal pronouns *I*, *me*, and *my*" of any character. Like Jacques and Silvius, Orlando "turns everything toward himself" until he sees Celia and Oliver fall in love so quickly and completely.[67]

Strout understands Rosalind's inability to sway Orlando entirely away from his self-involvement as her recognition of the "uncertainty of ever knowing the full truth about what is going on in the 'unexpressed interior' within another person's 'theatricalized exterior'". Strout attributes Rosalind's trepidation to the "unequal" nature of mutuality ever present in Shakespeare's "hierarchical world". Despite her brilliant wit and unmatched intelligence, Rosalind always must "acknowledge the authority of Orlando for the relationship to be mutual",[68] even if their marriage is a mutual choice. The "As You Like It" that Shakespeare emphasizes throughout the play, then, involves not a cynical acquiescence to his audience's rather pedestrian tastes; instead, it "expresses the freedom we have to choose whether we like or do not like a play or a person".[69]

Linda Woodbridge

In recent years, critics have "heaped scorn upon the bucolic realm of pastoralism",[70] Linda Woodbridge (b. 1945) argues in "Country Matters: *As You Like It* and the Pastoral-Bashing Impulse" (2004). Woodbridge cites New Historicists such as Louis Adrian Montrose (see discussion of Montrose in Chapter 6), who deem pastoral writers agents of legitimizing and sustaining a governing structure's hegemony.[71] Even those authors who escape direct charges of compliant agency suffer from accusations that they fail to portray rural life realistically.[72]

Woodbridge offers a strikingly different perspective, and declares that pastoral writers frequently attacked "specific abuses of power" and challenged "the power ethic itself".[73] Pastoral writers build their case against capitalism and "worldly values" by creating characters who remove themselves from morally diminished spheres such as the court and deny themselves the power and material comforts found only in the court. In short, these characters "gain moral authority through asceticism".[74] We should re-conceive pastoral, then, as the "wealth-eschewing genre", one opposed "to the new capitalism".[75]

Essentially, in Woodbridge's view, pastoral challenges the "assumption that power, public life, hard work, and success are everything". *As You Like It*, for example, "represents the world of power in Frederick's court as literally repulsive":[76] Shakespeare depicts it as "paranoid, twitchy, a world of hasty political decisions, its frenetic pace neurotic, born of the knowledge that its power is illegitimate".[77] In this court, Frederick and Oliver "project onto powerless siblings their own murderous impulses" and treat loyal servants such as Adam like animals.[78]

In contrast, the pastoral world of Arden features Duke Senior, who "listens attentively to people, replacing Frederick's banishments and repulsions with hospitable welcomes". His forest realm even lifts animals "to the human level", which differs radically from the animalization Adam and Orlando undergo at court.[79] As the play moves towards marriage and reconciliation, politics becomes "entirely replaced by love. Interest is deflected from public to private", and the pursuit of power lessens in importance as Arden pushes it "out of sight". The "exclusionary circle" maintained by Frederick gets replaced by an "inclusionary" movement towards "living happily ever after in a world of love".[80]

Throughout her argument, Woodbridge draws parallels between Duke Frederick's troubled court and our own world, and through these parallels explains why contemporary critics dismiss pastoral so categorically. As in Frederick's proto-capitalistic dukedom, our "workaholic age suffers entrenched resistance to relaxation".[81] We also prefer "action over contemplation", and valorize "public over private life":

> ■ Such devaluing of private life has gender implications: the domestic sphere has long been constructed as female and great ideological work has gone into confining women to the home.[82] □

Chris Fitter

In "Reading Orlando Historically: Vagrancy, Forest, and Vestry Values in Shakespeare's *As You Like It*" (2010), Chris Fitter describes Shakespeare's play as a "protest play", especially in terms of its "topicality" and its "constructed performance latencies". The play foregrounds "anti-Arcadian perspectives" and "political ills", and challenges "harsh contemporary attitudes" towards the poor.[83] More specifically, the play responds to a contemporary legislative "demonization of vagrancy" and the "intensification" of what Fitter calls "vestry values" developed and embraced by prominent local householders.[84]

As do Richard Wilson (see Chapter 6) and others, Fitter notes the myriad carnivalesque qualities informing *As You Like It*, and links these features to a popular reaction against "a now extraordinarily tight embrace between central authority and local elites". Shakespeare's stage participates in this reaction, and, through the implementation of certain "political performance secrets", seeks to "outflank mounting censorship pressures" and "activate on the stage transformative dimensions of meaning preserved invisible on the page".[85]

Fitter outlines *As You Like It*'s:

■ response to a nationwide *institutional* development: the authoritarian alliance of the state church with divisive parish oligarchies – a union legislatively empowered, distinctively repressive, and expressed above all in an *intensifying campaign to exalt local hegemonies by extirpating folk revels*. [Fitter's italics][86] □

This tightening of authority and increased censorship took place just prior to the play's composition in 1598 or 1599, and included a "hardening prosecutorial climate" towards underemployed labourers.[87] Fitter identifies local churchwardens as "the crucial arbiter of fluctuating social status in the parish". Under the new statutes, the local churchwarden simultaneously could "report and prosecute the culture of revelry", and served as overseer of the poor. The result of these changes involved, first, a circumstance where poor relief became a "means of control" over the poor,[88] and, ultimately, "a clash of cultures" that permeated performances on the stage.[89]

Critics frequently discuss Orlando's overall unsuitability as companion to Rosalind, but Fitter takes an even darker view of him. To Fitter, Orlando stands "at odds with audience values" and reveals "correspondingly abusive" attitudes towards the lower social strata. "Most tellingly of all", Orlando "is shrill with self-pity because he is not rich enough". His 1,000 crowns inheritance (£250), however, according to Fitter, is equivalent to £125,000 in 1599 money.[90]

Beginning with his brother's treatment of him in the first scene, Fitter argues, Orlando, and "gentlemanly self-pity, are being set up by Shakespeare for what we might call carnival targeting".[91] In continuing examples "of brilliantly scripted stage ambiguity", Shakespeare creates scenes where Oliver and then Rosalind can initiate "a deixis that renders Orlando the butt of audience mockery". His "ideological posture, defined through his loud class superciliousness, is being punished as misfit", in other words, and he remains "apparently unaware of the spectators'" existence or negative reaction to him.[92]

At the same time, however, in Orlando, a "thwarted pretension to class superiority becomes paradoxically articulated through a discourse that smacks of underclass rebellion", Fitter claims. Orlando, then, stands "on familiar ground for many in the audience when he complains" of his brother's treatment of him.[93] And yet, while Orlando may voice the "language of underclass resentment" and embody "the exciting spirit of active resistance", he nonetheless "will prove for nearly the length of the drama the dupe and doting puppy of overmastering Rosalind". His "sneering hubris" must be "humbled",[94] and his experiences connote a *"purgatorial"*[95] ambiance, so that he and his "ambiguous class position" finally become "incorporable into the playhouse's community of revelers".[96]

Adam, too, comes under scrutiny. His lifelong practice of thrift – he has 500 crowns, or £62,500 – problematizes his desire to remain in Orlando's service: "The moment must surely have been close to incomprehensible to many of the humbler spectators", because servants typically suffered horrible treatments from their masters: "Adam's gesture looks less like Christian generosity than potentially suicidal recklessness, coupled with bizarre preference for abasement over personal freedom".[97] Adam's preachy autobiography, and warnings against "sexual and alcoholic license", furthermore, not only assail "youth culture" but echo "the refrain of local elites and parish officers". Fitter doubts that Shakespeare's audience would have welcomed such a posture.

Both Adam and Orlando "embrace in a tender duet of vestry values: unconquerable servility in a joyless work ethic kneels to hierarchism's calm deserving of feeless underlying duty". An audience should perceive them as "oligarchy's newlyweds, melting into a marriage made in the very heaven of early capitalist accumulation".[98]

Fitter also sees in *As You Like It*'s "opposition to state authoritarianism" a "humane counter-valuation of the condition of vagrancy". Again, Shakespeare employs Orlando as the example: he is "capable of work yet without it – and precisely the category of vagabond against whom Elizabeth had issued a proclamation in 1598" and again in 1600.[99] Shakespeare's "treatment of rural refugees and the dispossessed", furthermore, constitutes a "politically charged departure from both political and literary norms". Most surviving Elizabethan "patrician attitudes consisted in a well-nigh pathological hatred of the roaming and propertyless". The parliament of 1597–98, for instance, considered 15 bills to help the poor and vagrants, but "so incorrigible proved gentry self-interest that parliament diluted the bill to suppress enclosures".[100]

Fitter focuses on 2.5–2.7, where a feast is set out for Duke Senior but his men leave it to find him. When reassembled, the courtiers are confronted by Orlando, wielding a weapon: "First, the spectacle of a laden board juxtaposed to terminal starvation must have formed a graphic, visually dominant tableau of contemporary social injustice." While the setting accentuates Orlando's "alienatingly censorious and moralistic" attitude towards those he initially views as uneducated and unpropertied forest dwellers,[101] it also "grants the audience delicious 'punishment'" of such a view, because "Christian duty and hospitality" undergird Duke Senior's welcome, and "his calm and remarkable mercy works as a humanitarian rebuke to the hardened heart of Elizabethan officialdom".[102]

"Unaccommodated Orlando", then, who bumbles upon the Duke and his company, now must redefine "in desperate hunger what it means to be a gentleman". Starvation and "outcast status" now "decimate" Orlando's "brusque class haughtiness". Once these scenes end, furthermore, "Puritanical Adam disappears from sight, and Orlando ceases to be a disapproving, anti-carnival figure".[103] According to Fitter, the "values" Rosalind and Celia espouse overpower those of Orlando and inform those of *As You Like It*. While the two cousins inhabit the play as "bearers of carnival values", the forest can be seen to "signify the Globe and its creatures":[104]

■ The identification of the new theater with merry greenwood refuge thus underscores its chosen political identity: a realm of countercultural freedom and flourishing satire, of antiauthoritarian populism.[105] □

Shakespeare, moreover "can be seen to infiltrate subtexts of subversion through a stagecraft of stealth", as the play "celebrates the impunity enjoyed in the liberty of Bankside, and consolidates its constituency, to sure commercial advantage, through the potent spell of deictic revel".[106]

As its name denotes, Cultural Studies brings to the fore matters of social practice and tradition, justice and fairness, gender and sexuality, and subjectivity and identity; and as the essays included herein illustrate, *As You Like It* accommodates all these issues and more. The play is so rich, in fact, that, as critics begin to explore more specific areas of interest and to create new terms to define their interests, including New Historicism, Gender Studies, and Queer Theory, *As You Like It* continues to substantiate these critics' claims with its complex relationships and freighted settings. The following chapters provide several prominent examples of these more closely focused interests and claims.

CHAPTER SIX

1980–Present: "To Mutiny Against this Servitude": New Historicism

One of the most influential literary theories to arise in the aftermath of Cultural Studies, *New Historicism* stands unique in that its first proponents focused their studies primarily on Shakespeare and early modern literature. Stephen Greenblatt (b. 1943), whose *Renaissance Self-Fashioning* (1980) and *Shakespearean Negotiations* (1988) changed the way our culture reads and discusses early modern texts, especially Shakespeare, coined the term "New Historicism". Cultural Materialism, an English counterpart, of sorts, to New Historicism, approaches the text somewhat differently.

As did Cultural Studies before it, New Historicism confutes New Criticism's insistence that a literary work is isolated from its time and historical circumstances; instead, a New Historicist urges the reader to perceive the text as a product of the culture surrounding its composition. More precisely, New Historicists understand the text as simultaneously produced by its culture and as an influence upon it; the text, in other words, constantly refers to, and comments upon, its culture while the culture always responds to it. A New Historicist's task, then, involves the recognition and explanation of the several dialectics occurring between the text and social process.

While many critics from the 1920s until the 1960s, including those discussed in Chapters 3 and 4, sought and found links between a literary work and its historical and political contexts, New Historicism distinguishes itself in its adoption of tenets associated with several pre-existing literary theories: Cultural Studies, feminism, Marxism, psychoanalysis, structuralism and deconstruction, among others. The theories and observations of Michel Foucault and Roland Barthes, as well as anthropologist Clifford Geertz, cultural critic Walter Benjamin (1892–1940), and semiotician Mikhail Bakhtin, especially as concerns power, governance, hierarchy, transgression, repression, and subjectivity, appeal to the New Historicists.

As do these theorists, New Historicists also tend towards a broader conception of history, and resist seeing it as positivist, a systematic progression towards the here and now. Assuming a more sociological and anthropological purview, New Historicist literary analysis focuses on the text as an "artifact", an object imbued and informed by cultural, political, religious, and folkloric realities. New Historicists also recognize that events such as the performance, publication, or censoring of a text seldom stem from one cause or circumstance. Therefore, when a critic discusses that particular text, s/he always must remain "conscious" of his/her discussion's "status as interpretation", as Stephen Greenblatt phrases it in his Introduction to *Renaissance Self-Fashioning*.[1] There is no truth in history, nor in interpretation, in other words.

Greenblatt and most New Historicists after him embraced the contention of C.L. Barber (among others) that festive comedy – or, to employ a term frequently used by the New Historicists, "transgression" – flourishes only temporarily in a literary work. Once expressed, New Historicists argue, this written or staged act of defiance almost always ends up diminished and contained. The regime, or dominant power structure, then, emerges as monolithic in many New Historicist writings on Shakespeare and other texts.

Even while New Historicists acknowledge how the regime ultimately and consistently maintains a hegemony over the transgressive voices and forces of the "Other", they nonetheless pay significant attention to these disenfranchised, oppressed, and marginalized members of a given culture. As do the proponents of Cultural Studies, moreover, New Historicists draw parallels between the past and present, and concede "the impossibility of fully reconstructing and reentering" a past culture.[2] Because of this impossibility, the questions New Historicists ask of an earlier culture frequently embody the same questions they ask of their own.

Stephen Greenblatt

While Stephen Greenblatt devotes the bulk of Chapter 3 of his *Shakespearean Negotiations*, "Friction and Fiction", to *Twelfth Night*, his contention that Shakespeare "discovered how to use the erotic power that the theater could appropriate, how to generate plots that would not block or ignore this power but draw it out, develop it", and "return it with interest" to his audience, sheds valuable light on one's reading of *As You Like It*.[3]

Greenblatt argues that "all memorable representation of individuality in Shakespeare" is "marked by the prodigious", including boys' playing of women's parts on his stage.[4] "Theatrical representation of individuality" during the early modern era, he remarks:

> ■ is in effect modeled on what the culture thought occurred during sexual foreplay and intercourse: erotic chafing is the central means by which characters in plays like ... *As You Like It* ... realize their identities and form loving unions.[5] □

Greenblatt isolates "verbal wit" and, more specifically, "dallying with words" as "the principle Shakespearean representation" of this chafing. Shakespeare's plots "go out of their way to create not only obstacles in the lovers' path but occasions for friction between them".[6]

When Rosalind meets Orlando in the forest, for example, she "initiates an occasion for playful tension between them", Greenblatt observes. Instead of viewing Rosalind's interactions with Orlando as her testing of his love or his readiness for marriage, Greenblatt proffers that her "chafing functions rather as a symbolic enactment of the lovers' mutual desires and a witty experimental fashioning of Rosalind's identity".[7]

Greenblatt also suggests that Rosalind's "independence, her sharply etched individuality" while she inhabits the forest "will vanish, along with the playful chafing, when the play is done". Rosalind's "improvisational self-fashioning" gives way, once her union with Orlando is assured, to a "self-effacement and reabsorption in the community", which Greenblatt describes as a sure "sign of a social system that marks out singularity, particularly in women, as prodigious".[8]

Throughout "Fiction and Friction" Greenblatt develops and explains his belief that "the transformation of gender identity figures the emergence of an individual out of a twinned sexual nature". Greenblatt gathers texts contemporary to Shakespeare that suggest the human body is a "natural transvestite", hermaphroditic in its constitution and functions, and that any expressions of individual gender – even those as ebullient as Rosalind's – never involve "the absolute exclusion of the other" gender, and "the presence of both genders remains evident through adolescence".[9]

Louis Adrian Montrose

An important and oft-cited New Historicist reading of this play, Louis Adrian Montrose's "'The Place of a Brother' in *As You Like It*: Social Process and Comic Form" (1981) employs anthropological, feminist, Marxist, and psychoanalytic theories to consider and historicize the compromised state in which Rosalind finds herself at the play's close. According to Montrose, Rosalind's marriage to Orlando, along with the "atonement" between the play's perpetrators and victims that precedes it, incorporate this bride and groom "within a process that reunites man with man".[10] Orlando's union with Rosalind strengthens this young man's bonds to his older brother Oliver and also to Duke Senior, "who becomes his patron"[11] while it diminishes Rosalind's autonomy:

> ■ The comedy establishes *brotherhood* as an ideal of social as well as sibling male relationships; at the same time, it reaffirms a positive, nurturing image of *fatherhood*. And because family and society are a synecdoche, the comedy

can also work to mediate the ideological contradiction between spiritual fraternity and political patriarchy, between social communion and social hierarchy. [Montrose's italics][12] ▢

At this juncture in the play's critical history, nearly every commentator failed to see, or ignored, how Rosalind's marriage to Orlando weakened "her ties to her natural father" and to Celia, "who has been closer to her than a sister".[13]

Montrose first examines the "precise comic teleology" Shakespeare adopts throughout his comedies, and notes how they often "turn upon the points of transition in the life cycle – birth, puberty, marriage, death – where discontinuities arise and where adjustments are necessary to basic interrelationships in the family and in society".[14] In *As You Like It* more specifically, Montrose observes not only Orlando's gradual adjustment "from an impoverished and powerless adolescence" to an individual on the "threshold of manhood and marriage, wealth and title", but also the reconciliations between "elder and younger brothers, father and child, man and woman, lord and subject, master and servant"[15] that assist in his adjustment.

One social practice in particular spurs discontinuity in *As You Like It* to a degree that threatens nearly every interpersonal relationship within it: primogeniture, or the handing down of property and wealth to the eldest son, which Montrose claims England practised "more widely and rigorously" than anywhere else.[16] Montrose describes how the efforts of early modern England's gentle class to "aggrandize and perpetuate their estates led them to a ruthless application of primogeniture", and how its effects on the younger sons and daughters included "downward social mobility and relative impoverishment, inability to marry or late marriage, and fewer children".[17]

In *As You Like It*, Montrose contends, Shakespeare's "opening strategy" involves immersion of characters and audience in the consequences of this practice. By doing so, the playwright sets the "process of comedy" against the "seemingly inevitable prospect of social degradation" that Orlando's confrontation with his brother suggests.[18] More significantly to a New Historicist, perhaps, such a strategy also reveals Shakespeare's acknowledgement of the "high proportion of gentleborn younger sons" attending the play, as well as those "baseborn youths who were themselves socially subordinate apprentices and servants" who stood in the theatre alongside them. The contingent "personal projections" and "powerful feelings" Shakespeare registers in the play illustrate a New Historicist's conviction that Shakespeare's theatre continually rehearses – places before its audience representations of – its culture.[19] Montrose pushes his point further when he describes how Shakespeare altered his main source, Thomas Lodge's *Rosalynde*, in order to "intensify the differences between the eldest son and his siblings, and to identify the sibling conflict with the major division in the Elizabethan social fabric".[20]

Primogeniture "complicates" not just "sibling and socio-economic relationships": generational relationships and one's subjectivity, or the circumstances by which one acquires and experiences a consciousness of self, also undergo challenges and disruptions. *As You Like It* examines the "difficulty or impossibility of establishing or authenticating a self in a rigorously hierarchical and patriarchal society", Montrose posits: as Oliver "perpetuates Orlando's subordination within the patriarchal order" and assumes a role as both his brother and father, he also "usurps Orlando's selfhood" and initiates "an implied resentment" on Orlando's part towards his deceased father.[21] And as Oliver's actions blur fraternal and generational distinctions, the "conflict of elder and younger brothers also projects an oedipal struggle between father and son".[22]

After he identifies Orlando as a youth – "physically mature and powerful, but socially infantilized and weak"[23] – Montrose then describes how during Shakespeare's time youth (as much as half of early modern England's population) typically experienced radical "shifts of residence, activity, sexual feeling, and patriarchal authority", the same shifts Orlando and others undergo during the play's "triadic romance pattern of exile and return".[24] Shakespeare parallels their experiences and transformations in Arden, in other words, with that "dangerous period of the Elizabethan life cycle that is betwixt and between physical puberty and social puberty".[25]

While the Forest of Arden never eliminates the "hierarchy and deference" associated with patriarchy, the presence in it of Orlando, Rosalind, and nearly all visitors offers them a "relaxed" atmosphere where their transformations may take place.[26] As does Orlando, Frederick finds a "loving father"[27] here, and Oliver reconciles with Orlando in a "friendship freed from the material conflicts of kinship".[28] For Montrose, these fictive brotherly reaffirmations provide for the audience the illusion of painlessness in primogeniture. Shakespeare leaves no male character in defeat or defamation; instead, "the two families and two generations of men are doubly and symmetrically bound".[29]

An entirely different outcome awaits Rosalind, however. In the forest, Rosalind "wittily asserts her independence", and with Touchstone discovers that romantic communication "revolves around the issue of mastery in the shifting social relationship between the sexes".[30] In an echo of C.L. Barber, Montrose asserts that Rosalind's control over Orlando and others manifests only a "compensatory 'holiday humor,' a temporary inversionary rite of misrule":

■ Rosalind-as-Ganymede and Ganymede-as-Rosalind – the woman out of place – exerts an informal organizing and controlling power over affairs in the forest. But this power lapses when she relinquishes her male disguise and formally acknowledges her normal status as daughter and wife.[31] □

The "social institution at the heart of comedy", as Montrose calls marriage, not only "serves to ease or eliminate fraternal strife" but also "as a defense against the threat men feel from women".³² And in *As You Like It*, marriage also serves as the space where primogeniture "is reaffirmed in public and private domains", and where theatre assists in the containment of social tension while it simultaneously advocates social advancement.³³

Richard Wilson

Hailing from the English Midlands, Shakespeare "dramatized agrarian conflict" in *As You Like It*, claims Richard Wilson (b. 1950) in "Like the Old Robin Hood: *As You Like It* and the Enclosure Riots" (1992). More specifically, Wilson believes that "it is within the context of the subsistence crisis of the 1590s" that the play's "violent plot and implausibly romantic ending have their material meaning". No other of Shakespeare's plays "transmits more urgently the imminence of the social breakdown threatened by the conjuncture of famine and enclosure".³⁴

In typically New Historicist fashion, Wilson opens his essay with an account of Elizabeth I's 1592 progress to the West Midlands; he describes as well several rural uprisings occurring contemporaneously to 1599, the year Shakespeare wrote the play, and argues that Elizabethan pastoralism "could not ignore the resistance to enclosure of woodland commoners and squatters". In Wilson's opinion, *As You Like It* "is powerfully inflected" by the "narratives of" this "popular resistance, whilst its plot" comprises not only "the brutal story of Elizabethan social transformation" but also illustrates how the "'holiday humor' (4.1.65) of customary culture is disintegrating" because of the "stress of social mobility and competition".³⁵

The play's opening moments expose the "bitter contradictions of England's agricultural revolution", as well as "the break-up of the feudal household and extended family through the capitalization of English farming". Oliver's estate exemplifies the "intensive cultivation" happening throughout the Midlands:

■ Oliver's is the Elizabethan success story of the rise of the gentry by engrossing and enclosure at the expense of evicted relatives and tenants. The text locates its power on the cutting-edge of agrarian change, as it exposes the danger to the social order he provokes.³⁶ □

A representative of the "gentry rebel",³⁷ Orlando stands opposed to Oliver.

Historically, according to Wilson, the gentry enjoyed a reputation as the "backbone of revolts" and "remained crucial in the folklore of resistance".³⁸ Orlando invokes "audience appeal" because, as a "social bandit" in the vein of Robin Hood, he plays a "vital role" in the growing tensions "between capitalism and peasant society". In essence, he "upholds the collective values of the poor against the 'ambition' of the rich". He also "helps the weak, so the weak help him". His ultimate purpose, at least to his auditors, involves restoring the "clientage of master and servant".[39]

As "one of a cluster of plays written in the late 1590s that exalt the rank of Robin Hood to make him a gentleman", Wilson continues, *As You Like It* adapts "the legend" of the forest do-gooder to "the contemporary crisis by dramatizing the divided loyalty of the propertied". More specifically, the play "engages in the discursive revaluation of woodland that coincided with the sale and 'disafforestation' (the legal alienation) of the Crown forests".[40]

Migration of displaced people to forests "facilitated their enclosure", Wilson observes, and in *As You Like It* Shakespeare "predicts that the struggle between the regulated and market economies will be decided" in forests that included the one Shakespeare knew in Warwickshire. As a representation of this struggle, the play "transports its displaced characters to a wood pasture community where population influx had put intense pressure on customary culture".[41] Throughout *As You Like It*, "all the elements of the folk scenario are latent".[42] Their presence, though, pervades the play: in Celia's darkened face and Rosalind's cross-dressing, for example, lie hints of both carnival revelry and of transgressive behaviours such as charivari and skimmington raids – the text betrays an apprehension "that it is playing symbolically with fire". This transgressive posture lasts until that instant when Orlando violently interrupts Duke Senior's forest dinner. While Orlando's disturbance "restages the action of the early modern food riot, with its 'conservative' aim of reasserting the normative economy", it also "highlights the self-destructiveness of rural insurrection" because it is "perversely directed at" the Duke, who stands as "the figurehead of the old order".[43]

More significantly, Orlando's identification as "inland bred" (2.7.98) associates him with the gentry who withheld corn and grain from the ports, ostensibly in fear of famine. From the moment when he meets the Duke in the forest, and through his educative meetings with Rosalind, Wilson observes, Orlando evolves into a "yeoman" whose actions affirm "the alliance of England's nobility and gentry and their appropriation of popular laughter" as well as the imposition of enclosures and engrossments of land:

> ■ Contrary to Bakhtin's idealization of carnival, *As You Like It* thus reveals how discourses work through social change and are never indeterminate. In fact, the discursive function of Shakespearean comedy will be to depoliticize carnival, just as "in every society discourse is controlled and redistributed," as Foucault sees, "to avert its dangers and evade its formidable materiality".[44] □

In *As You Like It*, Wilson concludes, Shakespeare shows that "the fate of sylvan society will hang on London finance, as in actual Midland forests it was the city's projectors and monopolists who profited from improvement and enclosure".[45]

Cynthia Marshall

The wrestling match between Orlando and Charles in 1.2 of *As You Like It*, Cynthia Marshall (d. 2005) argues in "Wrestling as Play and Game in *As You Like It*" (1993), "functions theatrically to unsettle various oppositions between art and life".[46] Because of the match's "intertextuality" (Marshall describes the event as a "performance embedded in a highly mannered drama"), in other words, Shakespeare's enacted "spectacle" skews all the rules by which one may "define the game, its players, the play space", and even the "audience": while this scene attempts "to order reality in a morally intelligible way", it simultaneously "interrogates" the codes which order the "complex layers of theatricality separating the bodies of the performing actors from those of the observing audience". Once cognizant of these interrogations, an audience may begin to construe wrestling, as well as all human acts and motivations, as "closer to theater than spectacle".[47]

Because Shakespeare presents his audience with a mimetic representation of wrestling, not the "real" thing, the audience may perceive the action of the spectacle as fake. Accordingly, Marshall contends, they may view love and gender as represented in the play as fake also. Orlando, for example, whom audiences typically view sympathetically, validates his violent actions towards his brother Oliver as the only response to his compromised status. (Actually, he manifests violence on several occasions throughout the play.) Marshall, however, suggests that his "sudden rupturing of cultivated prohibitions on physical resolution of differences" may stem instead from his "overgrown and uneducated" nature: she later contends that Orlando "displaces onto Charles the aggression" he exhibited when confronting Oliver.[48] Oliver, moreover, having learned to manipulate to his advantage his brother's violent bent and arranging ahead of time for Charles to wrestle with Orlando, erodes even further "any firm sense" of what wrestling or even the characters actually represent in these scenes.[49] To Orlando, then, wrestling may offer "a means of expressing anger" and of "winning renown", but to others, including the audience, it may expose his physical, intellectual, and behavioural entrenchments in a lower social class.[50]

Marshall's research reaches deep into contemporary accounts of, as well as attitudes towards, wrestling, and she ascertains "clear class distinctions in the matter and manner of wrestling";[51] she also describes how wrestling functions "analogously to theatrical plays" and, as does wrestling, drama often evokes a suspicion that "the appearance" of realistic figures and situations on stage "is almost paradigmatically *not* truth".[52] "In absence", therefore, of the "absolute truth of the body" and of the motivations behind human behaviour, Marshall declares, the "construction of 'play' becomes deadly serious".[53] Through Shakespeare's depiction of the wrestling match, the:

■ changing styles people employ in killing one another affirm the constructed quality of expressions of human aggression, and suggest the importance of attending to the ways a spectacle of violence is framed and understood.[54] □

Everything "people do with their physical selves", Marshall determines, "is subtly and extensively codified", and all violence is performed.[55]

The "changeable rules" marking violence, expression, and theatre signal "the arbitrariness of social convention" and, in *As You Like It*, permeate not only the wrestling scene but its "interrogations of human illusion, its inquiries into pastoral, melancholy, romantic love, and gender", Marshall concludes.[56] Not only does Shakespeare employ the wrestling match as "the earliest and most spectacular challenge to the modes of bodily interaction presupposed by mimetic theater", he also exposes the threat of social codes: by "exposing the theatricality of physical conflict" the wrestling match "explodes the myth of a place in society where one could avoid living 'by thinking'".[57]

A. Stuart Daley

In his "Calling and Commonwealth in *As You Like It*: A Late Elizabethan Political Play" (1994), A. Stuart Daley refutes Louis Adrian Montrose's assertion that primogeniture and the sibling rivalries this practice initiates inform and steer the conflicts depicted in *As You Like It*. In distancing himself from Montrose, Daley points out that Duke Senior, his daughter Rosalind, and Orlando all rely on primogeniture to stake their claims as rightful heirs. The "ultimate restoration of the lands, revenues, and dignities" of these displaced people, therefore, "unarguably endorses the rightfulness of their inheritance".[58]

Daley urges readers to see *As You Like It* as the dramatic representation of a political problem, one that plagued England periodically throughout its history. Shakespeare's primary "subject" in *As You Like It* involves:

■ the problem of redeeming a sovereign dukedom from the tyranny of a usurper and, on the parallel level of an eminent family, the freeing of an orphan youngest brother from the oppression of his elder brother, now *in loco parentis*.[59] □

Daley describes the play's first act as Shakespeare's sketching out of "the infection of the body politic", as well as the "vices typical" of all tyrants: "ambitious pride", which Daley identifies as "the sin against God", and "anger, envy, and avarice", or "the sins against kinsmen and neighbors". Daley also suggests that, at the start of the play, both Oliver and Orlando "are guilty of treachery against country and kindred", for while Oliver "personifies Fraud" in his desire to kill his younger brother, Orlando symbolizes violence and "Force", as seditious as Fraud in Tudor political philosophy.[60]

As he draws on contemporary political and religious treatises to inform his view, Daley determines that, for the Tudors, the "theoretical cornerstone of a well regulated commonwealth" involved an "observance of the doctrine of calling or vocation".[61] Daley attributes the culture's prioritization of one's vocation to Biblical injunction and long-held social custom. Oliver's denial of Orlando's vocation, along with Frederick's usurpation of his elder brother's dukedom, both instances of "egoistic repudiation of the duties of vocation and degree",[62] usher in the malignancy that infects the dukedom because both acts negate someone else's calling.

In Daley's view, Shakespeare makes clear that the cure of this realm's malignancy lies in the "concept of mutual need and symbiotic obligation". Shakespeare peoples the play with representatives of all "rank and circumstance" to illustrate "the need of each for other".[63] The playwright even includes Jacques, a figure who, in opposition to Duke Senior, represents certain audience members' "skepticism about the regenerative efficacy of traditional hierarchical and altruistic ideals".[64]

Through Jacques, Daley notes, Shakespeare introduces three "analogues for the commonwealth that permeated Tudor political discourse".[65] The first, invoked through his discussion of deer, involves the "body politic", an analogue that equates the cooperation of all parts of the human body in its proper functioning with all citizens working together in the daily functions of the realm. Then, in likening the world to a "sick human being" in 2.7, Jacques invokes the "health" of a state, an analogue that surpasses in frequency of its use even those employed in Shakespeare's history plays. Finally, Jacques' introduction of the *theatrum mundi* [theatre of the world] topos" underscores the frequency with which Shakespeare fills the play with "theatrical terms, playlets, entertainments, and actors self-consciously adopting roles".[66]

For all Jacques' insight and usefulness in terms of his political representation, however, his obsessions with himself lose their appeal as the aristocrats Rosalind and Celia, in tandem with the servants Adam and Corin, work together to recover "the good old order" of "selfish friendship", embodied in Celia, "ethical conduct" and "mercy", embodied in Rosalind,[67] and "labor" in service to "the common good" as well as "holiness",[68] embodied in Adam and Corin. All these qualities constitute the "virtues" implicit in one's calling.[69]

Susanne L. Wofford

Susanne L. Wofford (b. 1952) argues convincingly in "'To You I Give Myself, for I Am Yours': Erotic Performance and Theatrical Performatives in *As You Like It*" (1994) that Shakespeare, by representing the wedding of Rosalind to Orlando onstage in 4.1, enters into an ongoing:

■ cultural debate about the power of fathers and of the state to control the language that gives such actions a social reality – in other words, that makes the language truly performative. Shakespeare's theater contests the control of the performative utterance by the crown, implicitly claiming for itself the right to do things with words.[70] □

"To focus on the rhetorical structure and social force of words uttered in a play is", Wofford continues, "to link a concern with the play's assertions about gender and cultural authority to the kinds of power such assertions have".[71]

Wofford problematizes earlier theories regarding "performative utterances" as well as "speech acts", especially as concerns their lack of attention to theatre; she asserts that the theatre exists as "one of the cultural spaces in which" certain "cultural conventions and social expectations" are challenged and "changes" to these conventions and expectations "are given palpable form". *As You Like It*:

■ provides an exemplary text for considering the ways in which the play and popular theater more broadly may contest the implicit claim of the crown to be the sole arbiter of who is the "proper person" to pronounce a culturally powerful speech act.[72] □

More specifically, Rosalind's "erotic performance" while in Arden assumes a "performative power", one that results in her empowerment.

Wofford describes various scenes in Shakespeare's comedies as possessing an apotropaic quality, that is, the scenes often serve to avert or ward off threatening instances or misfortune for a character or group of characters. While Rosalind voices her desire for "curing" Orlando's "infection" in 3.2, for instance, she also poses an implicit threat in her erotic performative utterances and speech acts.[73] For example, while Rosalind's eventual marriage to Orlando neutralizes the threat of "wrong" sex attractions – Celia's desire for Rosalind, Orlando's for Ganymede – it also affirms "a patriarchal order which is itself dependent on an unacknowledged homoerotic bonding between male characters".[74] Her union with Orlando also negates any potential threat of shrewishness or cuckoldry once Rosalind enters into marriage, yet the means by which she accomplishes such a feat – her "wit",[75] specifically – obviously require a powerful woman, one capable of expressing and establishing speech acts that concede her hegemony. Her tongue lies at the heart of her power, Wofford suggests:

■ If her erotic performance wards off the figure of powerful female language by evoking it, it also presents the threat that this enactment will become contaminated with what it represents—that Rosalind will become this dominating woman—at which point the only way to control her would be to "take her without her tongue".[76] □

Rosalind's feigned masculinity when posing as Ganymede, Wofford concludes, actually demonstrates how women lose "their tongues as women", and Shakespeare's only resolution involves reaffirming "a form of enacted gender undecidability". As You Like It seems uniquely "willing to countenance such a doubleness".[77] Rosalind's power remains "real" throughout the play, despite its being "carefully circumscribed by the fact of male possession and priority".[78]

Catherine Belsey

In *Shakespeare and the Loss of Eden* (1999), Catherine Belsey (b. 1940) employs several theoretical approaches, including structuralism, Cultural Studies, and Marxism, to register and examine various visual and literary "representations of the emergence of the loving family" in early modern England.[79] Throughout her career, Belsey has consistently eschewed the label "New Historicist"; in *Shakespeare and the Loss of Eden* she instead attempts what she calls a "cultural history" of the family and family values as they emerge in early modern England.

Throughout her cultural history, Belsey concerns herself with the "increasing perception of the loving family as a place of danger",[80] a perception that appears concurrently with the culture's codification of the "meanings and values" associated with the family.[81] Belsey claims that a cultural history records not what "individuals actually did" in a specific historic moment, "but more what people wanted to do, wished they had done, what they cared about and deplored". She adopts Marxist critic Louis Althusser's contention that a culture's "beliefs are inscribed in practices, particularly ritualistic practices",[82] and attempts to "represent" the "incursion of anarchy, cruelty and death into what is legal, affectionate and life-giving".[83]

In Chapter 2, Belsey focuses on *As You Like It* as one such representation. Belsey first notes the play's fairy-tale structure, and then explains how early modern academics embraced "chivalry, as well as poetry, music, and masques" as among the "arts of civilized living". She also declares that in the 1590s Shakespeare introduced a "new genre" to the English stage, "romantic courtship", and notes this genre "set romantic love leading to marriage at the center of the action, anatomizing the relationships between lovers".[84]

A major part of this action, Belsey continues, centres on the lovers' "deferral of consummation that is romance". Shakespeare presents throughout the play a "symbolized" form of love in characters such as Orlando and Phebe, in other words, one:

■ indicated in the form of sighs, complaints, apostrophes, declarations, appeals, demonstrated by teasing and coaxing, and postponed by absences, misunderstandings, errors of judgment.[85] □

As do poets, then, *As You Like It*'s characters-in-love borrow their expressions of desire from the "poetic conventions of their culture" and thereby "assume an alien identity, reproduce an already familiar rhetoric and vocabulary, and put on display the inevitable citationality of desire". While the characters experience love uniquely and personally, they nonetheless express their experiences via "convention", and thus provide their audience with the "dual pleasure of recognition and distance".[86]

Through the behaviours and expressions Belsey describes, these characters also learn "to perform an identity which takes its place in a sequence leading on to full participation in the commonwealth".[87] The conventions that constitute one's expressions of romantic love serve particular social and gender-specific ends:

> ■ Romantic love and the process of courtship also integrate the young, and young men in particular, into their society, teaching them to reproduce, with whatever extravagance, the conventions of civility. From Ovid onwards, love is an art, to be acquired in the Renaissance by practicing the arts.[88] □

Orlando, for example, in his consistently bad poetry and increasingly woeful lamentations, "is not railing, but practicing the performance of civility", not only because he acknowledges some "room for improvement by the addition of nurture to an already gentle nature", but also because the marital relationship he strives towards "is the basis of civil society":[89]

> ■ As well as in art, love is thus a discipline, which tames and domesticates the human animal: desire is co-opted by social regulation.[90] □

Disguised as Ganymede, Rosalind first "deepens his desire"[91] and then teaches Orlando the "proprieties of courtship". In contrast to Orlando, Jacques "opts throughout the play for solitude and in the end for monastic celibacy".[92]

In much the same fashion as Jacques' emotional distance, Belsey contends, *As You Like It* on occasion appears "remarkably cynical about the joys of the condition it equates with a happy ending".[93] Not only does the play reveal the processes by which lovers "come to reproduce the conventions of their culture by learning to enact the identities it prescribes",[94] it also seems "almost preoccupied by the likelihood of unfaithfulness".[95] Love becomes "a discipline, which tames and domesticates the human animal", while "desire is co-opted by social regulation".[96] Touchstone's approach to obtaining Audrey, including his enlistment of Sir Oliver Martext, furthermore, suggests a sordidness underpinning the love bond. Belsey illustrates through Orlando and Rosalind how early modern culture simultaneously "embraced love as a humanizing force", marriage "as the divinely endorsed remedy for desire and the family as the source of civil society", while through Touchstone it also "recognized passion, even in its socially approved form, as all too human, and potentially dangerous and destructive".[97]

Mary Thomas Crane

In "Theatrical Practice and the Ideologies of Status in *As You Like It*", from *Shakespeare's Brain* (2001), Mary Thomas Crane (b. 1956) concentrates on the aspirant Lord Chamberlain's Men, Shakespeare's acting company from 1594 until his retirement from the stage (the company was renamed the King's Men in 1603, upon James I's accession). Organized under the patronage of Henry Carey, 1st Baron Hunsdon and Lord Chamberlain, the Lord Chamberlain's Men performed at the Theatre in Shoreditch, but because of a land lease conflict moved to the Curtain, also in Shoreditch, in 1597. Then, in 1599, the Lord Chamberlain's Men moved their operations from the Curtain to the new Globe in Southwark. This same year, the company dismissed their clown actor Will Kempe and replaced him with Robert Armin, who played Touchstone in *As You Like It*.

Crane outlines the Marxist and New Historicist inability to acknowledge the play's "emotional shading, the subtle inflection of concepts by complex social feelings"[98] surrounding the company's changes in 1599. To explain more comprehensively Shakespeare's mixed feelings towards Kempe's departure, as well as his company's pursuit of social ascendance via its new acting space, Crane couples these interpretive strategies with cognitive theory, and thus describes Shakespeare's participation in social mobility alongside his simultaneous "regret" that such a pursuit also signalled an "incipient rejection" of his theatre's "festive roots and established tradition of collaborative work":[99]

> ■ *As You Like It* thus takes us to the forest in order to sever, or at least to transform, the connection between drama and rustic festivity ... [T]he play uses the question whether "nature" or "fortune" plays a greater role in the attainment and maintenance of status simultaneously to obscure and reveal the real issue: that those terms and other status terms were changing in ways that could be beneficial to those who had the power to use them, with full awareness of their double-edged ironies, for their own benefit.[100] □

Shakespeare's employment of status terms such as "villain" and "clown" throughout *As You Like It* reveals an ongoing shift "from feudal to capitalist ideologies of social mobility and status hierarchy".[101] Along with "churl", these terms once merely denoted a man's social place; with the decline of feudalism, however, they slowly acquired "almost exclusively ethical connotations" and cast "moral disapproval" upon those labelled as such.[102] Shakespeare consistently uses "villain" throughout the play, for example, in "emotionally charged" moments and to identify a person of "gentle status".[103] To call a person of gentle birth a "villain" – as Oliver angrily calls Orlando in 1.1 – reflects an increasing resistance within the culture to accept that people "are born with qualities suitable to their permanent station in life".[104] Instead, we see the possibility that even "persons of lower status" not only "might possess the capacities for advancement" but may overtake the gentle born – if not in "fortune" (i.e., *money*) then in natural gifts of dignity, goodness, and love.[105]

Adam's frugality and temperance, for instance, rivals that of the "upwardly mobile merchant class",[106] and Corin appears a better man than his "churlish" absentee landlord, who "little reaks [cares] to find the way to heaven/By doing deeds of hospitality" (2.4.81–82). Both Orlando and Rosalind, likewise, are thrust into positions of subjection – Orlando to Oliver and Rosalind to Celia – but their wit and behaviour prove them superior to those materially above them.

Shakespeare's mediation of "clown" serves a slightly different semantic purpose. The term itself does not appear until the sixteenth century, Crane observes, and its emergence served to distinguish the high-born "villain" from the lowly born and uncultured country person. While the term "appreciated" in status and came to mean a comic actor at roughly the same time as Will Kempe's tenure in Shakespeare's company, his "rudeness and rusticity" solidified his identification with the word's original connotation. Disruptive and "tending toward an anarchic 'deconstruction' of the values of the main play", Kempe's jigs troubled Shakespeare and his company, Crane argues, not only because they tied their performances to festive revelry and lower-class interest, but also because their presence "assured that plays would be subject to interruption and qualification by unruly voices that were not under the control of the author".[107] When the Lord Chamberlain's Men left Shoreditch for Bankside, then, and when they parted ways with Will Kempe, they also may have left behind the jig. Either way, their move signalled "a point of upward mobility for the Chamberlain's Men and one of downward mobility for the excluded Kempe".[108]

Yet, because of a sense of remorse for what was left behind, as well as an awareness of his own upward social trajectory, Shakespeare frequently muddies distinctions between the values of the peasants and those of the bourgeois:

> ■ The play repeatedly hints at the counterideologies of the peasant or vagrant class but usually diffuses these potentially disruptive ideas either by shifting the class referent to gradations of status within the "gentle" classes or by means of a distancing and neutralizing layer of classical allusion.[109] □

Nonetheless, the play marks an "incipient rejection of the theatre's festive roots and established tradition of collaborative work".[110] And while cognitive theory suggests that emotions shape "human thought and conceptualization",[111] and thus its employment sheds a sharper light on what informs *As You Like It*, Shakespeare's guilt could not overcome his desire to climb the social ladder.

Matthew Kendrick

Over the past 25 or so years, readers of Shakespeare increasingly bristle at New Historicism's insistence that, no matter how subversive the text or performance, the dominant discourse under which the text or performance is produced ultimately will contain its transgressive proclivities. In "The Carnivalesque and Class Hybridization in *As You Like It*" (2010), for example, Matthew Kendrick urges scholars to seek instead the "complex relation of interarticulation between capitalistic and feudal elements" which inform both the play and the early modern period.[112] In more general terms, Kendrick offers a New Historicist reading of *As You Like It*, but one wherein he emphasizes how initially contested class and gender "perspectives enter into realms of articulation rather than mere conflict within the fantastic, carnivalesque green world" of Arden.[113]

Relying upon Mikhail Bakhtin's theories concerning carnival, and in particular Bakhtin's notion that the "playfulness of the carnivalesque as a mode of representation both deconstructs and reconstructs the social order",[114] Kendrick argues that the play negotiates simultaneously "the destabilization of the feudal order and the corresponding emergence of a capitalist class identity". Neither discourse dominates, and the play seeks a "hybrid social vision, neither purely capitalist in nature nor nostalgically yearning for a feudal past".[115]

Much of the negotiation, Kendrick suggests, centres on the marriage plot which drives *As You Like It*, and "which uses the highly classed romantic tensions between Rosalind and Orlando".[116] Orlando and Rosalind embody both sides of the class conflicts informing early modern England. Orlando demands recognition of his nobility, for instance, yet illustrates through his wrestling prowess that "self-determination and merit" can lift an individual's social status. His elder brother, too, recognizes through Orlando's popularity among commoners that "one's identity is not essential but relative".[117] Rosalind as well "must challenge the hierarchical imposition of identity to affirm her proper place".[118] Her and Orlando's attraction to each other challenges the traditional conception of marriage as an exchange of property: their coming together instead advocates "freedom of choice and affection" over the "rigid economic calculation behind patriarchal ideology".[119]

Rosalind's choice of dress while in Arden, furthermore, enhances her status as one of "the people", and mirrors Orlando's popularity among the workers on his estate, represented by Adam. Equally significant, her dress allows her to "determine", on her own terms, "whether or not Orlando would make a good husband":

> ■ Rosalind exercises independence in negotiating her relationship with Orlando. She is not an object on the marriage market but a subject who manipulates it to serve her own interests.[120] □

Through her interrogations of Orlando and clear-cut directives to him, furthermore, Rosalind shows a bigger concern for Orlando's "meritorious performance than with the establishment of property relations between families".[121] While the marriage ceremony that concludes the play seems to re-establish a "return to the normative order", Kendrick sees a "fragile balance" between the bourgeois and the feudal emerging: Orlando, for example, returns to the aristocracy, but only because he has "demonstrated his worth".[122]

New Historicist critics pride themselves on the resurrection and re-examination of long forgotten texts, documents, and accounts, often prepared by or attending to the marginalized or dispossessed. Vagabonds, outlaws, cross-dressers, hermaphrodites, or any other type of unaccommodated personage – frequently including playwrights, actors, and the characters they manipulate – through the New Historicist lens achieve a prominence traditionally enjoyed only by kings and potentates. More often than not, however, and in accordance with New Historicist belief, these characters enjoy their notoriety only because they have been identified, contained, and rendered insignificant by their culture. In much the same fashion, feminist and Gender Studies critics resurrect and re-examine both long forgotten authors and characters, but also provide a permanence and significance for the resurrected, as will be seen in the following chapter.

CHAPTER SEVEN

1965–Present: "If I Were a Woman": Feminism and Gender

Although the term began circulating widely in the 1960s, *feminism* (not to mention the issues associated with the term) has existed for centuries, and since the twentieth century has impacted every facet of Western culture. Our understanding and appreciation of *As You Like It* has been enhanced by the many feminist and gender-based discussions the play inspires, and these examinations' foci continue to widen as feminism influences and informs other theories, including *Gender* and *Queer Studies*. Appraisals of the play's representations of patriarchy, identity, gender, gender relations, and even of power abound: they constitute a valuable body of work that has made a considerable impact on how we read *As You Like It* and on how we view Shakespeare and his culture.

Beginning in the late 1970s, scholars grappled with the playwright's manipulations of gender, identity, and power through Rosalind and, to a lesser extent, Orlando, Celia, and Phebe. Rosalind's frustrations, stemming first from her powerlessness as the daughter of a usurped duke and as a woman, (seemingly) disappear in the Forest of Arden and as she becomes Ganymede. Just as she realizes the power she commands in the forest and employs it to help herself and others, though, she (seemingly) relinquishes it by handing control back to her father and Orlando. Her behaviours have sparked numerous debates as well as informative studies of gender, identity formation, and male–female relations in *As You Like It*.

Much like Cultural Studies and New Historicism, feminism and Gender Studies draw on several disciplines for their methods of textual analysis: historical criticism, psychoanalysis, Reader Response, Marxism, structuralism. Also like Cultural Studies and New Historicism, feminism and Gender Studies are anti-hierarchical; as such, they expose and interrogate the subordination of women to men as well as discrimination against non-binary sexualities across cultures and throughout history.

A major achievement of earlier feminist criticism involves the establishment of women's fundamental relationship to the patriarchy as portrayed in Shakespeare's plays – whether as subjects within it or engaged against it. Feminist readings began with Anna Brownell Jameson, Mary Cowden Clarke, and Helena Faucit Martin, nineteenth-century women who drew attention to the positive images of women in Shakespeare's plays, as well as the value they held as models for educated middle-class women (see Chapter 2). Their efforts, as well as the efforts of many others, culminated in the publication in 1980 of *The Woman's Part: Feminist Criticism of Shakespeare*, edited by Carolyn Ruth Swift Lenz, Gayle Green, and Carol Thomas Neely,[1] the first anthology of women's criticism devoted to feminist readings of Shakespeare. Dedicated to the memory of C.L. Barber, *The Woman's Part: Feminist Criticism of Shakespeare* (1980) was a product of the Special Session of Feminist Criticism of Shakespeare at the 1976 annual meeting of the Modern Language Association.

Since then, feminist criticism of Shakespeare has sparked several other methodologies of reading, including Gender Studies and, as discussed more fully in Chapter 8, Queer Theory. Because of the influence of psychology and cognitive studies, biology, and anthropology, moreover, most feminists and Gender Studies critics now discuss gender roles as culturally and textually constructed, as well as historically specific, rather than innate. As such, many practitioners of these and other theories capitalize on what Marianne Novy describes as Shakespeare's "flexible ego boundaries and ease of identification"[2] when examining his plays. Finally, and in the same spirit as the Cultural Studies critics discussed in Chapter 5, these critics also, and perhaps more significantly, diligently work to change established conventions, traditions, and perceptions as concern gender and identity. Feminists and Gender Studies critics establish and maintain links, in other words, to movements beyond the academy.

Nancy K. Hayles

In "Sexual Disguise in *As You Like It* and *Twelfth Night*" (1979), Nancy K. Hayles notes the increased attention her era's feminist critics devote to Shakespeare's use of sexual disguise and attributes it to "social concerns".[3] Recognizing that Rosalind's "ability to solve" the play's "problems" lies in her masculine disguise, and that these problems all stem from "the context of the social roles of each sex", Hayles contends that in *As You Like It* "fulfillment of desire, contentment and peace of mind" obtain when the "insistence on self-satisfaction" – a shortcoming suffered by both male and female – "ceases".[4]

Hayles attributes the strife between Orlando and Oliver to "male rivalry", and contrasts it with the "female intimacy" exhibited by Celia and Rosalind. Upon closer inspection, however, this easy contrast all but disappears when we note the "competition" that permeates Arden: Jacques challenges Duke

Senior's ownership of the forest, Touchstone sets himself at odds with several forest denizens, and Silvius finds himself lacking, in Phebe's eyes, when she meets Rosalind-Ganymede.[5] The impulses towards self-satisfaction and rivalry lie everywhere, according to Hayles.

Interestingly, as Rosalind adds layers to her disguise – transforming from Rosalind to Rosalind-Ganymede to Rosalind-Ganymede-Rosalind – the rivalries in both the forest and back at court intensify, Hayles maintains. And when she begins taking layers away from her disguise, which she does only after "claiming the right to be herself rather than Orlando's idealized version of her", Rosalind's "unlayering finally resolves that traditional tension between the needs of the female and the desires of the male".[6]

By Hayles' account, the needs of the female involve self-identification, where in males the need centres on autonomy. Because of these competing desires the woman often will project, out of fear, "phallic invasion", where a man will project onto women a fearful "female engulfment". Hayles sees both fears symbolized by the lioness and snake with which Orlando grapples in the forest: his relinquishment of his desire for revenge on his brother signals his "triumph over threatening aspects of masculinity and femininity", while Rosalind's fainting at the sight of Orlando's blood signifies her abandonment of "manipulative control over Orlando". *As You Like It* "suggests that control is necessary to state the legitimate needs of the self, but also that it must eventually be relinquished to accommodate the needs of another". The rivalry between a woman's "self-image" and a man's "desires" diminishes only when men and women replace "self-interest" with cooperation.[7]

Clara Claiborne Park

Among the many groundbreaking essays on Shakespeare in *The Woman's Part* is "As We Like It: How a Girl Can Be Smart and Still Popular" by Clara Claiborne Park (1923–2010). Symptomatic of writers participating in the first wave of feminist criticism, Park grapples with Shakespeare's attitudes towards women. Park concedes that "Shakespeare liked women and respected them",[8] yet she also notes that among the "secrets of his perennial appeal" lies Shakespeare's ability to "create women who were spunky enough to be fun with, and still find ways to mediate their assertiveness so as to render them as nonthreatening as their softer sisters".[9]

In his middle comedies especially, Shakespeare excels in glorifying "the image of the bright young girl" in constructing for his audience young women with "beauty, vigor, self-confidence and wit".[10] And yet, all this "glitter" drawing us to these women "obscures" the myriad means Shakespeare employs "to reduce the impact of [their] self-confidence, to make sure that equality is kept nominal". Above all else in Shakespeare's delineations of women, they make no one "uncomfortable".[11]

In Park's estimation, Rosalind emerges as one of only three Shakespearean heroines (along with Portia in *Merchant of Venice* and Beatrice in *Much Ado about Nothing*) who can "control events in the world around her". More significantly, Rosalind is the only woman who shapes "the world of men" and thereby claims as her own the play in which she appears.[12] Without "making the ladies censorious or the gentlemen nervous",[13] Rosalind singlehandedly choreographs the steps that bring each of the four pairs of lovers together in marriage.

Rosalind can accomplish all this, however, only by assuming male disguise, Park argues. Once in male attire, Rosalind "can be as saucy and self-assertive as she likes", and any threat of "aggression" reduces itself "into simple high spirits".[14] Park explains this situation by echoing C.L. Barber's contention that Shakespearean comedy affirms disruption as temporary, as eventually giving itself back to order. As soon as Rosalind brings the lovers together, and makes certain that Orlando will pair himself to her, she gives over all control by re-assuming a woman's dress and behaviours. In an interesting, if somewhat dated, conclusion, Park uses the 1970 film *Love Story* to illustrate how late twentieth-century culture adheres to the same gender constructions and reliance upon male dominance.

Barbara J. Bono

Grounding her essay "Mixed Gender, Mixed Genre in Shakespeare's *As You Like It*" (1986) in contemporary psychoanalytic and sociological models, ones that locate "the mother as socializer"[15] in a child's identity formation, Barbara J. Bono argues that "the patriarchal, oedipal crisis" encountered in the first act of *As You Like It* "is displaced back onto its preoedipal ground" once the characters escape to Arden. In the forest, Shakespeare "can represent both the male struggle for identity" as well as the "female 'double-voiced' discourse" (a term drawn from Elaine Showalter (b. 1941), who takes it from Bakhtin) which "simultaneously acknowledges its dependence on the male and implies its own unique positive value – within it".[16]

In order to accomplish both tasks, Bono argues, Shakespeare engages "the mixed genre" of the pastoral tradition, essentially because it criticizes the "larger culture" from which it came:

> ■ Orlando's masculine heroic quest, couched simultaneously in the language of biblical typology and classical epic, is resolved within Arden's "sweet style." There Rosalind, fully acting out romance's conventions of disguise, transforms the social

perception of woman from the Petrarchan conventions that both idealize and degrade them to a new convention of companionate marriage. Unlike Orlando's simpler quest, Rosalind's "double-voiced" discourse, criticizing the subject of which she is a part, can thus offer a method for cultural change.[17] □

Rosalind's masculine disguise, in other words, takes on a greater significance than mere romance convention: it challenges masculine assumptions of femininity and provides an avenue for change.

According to Bono, the "parricidal rage" plaguing Orlando (Duke Senior experiences this as well) creates a "void in his identity"[18] which, until the point when he overcomes Oliver, we perceive as innately gentle. Only when he meets the Duke in Arden, and encounters the gentility he once associated with himself, does Orlando "play seriously at the civilized game of love without threatening his basic male heroic identity".[19]

One of Bono's more compelling points involves the Duke's "seemingly benign verbal control over" his compromised situation and habitation in the forest; Bono equates his kindly and paternal demeanour with Rosalind's own "playfulness", despite her containment within "an overt masculinist sexual ideology".[20] Rosalind engages in this playful banter through her disguise, which enables her "double-voiced" discursive habits: by adopting the appearance of the male, Rosalind can take part in "the dominant male culture, including its view of women, even while skewing it 'saucily' toward self-consciousness and criticism", while she keeps "a part of herself hidden and inviolate".[21]

Rosalind's most important contribution to the play, in Bono's view, involves her providing Orlando an opportunity to "test" his love "within the relatively nonthreatening limits of supposed male discourse about women, and attempts to exorcise her own fears about giving herself into such a discourse". Rosalind, too, suffers an "oedipal crisis" at the play's beginning, and must resort to "nature"; she does not, however, "experience this preoedipal nature as harshly threatening".[22] Instead, she:

■ discovers a female identity that will allow her to complete the difficult, triangulated resolution of a girl's typical oedipal crisis: differentiation from and continuity with the mother and transfer of affection from the father onto an appropriate heterosexual love object.[23] □

In sum, Rosalind's time as Ganymede accommodates Orlando's vulnerability and tests his worthiness as her lover.

While Orlando never acquires a "sophisticated understanding of women's ambiguous position in the world", he does forego the restrictive Petrarchan conception of women and seek instead a "chaste wife" and "companionate marriage".[24] Rosalind's actions open "a world of possibility for the continued negotiation" of the differences inherent in sexual relations, Bono believes.[25]

Marjorie Garber

Unlike Shakespeare's other comic heroines who cross-dress in order to obtain their respective play's harmony and marriage, Rosalind does not need her disguise once she meets Orlando in Arden, Marjorie Garber (b. 1944) observes in "The Education of Orlando" (1986). Why does she remain in her male garb, given that she "does not have to learn much, if anything, about love, or about the quality and depth of her own feelings", nor does "she really need assurance"[26] that Orlando desires her?

Several readers of the play, including Garber, concur that Rosalind teaches Orlando how to love properly, but Garber maintains that her teaching involves not so much the "technique" of love as its "substance":

> ■ Her disguise as Ganymede permits her to educate him about himself, about her, and about the nature of love. It is for Orlando, not for Rosalind, that the masquerade is required.[27] □

By falling in love with Orlando, moreover, Rosalind rebels "against patriarchal domination and the filial bond"; her love for Orlando, in other words, "banishes her to Arden" just as much as Frederick's disdain and distrust of her. Orlando's exile, likewise, serves as "a step toward independence and maturity".[28]

Garber identifies "three distinct stages in Orlando's development as a lover", and Rosalind successfully guides him through all three. The first involves Orlando's need "to communicate his feelings", and Rosalind teaches him to "speak to her in the natural language of men and women". Her disguise allows him to feel more comfortable than "he was at their first meeting". Orlando also must abandon his "self-absorption", a sure sign of "adolescent love".[29] As their interactions intensify, Orlando learns not only the "quick use of his wits" in communicating to her his feelings, but also to perform "acts of constancy".[30] Finally, he requires time to mature into an "other-directedness".[31]

The most significant representation of Orlando's transformation, Garber believes, lies in the bloody napkin that Oliver presents to Ganymede when he first meets "him", for it signifies a "love token of a very different kind from the superficial love poems" Orlando affixes to trees.[32] While Orlando progresses in his preparations for marriage to Rosalind, Garber cites one "subtle", perhaps "finical", instance that proves he remains "no match for Rosalind":[33] he conflates the two stories Rosalind tells him about, first, the "religious uncle" who has taught her to speak and to recognize the symptoms of love, and, second, the "magician" who teaches her magic. This magician, Garber suggests, is Rosalind herself; therefore, Orlando never can stand fully as her equal. Like Prospero in *The Tempest* Rosalind must find the proper moment to set aside her garment.

Phyllis Rackin

Phyllis Rackin (b. 1933) opens her "Androgyny, Mimesis, and the Marriage of the Boy Heroine on the English Renaissance Stage" (1987) by urging further study of the "theatrical representations of gender"[34] which occurred during the early modern era. As the term "gender roles" denotes, all women – not merely the boys who played women on Shakespeare's stage – act out their roles as women, Rackin adds.

Rackin then contends that a Renaissance theatre audience likely would have seen in the "sexual ambiguity of the boy heroine in masculine attire" a "widespread and ambivalent mythological tradition centering on the figure of the androgyne". Although this androgyne figure often evoked an image of "transcendence", of exceeding the bounds of normal human physical, intellectual, or spiritual achievement, this image "was replaced by the satirical portrait of the hermaphrodite, a medieval monstrosity or social misfit, an image of perversion or abnormality".

While Rackin devotes only limited space to *As You Like It*, her essay situates the play within early modern reconfigurations of marriage and gender:

■ Shakespeare refuses to dissolve the difference between the sex of the boy actor and that of the heroine he plays; and he uses his boy heroines' sexual ambiguity not only to complicate his plots but also to resolve them.[35] □

While Shakespeare will "vindicate" both "the power of love and illusion" at the play's conclusion, he also emphasizes the "reality principle",[35] the Freudian assertion that the mind can move beyond the pleasure principle and respond within the realities of the external world.

Rackin then discusses the diminished "status and opportunity" that early modern women encountered – she cites how women were removed from "work they had earlier performed", from "participation in economic, political, and cultural life", and from many areas of public life, ultimately restricted to the "separate, private sphere" of their homes, among other curtailments of their autonomy.[36] These shifting attitudes towards women relate to equally unstable conceptions of art, and the androgyne "becomes the fullest expression of both relations".[37]

Rackin argues that for Shakespeare, the:

■ relation between art and life is complementary as well as reflective: that is, it resembles the relation between two complementary angles, one growing as the other decreases. What is real in one world becomes unreal in the other, what is impossible in one world becomes possible in the other.[38] □

Art as well not only mimics the "defects of the real world" but provides "what is wanting" in it. The conditions Shakespeare creates in some comedies, then, allow the "true gender" of the transvestite heroine "to be feminine, the opposite of the real sex of the boy who played her part". Even more significantly, "the dynamics of plot" in *As You Like It* and other plays "make femininity a desideratum rather than the liability it was in actual life, and within the represented action female characters exercise power".[38] As did Neoplatonic writers, most notably Sir Philip Sidney, Shakespeare continues, and even refines, a tradition in which the androgyne represents the ideal. In doing so, Shakespeare contributes to contemporary beliefs that, like the woman whose unruliness required containment, an actor stood as a "dangerous anomaly in a hierarchical society".[39]

In Rackin's estimation, *As You Like It*'s epilogue, especially its reference to the "sexual transaction between the men and women" who compose the audience, "echoes" not only the "multiple marriages" that were realized only a moment before, but also "implies that the relation between the play and its audience is a kind of sexual transaction or marriage". In order to succeed, the play must conduct "a playful androgynous appeal that is most appropriately expressed by the ambiguous figure who no longer has a single name or sexual identity", Rosalind:

■ Refusing to collapse the artistic representation into a simple replica of the world outside the theater or to abandon that world for a flight into escapist fantasy, [Shakespeare] insists on the necessary ambivalence of his play as a kind of marriage, a mediation between opposites, which can be brought together only by the power of love and imagination.[40] □

Jean E. Howard

One of the most significant and influential discussions of gender, class, and early modern theatre to date, "Crossdressing, The Theater, and Gender Struggle in Early Modern England" (1988) by Jean Howard (b. 1948), opens with a simple question: "How many people crossdressed in Renaissance England?" Howard posits that, while we never will know the exact number of cross-dressers, we do know that cross-dressing – and, in particular, women dressing in men's garments – existed, and, more importantly, that the attention paid to it throughout the 1590s and early 1600s signified a "sex-gender system under pressure". Furthermore, cross-dressing "threatened a normative social order based upon strict principles of hierarchy and subordination, of which women's subordination to man was a chief instance".[41] Issues of gender *and* class, in other words, inform not only the incidence of cross-dressing, but the reaction of Shakespeare's culture to it.

Howard spends the first half of her essay outlining the circumstances that led women of all classes to adopt male dress – from the women in the aspiring classes who imitated the increasingly problematic fashions at court, to those who sought protection as they traversed London, to the lower-class women who prostituted themselves for survival. She also explains how clothes:

■ distinguished one social group from those both above and below; they were precise indicators of status and degree. To transgress the codes governing dress was to disrupt an official view of the social order in which one's identity was largely determined by one's station or degree—and where that station was, in theory, providentially determined and immutable.[42] □

Howard also explains the punishments and degradations women endured for assuming masculine garb, and discusses how women came under increasing patriarchal control – largely because of changing economic and social norms.

Clothing, Howard asserts, constitutes "a highly regulated semiotic system", and reflects not only one's class but one's gender.[43] Moreover, Shakespeare's era:

■ needed the idea of two genders, one subordinate to the other, to provide a key element in its hierarchical view of the social order and to buttress its gendered division of labor.[44] □

Gender relations are power relations, Howard claims, and one's dress marked one's gender and social situation. Men who dress as women effeminize, weaken, themselves, and place themselves "in a position of shame". Women who dress as men, however, "symbolically" leave "their subordinate positions" and become "masterless women", an act far more dangerous, for it signals "not only the breakdown of the hierarchical gender system, but of the class system as well".[45]

Howard devotes the second half of her essay to the theatre, and again begins by asking a question: Did Shakespeare's theatre, "with its many fables of crossdressing, also form part of the cultural apparatus for policing gender boundaries, or did it serve as a site for their further disturbance?"[46] Again, Howard concedes that no concrete answer emerges from the evidence. While many plays that include cross-dressing in their plot "are intensely preoccupied with threats to, disruptions of, the sex-gender system", they offer no consistent stand on the issue. Like cross-dressing itself, the theatres were "controversial and ideologically volatile",[47] and intermittently provided plots that contained women's transgressions or that rewarded women for their behaviours. Howard then shifts to plays that feature women who dress as men, and she notes that, often, these plays "contain, they vitiate, challenges posed to masculine authority and the traditional gender hierarchy". Some, however, allow "for challenges to the most repressive aspects of patriarchal ideology".[48]

As You Like It, Howard believes, falls somewhere in the middle. While it confirms the existing "gender system", it nonetheless perfects it "by making a space for mutuality within relations of dominance". As the play concludes, Rosalind "retains a properly feminine subjectivity". She will "accept the position of wife", but not before she manipulates, while in her male clothing, her situation to the point where she can "redefine (albeit in a limited way) the position of woman in a patriarchal society".[49] Unusually for women who dress as men:

> ■ Rosalind impersonates a woman, and that woman is herself—or, rather, a self that is the logical conclusion of Orlando's romantic, Petrarchan construction of her. Saucy, imperious, and fickle by turns, Rosalind plays out masculine constructions of femininity, in the process showing Orlando their limitations.[50] □

In short, Rosalind "acts out the parts scripted for women by her culture", and then "reveals the constructed nature of patriarchy's representations of the feminine", all to illustrate "how to get beyond certain ideologies of gender to more enabling ones". Howard describes *As You Like It* as deliberate in its "attention to the destabilizing fact that it is boy actors playing the roles of all the women in the play". It does so in order to destabilize "those boundaries separating one sexual kind from another", as well as unsettle "those powers and privileges assigned to the hierarchically superior sex".[51] The play's epilogue in particular brings these challenges to light.

Carol Rutter

While the boy actors who played Portia, Viola, and Rosalind on Shakespeare's stage "cannot tell us" how they played their parts, "we *can* record how our own actresses have interpreted those lines", Carol Rutter (b. 1950) declares in the Introduction to her *Clamorous Voices: Shakespeare's Women Today* (1989; Rutter's italics). Actresses "have become critics" in an age where many scholars tend "to see plays as scripts for performance and each production as a fresh act of interpretation".[52]

In Chapter 5, "Rosalind: Iconoclast in Arden", Rutter allows Juliet Stevenson (b. 1956) and Fiona Shaw (b. 1958), who played Rosalind and Celia, respectively, in the production of *As You Like It* that Adrian Noble (b. 1950) directed for the RSC in 1985, to speak for themselves. Juliet Stevenson states:

> ■ I'd always suspected that there's a much more dangerous play in *As You Like It*. A subversive play, one that challenges the notions of gender, that asks questions about the boundaries and qualities of our "male" and "female" natures.[53] □

Stevenson also notes the "snatches of a wonderful relationship between two women, Celia and Rosalind". For her, the play "is about love, love in all forms".[54]

In Stevenson's eyes, the court stands for our world: violent yet ordered, and "structured around male values".[55] As a member of this court, Rosalind introduces herself as someone "nearing the *end* of her endurance [Rutter's italics]".[56] She mirrors Orlando in his opening scene: while she remains incapacitated, immobile, he repeatedly voices the desire to do something about his situation. Orlando takes, however, "the most parodic male way out" of his predicament: he fights.[57] Rosalind recognizes something of herself in his struggle, and then begins to act.

As with so many of Shakespeare's women, Stevenson observes, "adverse experience makes Rosalind self-determining" as her "tenacity" becomes restored.[58] While acting as Ganymede, Rosalind finds a "muscle exercised for the first time".[59] As her interactions with Orlando bring them closer to one another, gender roles become "turned on their heads":

> ■ Orlando plays the conventional woman's part in the play. He doesn't initiate any of the action in *As You Like It* (except at the very end). He isn't the pivot or the motor of the play. He's there entirely in relation to Rosalind; his role as her lover is his identity.[60] □

In his subservient role, Orlando slowly learns to dispense with the "pedestal he's erected" for Rosalind.[61]

As the play nears its end, Rosalind, too, becomes "exposed" as no longer in control of what she has begun, Stevenson claims. Through "role-play", Rosalind channels the situations she creates "into something controllable".[62] She also reveals several "contradictions", which Orlando will begin to discern as "part of his future".[63] Rosalind also "discovers herself", and realizes that the love she feels can be dangerous – not only to her emotions, but to her as a woman. What emerges from this discovery involves "breaking through" Orlando's "carapace of expectation and prejudgement to liberate the woman – warts and all".[64] Much of the conversations between Ganymede and Orlando, therefore, actually become conversations between Rosalind and Ganymede.

Fiona Shaw, on the other hand, believes that Celia begins the play "thinking" it is "about her. But when she gets to Arden, she finds that she is no Lord Hamlet, but an attendant lord in the land of love".[65] Nonetheless, Shaw decides that any scenes involving Rosalind, Celia, and Orlando ought to be played as "trios". The "problem is, Celia never speaks to Orlando in these scenes".[66] Celia faces the reality of becoming a "chaperone" and losing her relationship with Rosalind: Rosalind has, unfortunately, "outgrown Celia".[67]

Kay Stanton

Shakespeare's attitudes towards patriarchy and sexual politics are "inextricably bound up with the concept of remembrance", argues Kay Stanton in her essay, "Remembering the Patriarchy in *As You Like It*" (1989).[68] Stanton cites Orlando's and Rosalind's stubborn memories of their fathers, and contrasts their motivations with Celia's:

▪ Whereas Orlando and Rosalind are nostalgic for the past's benevolent patriarchy, subverted in the present, Celia makes little distinction between past and present representatives of patriarchy.[69] ☐

To Celia, Stanton adds, "any patriarch can abuse power; one can only trust in female solidarity".[70]

At the play's beginning, Celia places her full faith that "matriarchy" can and will "rectify the evils of the present patriarchy" involving her father. She plans to inherit Frederick's dukedom and then turn power over to Rosalind. While statements such as these, along with acts such as her leaving the court to accompany Rosalind, signify Celia as "the play's source of feminism", Rosalind, conversely, "continually sees herself in relation to a man: obsessed with her father until she meets Orlando, from then on she is obsessed with Orlando".[71] In contrast to Rosalind, who subconsciously may seek to "effect the reinstatement" of her father through marital "alliance" with Orlando,[72] Celia repeatedly "reinforces her negation of patriarchy's powers" and interprets "the course of human life as determined not from men's acts but" from herself.[73]

Stanton records several instances of "male violence against nature", which she categorizes into three distinct forms: "man against man", as occurs in the wrestling match; "man against animal", as in the hunting carried by out by Senior's courtiers; and "man against vegetation", as we see in Orlando's defacing of trees. The point lies in the fact that "men continually make violence a part of their lives, even when in love". Orlando even diminishes "Rosalind's humanity" when in his poetry he describes her as "goddesslike and as a composite of the better parts of famous females".[74] While many of the men occasionally reveal feminine qualities – Jacques weeping for the deer, Duke Senior welcoming Orlando, or Orlando caring for Adam – Stanton contends that men "will abandon" these "'feminine' qualities" any moment "an opportunity arises to demonstrate or celebrate 'manliness' though violence".[75]

All along, Celia rarely worries over patriarchy, but when she falls for Oliver she "suddenly remembers it" and "chooses to marry a man who is exactly like her father, except he has been redeemed". From that point on, she does not speak again. Rosalind, too, forgets the pains of her past while in male disguise in the forest, and grows in strength and confidence, but she remembers "that she is a woman after all" when Oliver presents her the bloodied napkin.[76] After their respective marriages, both women "become simply wives", much like Audrey or Phebe.[77] While Rosalind and Celia both surrender "to the strength of patriarchy", though, Shakespeare "does not allow the play itself to do so", Stanton claims. Instead, *As You Like It* shows "through Celia that women could rule successfully, and through Rosalind that a woman can do anything that a man can, with the possible exception of personal exertion of force".[78]

Lesley Anne Soule

"There is an inevitable connection between the ideality of the character and its gender" Lesley Anne Soule states in "Subverting Rosalind: Cocky Ros in the Forest of Arden" (1991), and, in Soule's view, "the myth of Rosalind encompasses a myth of the ideal female". Informed by "received notions of what social and sexual roles" for a woman ought to be, the various staged representations of Rosalind also carry with them "corresponding ideological notions of the nature and functions of the actor/actress".[79] For both Rosalind and the actress playing her, the "social ideal of ingratiating behaviour" she displays becomes mixed with the "individualist fantasy of sexual gratification in ownership".[80]

These myths and traditions associated with Rosalind, however, stem from an "incomplete perception" of both the play and its theatrical history. Soule urges readers to consider that nearly all appraisals of Rosalind (as well as of the play) are based on "thematic rather than theatrical" notions, and they almost always view Rosalind's character as one acted by a woman: "casting a female in the role effectively destroys the character-actor relationship on which the performance and much of the meaning of the play depend".[81]

Throughout the play, Soule suggests, the "actions of both a fictional character and a stage performer are described", and the play's text emphasizes an "ironic counterpoint between" these two identities. The romance between Rosalind and Orlando, for example, as well as the political intrigue between Duke Senior and Frederick, are "continually interrupted by obviously theatrical digressions, in which empathetic concern with dramatic characters is sacrificed to achieving greater rapport between performer and audience".[82] Rosalind's character in particular, played by the boy actor whom Soule calls "Cocky Ros", is nothing more than a "stage presence who alternately represents and presents, impersonates and plays with Rosalind".[83]

When Rosalind leaves the court and adopts her male disguise, she effectively severs herself from all "social and fictional attributes", including "family circumstances, residence, rank, name, dress, and sex". She then becomes a "creature of words", a "literary-fictional Other", a character "mediated" by the boy actor Cocky Ros. With the character shift comes a dramatic shift as well:

> ■ This actor-figure becomes the primary focus of an audience's engagement with the stage action – this action now being determined by the motivation of the new central figure [Ganymede], which is to play-act and to mock. With the resultant marginalization of fiction and of character, popular performance holds sway over love as the audience's interest is shifted from fictional romance to stage entertainment.[84] □

When "Rosalind" returns to marry Orlando, she returns as "an abstract emblem of realized fantasy – without personality, and with only two formulaic speeches". She becomes, in effect, a "masque figure for male appropriation".[85]

Soule situates the "actor-persona" who plays Rosalind-Ganymede in several traditions, including the *eiron* hero of Aristophanic comedy (a hero typically self-deprecating and aware of irony around her), the devils of medieval cycle plays, the "impertinent pages and apprentices of the earlier Elizabethan drama", and, most significantly, the vice figure. She then explains how these types of characters, as well as of actors and adolescents, all, in their "liminality", share common traits, including that of defiance, in matters such as "mockery of and playful experimentation with adult sexual role-playing".[86] Defiance in *As You Like It*, however, remains in the actor – "eternally adolescent, liminoid, even slightly demonic" – while Rosalind prepares herself for marriage.[87]

Juliet Dusinberre

Juliet Dusinberre's "As Who Liked It?" (1994) illustrates how feminist critics occasionally manifest the same uncompliant tendencies as those who practise Cultural Studies, and often arrive, as do New Historicist critics, at the conclusion that a regime ultimately will regain control over a defiant voice within its dominant discourse.

Dusinberre begins by blaming *As You Like It*'s consistently lacklustre performance history on directors' and actors' inability to coax out the play's transgressive elements, which she locates in Shakespeare's creation of "fictions of sexuality which could speak to women" audience members and readers.[88] Citing Elizabeth I's "elaborately constructed fictions of chastity and desire",[89] as well as her failure to diminish "the male narrative"[90] that dominated her culture, Dusinberre explains how Shakespeare, through Rosalind, challenges this narrative. The play:

■ seems to me to rewrite the record of female desire so that women want to read it. The agent of rewriting is Rosalind. This dominant heroine with, in the end, magical skills, creates the parameters within which the danger of Shakespeare's play can be recovered, because she is so closely identified in the play with Elizabeth I.[91] □

As the play unfolds, Rosalind catalogues several "inherited narratives of desire", remarks on "the peculiarities of the male imagination", and then "offers" women an "opportunity to rewrite" the "language of desire" in a manner that insists upon "reinstating the body at the center of culture".[92]

Dusinberre attributes the play's tendency to depict women as the "inventors of the fictions in which they must play a part"[93] to the influence of Elizabeth's godson, John Harington (1560–1612), translator of *Orlando Furioso* [*Orlando's Frenzy*] by Ludovico Ariosto (1474–1533), author of *The Metamorphosis of Ajax* (1596), and admirer of *Pantagruel* (1532) and *Gargantua* (1532) by François Rabelais (1494–1553). Using Harington's examples, especially those he found in *Ajax* and *Gargantua*, Shakespeare reconfigures his culture's "inherited narratives", particularly those surrounding "women's desire".[94] Through Jacques and, more aggressively, Touchstone, Shakespeare offers a more vernacular and at times even subversive reaction to Elizabeth's expressions of authority, language, faith, and tradition.

The strongest example Dusinberre provides involves the play's title, *As You Like It*, which she believes Shakespeare extracted from the motto which hangs over the Abbey of Thelema in *Gargantua*: "*Fay Ce Que Voudras*", or "Do what thou wilt". Depicted in *Gargantua* as an affront to the restrictive Catholic faith, the abbey welcomes both men and women and celebrates "perfect liberty": its entrants are "wealthy, free and chaste – not as celibates, but as people who will in due time marry and go back to a world they will transform through their vision of concord between man and woman".[95] Shakespeare's Forest of Arden encourages the same freedoms, as witnessed in Rosalind's liberation once she enters. And in Dusinberre's eyes the effect would have carried over and impacted his women audience members who, if only for a moment, would have experienced the liberation Rosalind feels while in the forest.

Penny Gay

As She Likes It. Shakespeare's Unruly Women (1994), by Penny Gay (b. 1945), signals a departure, of sorts, from the impressive outpouring of feminist textual studies that came after Lenz, Green, and Neely's *The Woman's Part*. It stands as one of the first feminist theatre histories of Shakespeare, and offers essays on *As You Like It*, discussed in Chapter 2, and other plays. In her Preface, Gay explains the significance of her study of various Royal Shakespeare Company productions of these plays from the early 1950s to the early 1990s:

■ To study its performance of Shakespearean comedy is to encounter a continuing dialectic between theater practice and English social and political history, since theater will always in some way reflect the general culture of which it is a part.[96] □

Gay challenges the longstanding consensus that watching Shakespeare on stage instead of reading him lessens the likelihood of registering the play's transgressive or defiant qualities. With *As You Like It*, a belief prevails that an audience may "enjoy its fantasies of disruption" as Rosalind has things her way in Arden, but then "settle back into the regulated social order of patriarchy" as she surrenders herself first to her father and then her husband.[97] This tendency may hold true in certain readings of the text, Gay counters, but any given performance of the play "must respond in subtle (or not so subtle) ways to the changing Zeitgeist", and therefore we must understand performance as always "potentially disruptive of received readings".[98]

Gay emphasizes the particularly transgressive potential of women in Shakespeare's dramatic oeuvre:

■ "Woman", especially because she is the unknowable Other of patriarchy, can make her marginal position a source of disruptive power: though politically powerless, she can refuse to obey the rules of appropriate gender behavior, flaunting her sexual mystery as if to point out that the patriarchy cannot do without her.[99] □

"It is around such transgressive female figures that Shakespeare chose to center" the comedies that Gay discusses in her text. Gay considers the control of women's images, either through fashion, body language, or interactions with other characters, as well as the politics of a production's director and actors – Gay faults the RSC for the "dominance of men in all areas of decision-making".[100] She also draws attention to the dire need for feminist theatre historians, in order to transform the idea of what "good theater" is and should be.[101]

In the short prefatory note to her discussion of *As You Like It* in Chapter 2, Gay states that, from the 1950s to the 1990s, the play "reflects most strongly our culture's fascination" with the "marriageable daughter"; it also "responds to a changing view of the nature of social bonds".[102] Gay's coverage begins with a discussion of the 1952 production by Glen Byam Shaw (1904–86), featuring Margaret Leighton (1922–76) as Rosalind and Laurence Harvey (1928–73) as Orlando, and then focuses on the 1961 production starring Vanessa Redgrave (b. 1937) as Rosalind, a depiction which, for the next 30 years, enjoyed distinction as featuring the definitive Rosalind. Throughout the performance, Gay states, Redgrave "forced" critics:

> ■ to recognize that the part of Rosalind is there to be filled out by an actress who can put into it her own sense of what it is to be a young woman "fathom deep" in love. But she is also a character thrown on her own resources when exiled by an authoritarian state.[103] □

Gay describes as "appropriate" the fact that Redgrave, just after this production, became "a political activist",[104] and discusses the impact of C.L. Barber's *Shakespeare's Festive Comedy* on readings and performances of Shakespeare's comedies from this point on. She also notes that Ian Bannen (1928–99), playing Orlando, hinted at the character's possible bisexuality and that Max Adrian (1903–73), playing Jacques, "emphasized" his role "as cynical commentator" on the pastoral; "no longer could the actor of Jacques get away with being either slightly daffy or a sonorously venerable court philosopher".[105]

Gay covers two 1967 productions, one of them by David Jones (1934–2008), which garnered mixed reviews until a 1968 revival attracted attention because it costumed Rosalind and Orlando "almost identically", suggesting that "gender differences and the power-structures based on them were simply irrelevant".[106] The second was an all-male production at the Old Vic, directed by Clifford Williams (1926–2005). Gay then examines the 1973 "Hair" production, directed by Buzz Goodbody (1946–75). Described by Gay as a "defiantly feminist"[107] endeavour, the production was labelled "Hair" because of the hippy clothing and long hair of the actors.

In 1977 Trevor Nunn (b. 1940) attempted a musical, masque-like, rendition, and his set and costumes reflected on French cultural dominance in England during the seventeenth century. While applauded for its spectacle and music, the production suffered for lack of individuality in its characterizations of Celia, Touchstone, and Jacques. Critics also felt that Kate Nelligan (b. 1950), who played Rosalind, should have shown more change – and sexual suggestiveness – when shifting from Rosalind to Ganymede.[108]

Director Terry Hands (b. 1941) emphasized the play's "festive comedy" in his 1980 production: the play opened in a "pessimistic" winter and moved into "spring's optimism" in its second half.[109] The production featured an "up-front physicality" that critics praised, and Hands made Celia "a sexual competitor" to Rosalind.[110] Susan Fleetwood (1944–95) as Rosalind "produced more enthusiasm among the critics than anyone" since Redgrave, largely through her "physical" and "sexy" performance.[111]

Adrian Noble's 1985 production "psychoanalyzed the fairytale in a contemporary (modern-dress) reading, set in the country of the modern mind". Juliet Stevenson played Rosalind, and the programmes included texts "related to the thematic idea that to enter the 'woods' is to enter a dream or fantasy".[112] Critics gushed over a pronounced feminist (and Jungian) interpretation: for the first time, the play emphasized the relationship between Rosalind and Celia, played by Fiona Shaw, and deconstructed gender roles by presenting "the feminine in the masculine, the masculine in the feminine".[113]

The 1989 production by John Caird (b. 1948) opened in a "1930s cocktails-and-tango party": the effect "was overwhelmingly funereal, not to say sinister".[114] Everyone was rich and jaded, and Rosalind, played by Sophie Thompson (b. 1962), appeared as a "bored young sophisticate".[115] The "sources of power and energy" came not from Rosalind or the forest, but from the "world of macho games ruled by the men in suits".[116] Reviews were mixed, partially because little "sexual excitement" inhabited the performance.[117]

Cynthia Lewis

"Repeated references to hunted stags and their horns", avers Cynthia Lewis in "Horns, the Dream-Work, and Female Potency in *As You Like It*" (2001), register a male fear of cuckoldry which resonates throughout the play. This fear reaches its apex in 4.3, when Oliver relates his rescue from the serpent and lioness by Orlando and his subsequent "conversion". Lewis describes Oliver's narration as so fraught with "cryptic" allusion and allegory that she enlists "Freudian dream analysis" to explain these undercurrents of fear, and to illumine the play's alertness to "female potency".[118]

While threats of betrayal – familial, political, and sexual, particularly as concerns cuckoldry – appear "continually displaced, defused, or indirectly represented", they nonetheless inform the play with a "sober preoccupation with keeping faith", Lewis argues.[119] The only way out of this threat, as evidenced in Touchstone's nonchalance towards Audrey's (or his own) marital loyalty, comes through language; the inability to respond in words and to counter through language any perceived transgression denotes "impotency and physical failure".[120] The "less talkative, less verbally facile" Orlando, for example, whose "fear of cuckoldry as a would-be groom is more deep-seated than the clown's", can muster no words to manoeuvre his way through the early onset of love or the wit-filled admonitions of Rosalind.[121]

As You Like It's plot development includes Rosalind's quick acquisition of the ability to exploit "patriarchal structures and expectations to her own benefit, although often at some risk to her appeal", Lewis observes. At court, she, too, reveals an uneasy reticence, but in the forest she learns to manipulate and incite "the very male fear of cuckoldry" that pervades the play. She steers things her way so effectively that by the end of the play she "achieves a balance of power with her new husband and, by extension, with male society at large".[122] "In this light", *As You Like It* "is less a comedy of subordination than one of inclusion".[123]

What Rosalind enacts in the forest with Orlando, Lewis posits, involves a "methodological intensification of Orlando's love-madness", one that serves to "deepen his anxiety toward women",[124] Fear of her own betrayal at Orlando's hands may underlie her actions; however, her strategy remains strictly focused on instilling in Orlando a fear of marital disloyalty. Performing in this fashion, Rosalind "attributes humanity to women by acknowledging that they have desires for themselves separate from the husbands".[125] Without their freedom, Rosalind illustrates, women will seek alternatives to the marriage bond.

Rosalind, according to Lewis, insists that Orlando treat her well: he should show up on time and allow her a voice of her own within marriage. Orlando's misperception of Rosalind – her ideal state, which in his mind precludes any verbal challenge on her part – simply must go. Because of Orlando's inarticulate nature, Shakespeare enlists Oliver's narration of Orlando's rescue to demonstrate Orlando's working through of his anxieties. In dream-work, of course, one character may – and typically does – represent multiple characters: in Oliver's dreamlike story, he represents, at various times, himself, Orlando, and Rosalind. First, Oliver's experiences in the forest awaken him "to his own viciousness".[126] Oliver's struggles with the lioness (a recurrent symbol of sexual appetite) and serpent, furthermore, represent both Orlando's fear of cuckoldry and, in the instance of the serpent, his "vulnerable brother, overwhelmed verbally and physically by a possessive, loquacious, and potentially spiteful bride".[127] This "condensation" of multiple personages, along with the "displacement" of one character for another, eventually creates a sense where Orlando, in defeating the serpent and lioness, and in overcoming his anger at Oliver, actually defeats not only Oliver and Rosalind but also his fear of betrayal by Rosalind. The bloody napkin Oliver brings to Rosalind, moreover, comes to represent Orlando's newly forged commitments to both Oliver and Rosalind, no matter the price.

As You Like It, Lewis concludes:

> ■ resists the misogyny that might be directed at a woman taking control and also softens the cynicism that a woman's taking control through sexual manipulation might ordinarily provoke. In particular, the play understates and obscures Rosalind's considerable agency.[128] □

Moreover, by "assuming the role of wife" in the manner she does, Rosalind "redefines it to her satisfaction".[129]

As feminism and Gender Studies extend their influence over how we read and assess *As You Like It*, some critics shift their focus more towards matters of sexuality and identity. The following chapter includes discussions of those studies concerned with these issues.

CHAPTER EIGHT

1981–Present: "She Phebes Me": Homoerotics, Queer Theory and Identity

After establishing itself as a logical theoretical extension of feminism, Gender Studies expanded to include studies of masculinity and male desire; from these explorations of maleness and male desire emerged *Queer Theory*. As discussed in Chapter 7, nearly all Gender Studies practitioners maintain that gender and gender roles are culturally constructed and, therefore, malleable and manipulable by a subject's culture and the individual subject. Queer Theorists complicate this premise by rejecting the male/female binary construction – the belief, in its rudest articulation, that men are men and women are women. (Queer Theorists, incidentally, actually eschew most if not all culturally constructed bifurcations, including those of colour, faith, or politics.) In its place emerges the concept of a spectrum, where all males and females situate themselves onto varying measurements of maleness and/or femaleness. Within any given human being, in other words, there exists a fluidity of gender, and each human is free, as Shakespeare exemplifies in his depiction of Rosalind, to explore female or male identity, as well as desire and experience, at any moment.

Proponents of Queer Theory find an embarrassment of riches in the never fully resolved love relations and romantic entanglements taking place in Arden. For short intervals, Phebe obsesses romantically over Ganymede-Rosalind, while Orlando kisses Ganymede-Rosalind as a substitute for his love "Rosalind", who in his mind constitutes no more than an idealized version of the female he has concocted from Petrarchan poetic convention. Celia, too, seems to suffer from an unrequited attraction to her cousin Rosalind, and while Rosalind belittles Phebe's besotted advances, she never stymies Phebe's attraction to her. These various queerings of desire invite numerous readings of the play and create heretofore unconsidered possibilities of meaning and significance.

Robert Kimbrough

In "Androgyny Seen through Shakespeare's Disguise" (1982), Robert Kimbrough insists that gender is largely self-determined. Urging readers to view early modern drama both "historically and theatrically", Kimbrough also claims that audiences acknowledged that boys acted Shakespeare's female characters' roles: for any drama to succeed, the audience must accept any "sex, age, and cultural origin" an actor portrays.[1] With this said, Kimbrough suggests that Shakespeare's employment of boy-actor-into-woman-character-into-boy-character stems from a conviction that the "ideal goal" of androgyny involves "unity, wholeness, harmony, and perfection within the confines of the human".[2]

Greek and Judeo-Christian archetypes of androgyny, according to Kimbrough, connote a time and experience before the duality of male and female rendered feelings of division or incompleteness among individuals. Living at a time when gender roles and relationships between woman and man undergo increased scrutiny, Shakespeare advocates an acceptance of the "complete humanity of women" as well as men's adoption into their own psyches of "female graces" such as compassion.[3] Female characters such as Rosalind illustrate the developmental path all humans should take, for, in disguise as men, they realize much fuller expressions of the human: male and female harmoniously combined. In Celia's company, Rosalind can reveal "intellect and wit" while she also can be "relaxed, giddy, and giggly"; in man's disguise and in Orlando's company, she just as easily may exude aggressiveness and salaciousness; and in Phebe's presence, Rosalind illustrates the maturity and wisdom she has reached through the liberation her disguise provides.[4]

From the start, Rosalind seems to understand the restrictions her culture imposes on her through gender bifurcation, and she welcomes the opportunity to eliminate them through masculine dress. Her eagerness, Kimbrough posits, shows in the redundancy implied in requesting Touchstone's accompaniment in the move to Arden: his presence "negates" the need for protection that male habiliments may offer to her and Celia. While in the forest, furthermore, Rosalind avoids contact with her father, who, if he recognized her, certainly would force her to re-assume her identity as Rosalind. Finally, Rosalind remains in disguise even after she discovers that Orlando resides in the forest near her.

Kimbrough encourages his readers to construe the anti-feminine remarks Rosalind unleashes while speaking with Orlando or Celia as a means of "wrestling with attributes created for women"[5] by her culture; in essence, she challenges these constrictive attributes and reaches "toward a fuller realization of her humanhood, or potential for androgyny".[6] Through a closer examination of this play, we see how androgyny "is not a physical state, but a state of mind".[7]

Bruce R. Smith

In Chapter 4 of his *Homosexual Desire in Shakespeare's England* (1991), Bruce R. Smith (b. 1946) states, "Amid the high spirits of folk festivity, playing about with gender roles could easily turn into playing about with sexual roles".[8] Smith's claim ushers in discussions of the relations between genre and expressions of sexual desire, as well as between different social classes' written and/or performed expressions of this desire.

In *As You Like It*, Smith argues, Orlando and (especially) Rosalind woo each other through "some audaciously direct talk about sex".[9] This dialogue, spoken and presented on Shakespeare's stage by an adult male actor (playing Orlando) and "a boy actor dressed as a woman dressed as a boy" (playing Rosalind), would have been perceived by the audience as "a man and a boy flirting with abandon and getting away with it".[10] This staging of homosexual desire models itself on two traditions. The first, Greek romances and eclogues and then Ovidian narratives, where boys often stood as the "object of desire",[11] permeated and influenced early modern English tradition through Christopher Marlowe (1564–93) in "Hero and Leander" (1598), Francis Beaumont (1584–1613) in "Salmacis and Hermaphroditus" (1602), and even Shakespeare himself in "Venus and Adonis" (1593). These texts fixate on "a male youth who is innocent of both sexual experience and gender identity" wherein readers "discover an erotic allure far stronger than that of heroes and heroines whose gender is certain". The effect lies in a vertical as well as horizontal "male bonding": these young men:

> ■ inspire in other men, especially in older men, a desire to initiate the youths into maleness, to *incorporate* them, physically, into the male power structure. [Smith's italics][12] □

These "bisexual fantasies", in other words, offer a "temporary freedom" to the young men before inculcating them into the norms of the culture.[13]

The second tradition involves rural English folk festivities and plays, which likewise often gave licence "for homosexual shenanigans",[14] in this case to a wider circle of participants: "While gentlemen were reading about" homoeroticized young men "in their libraries", Smith observes, "villagers were acting them out" in mummers' plays, morris dances, Robin Hood legends, and romance dramas.[15] Although all "impulses that run counter to social rules", including "male-male sexual desire", are "allowed expression" in these folk festivities, "they must be played out within carefully prescribed boundaries"; these "moments were totally contained by the power structure of Elizabethan society", and whatever "might happen on that special Sunday, the normal rules of society obtained on Saturday and Monday".[16] Thus, while the activities gentlemen read about and commoners watched stimulated sexual desire, and even enlarged the parameters whereby "the sexual desire that men feel for each other"[17] could be intensified, they did so to stifle these behaviours.

In *As You Like It*, Shakespeare challenges gender roles in two ways, Smith contends. First, he "lets the woman play the role of sexual aggressor". He also allows "the confusion of gender roles" to spiral to the point where Orlando eagerly pursues an erotic interaction with a boy.[18] In both instances, Shakespeare "seizes the chance to play up the artifice of acting and the sexual ambiguity of the actor".[19] He realizes that cross-dressing and other methods of gender confusion constitute "a particularly volatile symbol of liminality, a relaxation of the social rules that hold man's animal passions in check".[20] Romance, that tradition from which *As You Like It*, the Greek and Ovidian narratives, and many of the folk festive dramas derive, provides "a way of indulging homosexual desire and yet not indulging homosexual desire". *As You Like It*'s "conventional" ending in marriage, for example, separates the reader-auditor "from the fantasies in which he has reveled", but it even may push further, in that the "androgynous flirt" who delivers the epilogue "invites us to take with us as we leave the theater some of the liminal freedom we allowed ourselves during the play".[21]

Valerie Traub

The practice of employing boys as actors on Shakespeare's stage "made possible complex desires and fantasies, and mediated cultural anxieties"[22] concerning not merely gender but sexuality, Valerie Traub (b. 1958) argues in Chapter 5 of her book, *Desire and Anxiety: Circulations of Sexuality in Shakespearean Drama* (1992), one of the most insightful studies of gender and sexuality in early modern England. Traub proposes that boys acting in Shakespeare's comedies worked "for both actors and audiences as an expression of non-hegemonic desire within the confines of conventional, comedic restraints".[23]

Various Shakespearean texts, *As You Like It* among them, not only "display a homoerotic circulation of desire", Traub continues, but also demonstrate how, in the playwright's culture, "homoerotic energy is elicited, exchanged, negotiated, and displaced as it confronts the pleasures and anxieties of its meanings".[24] Traub prefers the term "transvestism" over disguise or cross-dressing, and notes the frequency with which early modern opponents of Shakespeare's theatre deemed the boy actors' transvestism an affront not only to "status and gender boundaries, but erotic boundaries as well"; as such, clothing stood as "an important indicator of one's sexual stance", for it denoted "erotic availability or lack thereof".[25]

"Gender anxiety is no more, and no less, constitutive of homoerotic desire than it is of heterosexual desire",[26] Traub reminds readers; "homoerotic activity", furthermore", which is "predicated on, but not identical to, the presence of boy actors playing female parts", provided "a de facto homoerotic basis upon which to build structures of desire" which the theatre "made available" to both male and female auditors. As You Like It, for example, demonstrates "that within the early modern erotic community the homoerotic relation to desire could be represented as both celebratory and strained".[27] And because Shakespeare presents Rosalind/Ganymede as "a multiply sexual object", Orlando's desire for her/him "prevents the stable reinstitution of heterosexuality, upon which the marriage plot depends".[28]

In other words, the "reinstitution of gender role (and Rosalind's political subordination under her husband's rule) is incommensurate" with the "rigidification of sexuality" one would expect in a play that ends in so many marriages, Traub avers.[29] By the time she weds Orlando in her father's presence, Rosalind instead has led "the play into a mode of desire neither heterosexual nor homoerotic, but both heterosexual *and* homoerotic [Traub's italics]". Rosalind "thus instigates a deconstruction of the binary system by which desire in subsequent centuries came to be organized, regulated, and disciplined".[30] As she does with Orlando, Rosalind "*elicits*" Phebe's homoerotic desire as well, one "which falls outside (or on the cusp) of the binarism of gender [Traub's italics]".[31] In addition, Rosalind basks in "her sense of power" over Silvius that she experiences while posing as a male.[32] The play's "investment in homoerotic pleasure" extends as well to the courtship of "Rosalind" which Orlando enacts, where his "ability to hold in suspension a dual sexuality that feels no compulsion to make arbitrary distinctions between" male and female comes to the fore. We witness an even more explicit instance of a diminished "distance between Rosalind and Ganymede" in their mock marriage, where:

■ distinctions between homoerotic and heterosexual collapse as well. As the woman and the shepherd boy merge, Orlando's words resound with the conviction that, for the moment, he (as much as Rosalind and the audience) is engaged in the ceremony as if it were real.[33] □

Here, Traub, suggests, the:

■ subversiveness of this dramatic gesture lies in the dual motion of first, appropriating the meaning of matrimony for deviant desires; and second, exposing the heterosexual imperative of matrimony as a reduction of the plurality of desire into the singularity of matrimony.[34] □

By the time Hymen actually unites them in marriage, the "text's devotion" to any "simultaneity" between heterosexual union and homosexual desire "would appear to be negated".[35]

Instead, the text playfully explores the various possibilities implicit in "if", the word Touchstone introduces just as the marriages commence. No character in the play, then, is "homosexual", Traub continues, or in any way a threat because of his or her sexuality. Instead, "at various moments", several characters "temporarily inhabit a homoerotic position of desire".[36] In the scene involving Oliver's encounter with the lioness and snake, however, Traub notes that, while *As You Like It* "seems less interested in the threat of a particular mode of desire (hetero/homo)", it does register the "dangers desire *as such* poses to men [Traub's italics]". Sexual "danger", then, in Traub's estimation, "is encoded as feminizing to the object persistently figured as male".[37]

Homoeroticism only becomes "problematic" when it is not mutual[38] or, more significantly, when "homoerotic exchanges threaten to replace heterosexual bonds, when eroticism is collapsed into anxiety about reproduction", Traub concludes. In these instances, homoeroticism "is exorcised at the same time as the female gender is resecured into the patriarchal order".[39]

William Kerrigan

"Courtship is a time of liminal experimentation for a woman", William Kerrigan (b. 1943) asserts in "Female Friends and Fraternal Enemies in *As You Like It*" (1994), as well as a "time of woman's greatest power and liberty".[40] Perceiving the girlhood "twinship" between Rosalind and Celia in Freudian terms, Kerrigan argues that both women "attempt to achieve a completeness and self-sufficiency" before they reluctantly cross the "threshold" into "mature sexuality" and marriage.[41] Largely through Rosalind's industry, these women reprove any harm to the narcissism that, according to Freud, commences and accompanies the female Oedipus complex. While both women "choose marriage over female friendship", then, they also find a way to "elevate their cousinhood into sisterhood", which becomes a "best-case situation for preserving their old oneness in the adult context of marriage".[42]

Kerrigan observes in Rosalind's cross-dressing an indulgence, an eagerness, to "explore" the disguise that male clothing offers her, at times to the point where "this indulgence acts as a drag on the destined resolution of the comedy". He suggests that the "liminality" Rosalind's disguise affords her, a "state" where she is "neither man nor woman, betwixt and between",[43] parallels the positions in which courtship situates both young men and women:

> ■ During courtship some of the major dichotomies in life are experienced at the same time. The participants in a wooing may exchange vows and love tokens, at once married and not married; in the Renaissance this sort of doubleness flourished in the time between troth-plight (*sponsalia per verba de futuro*) and the

exchange of performative vows completing the marriage (*sponsalia per verba de praesenti*). Wooers are also chaste and sexual, settled and unsettled, adult and not fully adult, sane and mad."[44] ☐

In addition, courtship involves "the feeling of being in disguise": the person attracted to you "does not know you, and couldn't possibly love *you*, so it must be that some disguised version of yourself is loved [Kerrigan's italics]".[45]

Because *As You Like It* concerns itself "with the place that might be assigned in the ages of woman to the radiant friendship" between Rosalind and Celia, it contrasts these women's "great but unsentimental intimacy"[46] with the male sibling rivalries around and impacting them, Kerrigan asserts. Noting the "literacy" of the Forest of Arden, a forest "teeming with heteroglossia", Kerrigan believes this forest acts a place where Orlando, Oliver, Frederick, and Duke Senior encounter "a set of problems that stand prior to" the Oedipal issues more easily averted by Rosalind and Celia, a space beyond Lacan's "paternal" language order and one "embryonically a part of the mother/infant dyad".[47]

■ Both sets of exiles discover that, in order to get to Arden, one must nearly starve; hunger in infancy is what calls forth the mother, transforming her absence into presence. These cues suggest that the flight to Arden is at some level a flight to the mother of infancy.[48] ☐

Represented by the serpent and lioness, however, this mother simultaneously proves a menace, who threatens engulfment. Orlando's "nature" and "kindness" towards Oliver "defeat" the elder son's "deep motive" of "revenge and justice" for Orlando's displacing him from maternal favour, and Oliver suddenly becomes "excessive in beneficence". Oliver thus sees the "good" of freedom from "that mother" and "immediately the sibling rivalry is over".[49]

Kerrigan extends the "primeval mother" representations even further, as he describes how Orlando, too, overcomes a "dread of being overmastered by the wit and bossiness of" Rosalind, his "dominant wife".[50] Acknowledging that, because of his inability to speak when he first falls for Rosalind, Orlando "will be the submissive partner in his love match"[51] with her, Kerrigan explains how his defeat of "the most savage early mother, the hungry dry-dugged lioness", proves him now "fit for marriage".[52]

Kerrigan concludes by challenging earlier critics' conjectures concerning the play's homoerotic proclivities: *As You Like It* "does indeed accumulate a charge of homoerotic feeling", Kerrigan states, "but it is not to be enjoyed as readily as some modern interpreters imagine".[53] The "heterosexual declaration" implicit in the marriages that end the play is answered in the epilogue, which "balances the theme of female friendship with good spirits between men", and "homosexual desire surfaces in the kisses" that the actor who played Rosalind "would plant on the audience's most attractive faces".[54]

Cynthia Marshall

Situating her essay on the "divide" between structuralist and poststructuralist discourse, and employing "the psychoanalytic concept of negation" in order to examine *As You Like It*'s "structure" and "particular fixations",[55] Cynthia Marshall focuses, in "The Doubled Jacques and Constructions of Negation in *As You Like It*" (1998), on the two Jacques inhabiting the play. She believes the "melancholy Jacques", who accompanies Duke Senior and his exiles into the forest, actually serves as a "double" for Jacques de Boys, middle brother to Oliver and Orlando:

> ■ In a play so intimately concerned with names and with situations, this elliptical blocking of an absent Jacques with a present one provides a signal instance of the symbol's capacity to compensate for loss.[56] □

The melancholy Jacques' "crucial" purpose in the play involves the "undertow of sadness" throughout *As You Like It*, one "that is brilliantly held at bay by a Shakespearean game of *Fort/Da*" (see below). The "unconstrained gender play in Arden", moreover, along with "other sorts of liberty within the play" are linked to this Jacques as well.[57] Jacques represents "the most obvious example of the structural and linguistic compensations the play repeatedly makes". Marshall's intent here involves extending:

> ■ the classic understanding of the compensatory nature of comedy by showing how language is imbricated in comic structure, using contemporary psychoanalytic theory to probe the connections in early modern texts between melancholia, gender, and language.[58] □

After reminding readers that Jacques actually "shows little sad or brooding affect [emotion]" throughout the play, Marshall encourages us to view this character as a "placeholder, standing in" not only for the de Boys brother but, more significantly, "for the acknowledgement of loss and sadness missing in Arden's merry crew". Jacques may "forestall the threat of melancholia" in Rosalind, Orlando, and others, but as he does so he "also figures melancholia's threatening estrangement of self from self".[59]

What Marshall means by all this involves Sigmund Freud's concept of *negation*, a means of "taking cognizance of what is repressed" and allowing "the content of a repressed image or idea" out into consciousness "on condition that it is *negated*", as Marshall quotes Freud [Freud's italics].[60] Marshall identifies negation as a "central" element in the "functioning of comedy", and connects it, albeit advisedly, to Freud's *Fort/Da* game, wherein Freud associated *"Fort"*, or "Gone", and *"Da"*, or "There" – the two terms his grandson used to describe a toy the boy repeatedly threw and then recovered – to explain people's compulsion to repeat past traumatic experiences.

Because negation "fails to deliver mastery of what is repressed", the subject "must appeal to language in order to trick herself".[61] And because of this failure, Marshall modifies Freud's conjectures as concerns the *Fort/Da* game to incorporate Jacques Lacan's concept of the "split subject", where Lacan investigates how totally a "subject may invest itself in others and how divided its emotional life may be" as a result. What this means as regards the *Fort/Da* game involves the symbolic value of the toy thrown by the child: to Freud, it represents the mother, but to Lacan it represents "a small part of the subject that detaches itself from him while still remaining his, still retained".[62] The significance of this lies in the melancholia Jacques manifests.

While Jacques claims melancholia as his defining feature, he actually uses the malady "to veil an inaccessible zone, a 'reality that is other than what we are allowed to see'" (Marshall quotes Joan Copjec). His use of language in this manner mirrors an important tendency Marshall observes throughout the play:

> ■ *As You Like It* returns again and again to the ability or propensity of language, and in particular of names, to veil an inaccessible zone, a "reality that is other than what we are allowed to see" and is taken for reality precisely because we are unable to see it.[63] □

The "play's world" becomes one of substitutions much like the one Jacques enacts, and Rosalind "is the showpiece of the play's set of substitutions".[64] Her veiling of identity by becoming Ganymede not only allows her a way out of her own melancholy (an example of negation) but also licenses her "and those who identify with her" to be male, while Orlando "and those readers or viewers who primarily identify with him" may "acknowledge the titillating possibility" of becoming "a boy lover". Her staying in disguise throughout the play, furthermore, signals the extent of "erotic play" within the drama: she simultaneously desires to engage in heterosexual coupling and to remain a boy who interacts with Orlando. Orlando, too, only pulls back from sexual union with the male Ganymede because, when Oliver claims Celia as his bride, Orlando "quails from continued 'thinking' of this free and enriched sort".[65] *As You Like It*, in essence, repeatedly expresses "troubling ideas" but then disguises them "so as to limit their impact".[66]

Marshall also delves into why Rosalind silences herself at the play's conclusion, having been "freed to practice the proliferating substitutions of happy linguistic function" as a result of Jacques "serving as the symbol for melancholia". She notes that, through Hymen's presence at the wedding ceremony, there appears "a correspondent movement away from parents and in particular from mothers", for Hymen's presence signals a "profound absence of mothers" in the play.[67] Their nonexistence is "because the primal bond with them occurs prior to linguistic acquisition".[68]

What *As You Like It* offers instead includes various manifestations of misogyny – found in Ganymede's, Celia's, and Jacques' statements – all of which suggest that "the play does not thereby create an ideal site of gendered or psychological equality".[69] Instead, it ends with Jacques "redistributing over the four couples" the melancholy that he claimed for himself. There seems to arise an "association" between melancholy and marriage, Marshall believes, one that arises because of marriage's "shutting down of gender play".[70] If Arden, "the place of banishment, is *Fort*", then "the arrival of the Second Brother would seem to announce *Da*, the completion of the pattern, the return to reality, and the end of the play".[71]

Jessica Tvordi

In "Female Alliance and the Construction of Homoeroticism in *As You Like It* and *Twelfth Night*" (1999), Jessica Tvordi differentiates *As You Like It* from *Twelfth Night* by noting the total erasure in *As You Like It* of the "nonmutual" yet "specifically homoerotic" alliance between Rosalind and Celia. *Twelfth Night*, in contrast, "preserves a mutual alliance" between Olivia and Maria, one that remains "erotically ambiguous" throughout.[72] Despite the ultimate elimination of homoerotic pairing in *As You Like It*, Tvordi believes that Celia represents a woman who "challenges masculinist constructs of feminine subjectivity by transgressing accepted boundaries of gender, sexuality, and power".[73]

Tvordi attributes Celia's compulsive attraction to Rosalind to "socioeconomic" factors just as much as to "emotional" and "erotic" factors,[74] and claims that these factors become more apparent when we recognize Celia's behaviour towards her cousin as "manipulative and combative".[75] While in her home, which also serves as her usurping father's court, Celia exudes both confidence in and control over her relationship with Rosalind: her demeanour illustrates this authority women exerted only within the early modern domestic sphere. Yet in her comparison of herself and Rosalind to Juno's swans in 1.3, Celia also reveals a degree of self-delusion, for her allusion connotes an everlasting bond between Rosalind and her, a vision that Rosalind does not share.

In actuality a "lukewarm participant" in their "alliance", Rosalind instead distances herself from Celia and pursues her "heterosexual desires"[76] for Orlando immediately upon their meeting – a behaviour Tvordi believes all female "transvestite figures in Shakespeare's plays" enact.[77] While Celia never fully comprehends that her power over Rosalind stems from Rosalind's compromised position at court, she does recognize Rosalind's sexual inclinations and begins a "desperate effort to recover" the relationship, one often more "transgressive"[78] in its homoerotic content than Rosalind's masculine disguise: she conducts "subtle forms of manipulation" as well as some more direct challenges to Rosalind's newfound "authority" by "bringing attention" to her "political power".[79]

As the play reaches its end, Celia becomes quiet, even "subservient", and her marriage to Orlando's recently converted brother Oliver serves as a "satisfactory substitute" for her lost relationship with Rosalind – and, in a larger sense, represents a woman's "compliance" not only with the "inevitability of marriage"[80] but also with a delimited "autonomy", both "socially and sexually".[81]

Carol Thomas Neely

In "Lovesickness, Gender, and Subjectivity: *Twelfth Night* and *As You Like It*" (2000), Carol Thomas Neely (b. 1939) argues that the marriages which conclude *As You Like It* reveal:

> ■ less a prescriptive imposition of a hierarchical patriarchy than an accommodation to subjects both male and female who negotiate within culture and ideology to attain their compelling desires.[82] □

Once Neely acknowledges the recently "uncovered evidence of women's initiatives, achievements, and disruptions both in Shakespeare's plays and in the culture", she then directs attention towards the early modern discourse of lovesickness as further evidence that, because "desire can strike anyone and fasten on anything, gender roles and erotic object choice are remarkably fluid, and the relationship between gender and sexuality is unstable".[83] Therefore "theatrical representations of love can license wayward desires", and "theatrical happy endings do not always reproduce rigid gender hierarchies and normative heterosexual marriages".[84]

Once considered a malady almost exclusive to men, lovesickness actually afflicted women in what appears equal measure, Neely observes. While lovesickness exposes men and women to "painful desires and strange fantasies", it also often initiates "passionate agendas" which can cause a man or woman to "resist or disrupt status roles, rigid gender hierarchies, and binary constructions of sexuality". Acknowledgement that lovesickness affects women as frequently as men also brings to the fore a clearer picture of the "multiple and fluid modern sexualities" manifest at this time:

> ■ In the discourse of lovesickness, gender is less polarized and sexuality less normalized than in many other early modern texts. Because the discourse is concerned primarily with the satisfaction of desires, only secondarily with marriage,

and not at all with reproduction, it includes without sharp distinction a wide and weird range of gender behaviours, erotic objects, and amorous styles.[85] ☐

Neely provides an extensive account of the symptoms associated with lovesickness, and identifies "unsatisfied desire" as the most prevalent of them. Two cures for unsatisfied desire arise as the most common, she also explains, both of which are prescribed only to men: "therapeutic intercourse" and "misogyny therapy", where other men close to the victim recount for him the ugliness and trouble that women bring with them into a relationship. Doctors, theologians, and philosophers rarely discussed women who suffered lovesickness, and when they did, they "occluded their satisfaction".[86]

During the Renaissance, though, attention to women who experienced lovesickness increased, Neely observes, and this attention began to focus upon "the instability of bodies, desires, and love objects". Discourse also began to blur "distinctions between normative and transgressive desires and between heteroeroticism and homoeroticism".[87] "Gendered object choice does not centrally define the boundary between acceptable and unacceptable sexuality",[88] and even fetishes involving inanimate objects entered the discourse. One's "inability to satisfy desires", Neely continues, "springs invariably from the love of inappropriate or unobtainable objects", and the fact that these objects "are homoerotic or heteroerotic is not of great importance".[89]

In Shakespeare's plays, including *As You Like it*, challenges to the normative abound, including representations of love: where "women's love is routinely represented as urgent, aggressive, and acted on", Neely describes, "men's love is more often passive, subordinating, or fetishistic". In addition, the gender of a love object almost always stands in diminished importance when compared to "age, class, or erotic roles or styles", and one's desire consistently gives a character, male or female, "momentum and energy".[90] Even when the play ends, women do not necessarily fall back into subordinate or compromised positions. "Individual satisfaction" takes precedence over what C.L. Barber and Northrop Frye labelled "social reconciliation"; and even when heterosexual marriage obtains, it "assures *neither* permanent satisfaction *nor* social harmony [Neely's italics]".[91]

In *As You Like It*, Neely believes, "love sickness discourse reveals how love can catalyse subjectivity and overturn normative gender and erotic roles". The play also illustrates how women pursue love "more aggressively" than men and represents "several gendered stereotypes" of desire,[92] which, when seen in aggregate, "call into question the possibility of normative desire, fixed gender roles, or stable marriages". Throughout the play, shifts "of character and allegiance are the rule". Frederick and Oliver "convert", while Audrey abandons William for Touchstone, Phebe shifts her affections from Ganymede to Silvius, and Rosalind and Celia "give up their affection for each other to become lovers of men".[93] Rosalind experiences the most changes, and also serves as the catalysing agent for others, largely:

- by putting into circulation multiple stereotypes of masculinity and femininity, of love and marriage. As these are ventriloquized through Rosalind, they are rendered comic and unstable.[94] ☐

Celia, in contrast, "is reduced to watching, mocking", and, through her hasty marriage to Oliver, "eventually mimicking Rosalind".[95]

With Orlando, Rosalind-as-Ganymede-as-Rosalind "exploits the conventions of the discourse of lovesickness" to fix his attentions on "her"; she "induces lovesickness by modelling for Orlando the symptoms of desire" and then helps him to rehearse "wooing", "kissing", and "marriage", all before enacting her cure via "the standard misogynistic denigration of women recommended by" former writers.[96] By the end of the play, she "subordinates" Orlando and imagines herself as "Rosalind", so that she can "alleviate her own anxieties about being subordinated to a lover or husband". Her misogynistic language and promise of "aggressive sexual promiscuity" remind not only Orlando and herself but the audience that "marriage does not necessarily provide a cure for love, produce a stable gender hierarchy, or lead to a happy ending".[97] Celia mimics Rosalind's actions when she calls "into question Orlando's looks, his kisses, his fidelity" in 3.4.

In contrast to the standard methods of misogyny therapy, Rosalind's version "does not eliminate desire but induces it", Neely explains.[98] Perhaps more significantly, the "multiplicity" of Rosalind's (as well as of the text's) "erotic styles and gender roles" proves "unsettling", for they "deconstruct any simple notions of gender and desire", despite their conventional natures.[99] They remain unsettling, even though the play ends in multiple seemingly heteronormative marriages, because the weddings' "highly formalized and ritualized enactment" hint that "this is just one more moment of roles performed", and is no more permanent than any other performance in the play.[100]

Valerie Rohy

"The language of conversion is striking in a play so profoundly concerned with mutability", Valerie Rohy states in "*As You Like It*: Fortune's Turn" (2011), especially when one considers that the "notion of conversion presumes that some aspects of character are inessential and impermanent – that is, contingent". Are heterosexuality and homosexuality, Rohy asks, "subject to the whims of fortune"?[101]

As do many recent readers of *As You Like It*, Rohy notes Celia's same-sex attraction to Rosalind, as well as her quick agreement to marry Oliver. Rohy likens her experience to Oliver's (as well as Frederick's) and calls it a "conversion experience".[102] She then compares Celia's change to contemporary "conversion therapy", a process advocated by several anti-gay, right-leaning organizations who believe that homosexuality is one's choice:

> ■ At stake in both queer and anti-gay claims is the possibility of desire's contingency; for both, the definition of desire as anything other than nature opens up the (threatening and promising) prospect of homosexuality's end.[103] □

The "problem" here, accordingly to Rohy, "lies in any narrative" that offers "only one conclusion – marriage and the reconstitution of social order – in pursuit of which it both promotes and denies desire's contingency".[104]

Any "narrative fantasy" that insists on heterosexual marriage as the normative ideological formation in a culture, in other words – including both *As You Like It* and a conversion therapy pamphlet or film – will subordinate "desire's contingency"[105] to itself, even when the narrative makes clear that love is subject to the whims of fortune. In fact, Rohy argues that neither *As You Like It* nor conversion therapy advocates "grant nearly enough" value to "fortune" when they consider the phenomenon of desire.[106] Rohy suggests that both queer theorists and the LGBT community consider "contingency" as a "third term", one that is "defined by neither voluntarism nor subjection".[107]

CONCLUSION

As discussed in the introduction to this guide, *As You Like It* suffered a long neglect, well into the eighteenth century, after its initial performances ended. Partially because of its examinations of gender and identity, however, which parallel our interests in these matters, the play now stands among Shakespeare's most popular comedies, and the most discussed in academic circles. And as becomes clear in several essays included in this guide's second half, discussions of gender and identity more and more drift into discussions of performance. As critics consider more thoughtfully Shakespeare's awareness of how actors who play the parts of others become potential proxies for any auditor or reader who questions his or her identity – because of gender leanings, ethical concerns, financial advancement, political aspirations, or personal fulfilment – the play likely will fill theatres and dominate scholarly discussions well into the future. Performance is becoming criticism, some would say.

Continuations of gender and identity study through performance

Performance studies began in the 1970s, and now ventures down myriad paths, including interrogations of a period's treatment of gender and/or gender roles. In "'Perfect Types of Womanhood': Rosalind, Beatrice and Viola in Victorian Criticism and Performance" (1979), for example, Russell Jackson acknowledges a "general enthusiasm" among Victorians for Shakespeare's "heroines as examples of womanhood at its finest", but also notes how certain female characters, Rosalind among them, "could not be accepted without some special pleading", primarily because they "enjoyed a freedom of speech and mind beyond what is proper in a well-brought-up Victorian girl".[1] Jackson examines critics' often uneasy appraisals of Rosalind, and explains how the construction of her costume straddled the "demands of historical consistency and feminine modesty".[2] When staging performances of *As You Like It*, furthermore, Jackson notes how critics and actors "established a subtext in which" Rosalind "found happiness through marriage", which ultimately contained her autonomy.[3]

In "Touchstone for the Times: Victorians in the Forest of Arden" (2003), Richard Foulkes revisits Jackson's contention that Rosalind's character required

CONCLUSION 133

tempering before consumption. Helena Faucit Martin's portrayals of Rosalind, occurring from 1844 to 1879, bear all the attributes Jackson describes, as she purposefully embodied the "Victorian gentlewoman".[4] Citing 32 productions of *As You Like It* between 1871 and 1911, however, Foulkes argues that the play's growing popularity stems from the "physical appearance of Rosalind as Ganymede".[5] Several actresses, including Lillie Langtry (1853–1929), who played Rosalind in 1882 and 1890, emphasized "the more assertive side of Rosalind", a method that proved "as liberating for the actress" as for Rosalind.[6] The American actresses Mary Anderson (1918–2014), Ada Rehan (1857–1916), and Eleanor Calhoun (1862–1957) adopted and even embellished Langtry's style, and exerted significant influence over Rosalind's autonomous stage presence, a control which led to occasional all-female performances of the play.

More recently, studies have appeared that focus on the play's metatheatrical qualities and relationships to gender and sexuality. One example is Lina Perkins Wilder's "Playing Sodomites: Gender and Protean Character in *As You Like It*" (2012). The fact that one actor plays Rosalind/Ganymede instils in these characters an "embodiment of change", Wilder claims, and creates personas that "must be understood" not as character or actor, but as "both".[7] Rosalind's/Ganymede's "duality" throughout the play "speaks both to the quality of gender in the play and to the construction of character".[8] In early modern England, boys and women were deemed unstable, changeable; in much the same fashion, actors possessed this liminality. And just as actors failed to "abide by rules that govern stable gender identities", *As You Like It* "embraces" charges of "sodomy" in that its characters "become the very gender-bending actors who portray them".[9] At the end of the play, for example, when Rosalind provides for Orlando exactly what he desires – a woman dressed as a woman and who acts like a woman – she "transfers the gender-bending 'sodomite' that is the boy actor from a playworld to a social context" that takes on the characteristics of "the real world".[10]

Wilder discusses early modern anti-theatrical polemics, including the anti-theatricalists' conception of sodomy as "idolatry" and "theatricality", or instability of character.[11] Like Hamlet, Rosalind "adopts a deliberately deceptive mode of behavior",[12] one long associated with Proteus, and through which she changes "seamlessly from one passion to another" and "from one gender to another".[13] Because one's actions, like an actor's performance, may be genuine or not, one's identity also can become ambiguous; one's clothing, moreover, enhances this ambiguity. Rosalind and Celia manipulate their clothing and thus make "complex erotic play out of" what Wilder terms "actorly 'sodomy'". All "Rosalinds", including the "real" one who loves Orlando and laments her father's exile, constitute no more than "performance".[14] At any moment, Rosalind is a "creature of constant and unstable transformation whose changefulness, in this case, is a product of her/his gender identity both as boy and as woman".[15]

Even at the play's end, when marriage and Hymen's "magic" corral Rosalind's gender indeterminacy, Rosalind "need not embrace any of her multiple identities"; instead, she need only "assume one that will allow the plot to conclude". This continuation of indeterminacy even into the epilogue "becomes shorthand" for "the unclear boundary between character and actor".[16] Her protean sodomite status legitimizes for the audience a toying "with the idea of other endings than marriage".[17]

In "'Better Days': Cultural Memory in *As You Like It*" (2008), Indira Ghose takes performance theory in a different direction, as she argues that "through the repeated staging of cultural narratives", including staged plays, a "society's memory is created".[18] While *As You Like It* exploits the market for Robin Hood plays and the nostalgia they satisfied, it also "undercuts" this nostalgia "by deploying a range of countervailing strategies", including humour,[19] to establish a "covenant based precisely on the contractual relations" between theatre and its paying audience.[20] An "exploration of modes of laughter"[21] which includes the emergence of the wise fool, the play represents "a radically new development in the culture of leisure", one where "communal mirth" is stripped away from traditional folk festivities such as morris dances and maypole games and "transposed to entertainment, grounded in the relations of commodity exchange" that were the for-profit theatres.[22]

Britain's world dominance, the colonial experiment, and utopia

Richard Foulkes mentions in his "Touchstone for the Times" one final reason for the play's popularity: its "idealized evocation of rustic life in the Forest of Arden appealed" to those English men and women living in "far-flung colonial outposts who shared a powerful sense of nostalgia for their roots in Shakespeare's England".[23] By the mid-nineteenth century, moreover, as Inga-Stina Ewbank (1932–2004) observes, Shakespeare occupied both English and European consciousness as "a figure of the victory of poetic calling over bourgeois duty". Many Europeans came to accept English critics' contention that from Shakespeare's works emerged a "universal" portrayal of humanity.[24] English and Europeans alike immersed their colonized subjects in studies of Shakespeare in schools, and, in the same fashion as the English had done with their aspiring classes, positioned Shakespeare as a model for civilized behaviour.

As You Like It contains the seeds of these sentiments, Leah S. Marcus (b. 1945) explains in "Anti-Conquest and *As You Like It*" (2014). The play includes a "critique of incipient British colonialism", one that reveals a "strong preference for the 'inland' over the peripheral" as concerns the colonial experience.

Throughout *As You Like It*, Marcus notes a consistent fear as well as disparagement of the global, represented by Jacques, alongside a partiality towards all things English; "editorial treatment of the play over time", furthermore, intensified these disparagements and partialities.[25]

The "sole representative" of "early modern travel and colonization",[26] Jacques "stages a disjunct series of protocolonial postures in relation to the 'natives' of the forest, the deer",[27] which occur in 2.5 and 4.2. And in his interactions with Duke Senior's men, he "relates" to Arden as if it constitutes an "internal colony".[28] Although Jacques laments the deer's brutalization, he refuses to blur "the lines of demarcation" by which an animal defines what a human is not; he simply will not assimilate, as do Rosalind, Celia, Orlando, and Duke Senior's men, "with the ethos of the forest and its melding of human and animal identities".[29] Jacques represents "the colonizer", an "observer convinced of his own moral superiority"; his identification with the wounded deer, moreover, "without recognizing that his extravagant sympathy for its plight is essentially narcissistic", betrays a "displacement of his own feelings of unfair rejection at the hands of the dominant culture".[30] Marcus echoes Stephen Greenblatt in contending that Jacques' words in 2.5 and again in 4.2 represent a "stark contradiction between two incommensurable early colonial attitudes: the desire to admire and empathize with the newly discovered, and the desire to destroy or appropriate it as a proof of conquest".[31] Despite all his passionate rhetoric and emotional overflow, Jacques "presides over a celebration of the kill" later in the play (4.2), when the hunter returns with a dead deer. The horns his men wear when they commemorate the hunter's success symbolize "conquest".[32]

After examining differing opinions concerning the meaning of Jacques' "Ducdame, ducdame, ducdame!" in 2.5, and explaining how possible links between the phrase and Romany, Celtic, or other ethnicities' phrases signal a "filtering" of the play "through a colonial state of mind",[33] Marcus offers her own interpretation: "ducdame" means, through Latin, "Lead, O deer!" No matter how sarcastically Jacques says the phrase, it signals that in Arden the "normal rules of social hierarchy are suspended and the human" becomes "merged through figurative language with the animal". Viewed in this light, Jacques poses as a "proto-ethnographer – one who knows the tribal secrets and uses his arcane language skills to show his superior mastery of the culture".[34] Starting in the nineteenth century, Marcus contends, editors of Shakespeare avoided such a translation "because of their desire to separate Jacques off from the Forest of Arden, which they want to imagine" as Shakespeare's and as English – not as belonging to, or controlled by, the "suspiciously cosmopolitan" Jacques.[35]

"Ducdame" also may resonate with "dame" and its various European cognates, which links the phrase to "the leadership" of the play's "central female figure", Rosalind, and signals a "dissolution" in Arden "of ordinary social rules and limitations, even including the separation between the male and the female".[36] In the 1623 Folio edition of *As You Like It*, gender becomes even more fluid because, when Hymen tells the Duke to join Rosalind's hand with Orlando's, the god says, "That thou mightst ioyne his hand with his,/Whose heart within his bosome is". Such gender confusion suggests that Rosalind presides over an England blessed with a "special freedom for women", although Rosalind possesses an "innate sense of limit and proportion that keeps her from ever behaving inappropriately".[37]

In similar fashion as those nineteenth-century critics who enforced Jacques' segregation from the other characters, many critics purposefully misconstrue utopian fiction, Ryan Farrar states in his "*As You Like It*: The Thin Line between Legitimate Utopia and Compensatory Vacation" (2014). In many readers' minds, utopian literature "synopsizes its dreamworlds with places of perfection",[38] when in reality it depicts a person's "want for advancement", an effort to achieve "what he or she might lack".[39] The "place out of reach" that a utopia presents, therefore, "impresses upon people a desire to change themselves or be changed in hopes to achieve a better lived experience".[40] Because these desires often involve subjective, individually envisioned social or behavioural matters, "their design can place individual or exclusive interests over those of the commonwealth, even if those interests exist only in fantasy". And when a character's "lust for control, power, and advancement increases", dystopian states arise and "cause suffering for characters subject to the whims of oppressive vices".[41]

A utopian critic's task, then, lies in the discernment and articulation of the dialectic employed in a character's "pursuit of progressive ideas" and that character's self-serving "desire".[42] The critic must attend to a work's dystopic tendencies as well as its utopic ones, in other words, and Farrar sees both in *As You Like It*, particularly in the "language games"[43] played between characters. Duke Senior's insistent depiction of an egalitarian camaraderie existing between himself and the exiled courtiers, for example, runs counter to the actual rigid observances of social place that the reader cannot help but see, and problematizes all the forest relationships as the play progresses. His men's derisions of Jacques also belie the sense of "unity and harmony" of which he boasts. Farrar notes a disjunction between the bliss the Duke claims he feels in the forest and his eagerness "to return to the city" and his title once Frederick gives him back the dukedom. Instead of "carrying utopian potential", Arden "gets reduced to a mere vacation spot".[44]

Oliver's self-serving mistreatment of Orlando, as well as Frederick's exile of Rosalind, also mark a dystopia; even Adam's loyalty to the de Boys family "blemishes the utopic portrait of fidelity and harmony", for he experiences "very real pain" while he helps Orlando. At best, "the nature of utopia in the play is ambiguous", and characters such as Rosalind and Orlando possess and exert more healing power than the forest. Farrar argues that the play's title provides the key to its ambiguous portrayal of utopia: while Duke Senior's rush back to court offers a "satisfying conclusion"[45] to those conservative nobles who watch the play and expect a preservation of order, characters such as Jacques, who remain "pessimistically utopian", provide "hope for a better world achieved through satiric criticism".[46] The play, in other words, caters simultaneously to status quo culture and the desire for cultural change, and affirms "both an order that rewards privilege and one that redefines it".[47]

Pedagogy and As You Like It

One area of scholarship that has come into prominence involves the teaching of Shakespeare's corpus to undergraduates, many of whom have not received adequate training in close reading or analytical skills. Series such as the Folger Shakespeare Library's *Shakespeare Set Free* (1993–present), as well as journals devoted to Shakespeare and pedagogy, conference proceedings, and Festschrifts, have arisen to assist in teaching Shakespeare.

One of the first of these pieces is Elaine Hobby's "'My Affection Hath an Unknown Bottom': Homosexuality and the Teaching of *As You Like It*" (1991), where Hobby considers the "pedagogic usefulness of being openly gay, and of encouraging classroom discussion of sexuality and gender construction". Hobby concedes that *As You Like It*'s opening scene underscores a necessity for "familial stability" in maintaining a larger "social stability", but also observes how the play exposes family structures as unstable "social, ideological constructs".[48] She then locates the play's "central focus" in Rosalind and her challenge to "the stability of gender" through a "juxtaposition" of her "characteristics as a young woman with her behavior when playing the part of a young man" and "through a series of jokes about the actual gender identity of the actor playing Rosalind's/Ganymede's part".[49]

As Rosalind and Rosalind-as-Ganymede interact with Orlando and the others, a suggestion arises that "differences between male and female behaviour are" largely "arbitrary, the result of social circumstance – clothing, or the beliefs and behavior of those who surround us". Instead of emanating from our "essential nature", gender identity actually is a "social construct".[50] By choosing the name "Ganymede", which in early modern England could mean "homosexual" and was also used to describe the boy actors who played women's roles, Rosalind identifies herself as a "boy actor" as well as a "sodomite".[51] In doing so, she creates a "shifting identity" which provokes "humor, pleasure, and sexual titillation",[52] but which also destabilizes gender identity.

In "'For Solace a Twinne-like Sister': Teaching Themes of Sisterhood in *As You Like It* and Beyond" (1996), Jan Stirm explains her employment of *As*

You Like It to "examine how early modern writers construct sisterhood as a relationship that empowers women".[53] Stirm asks her students to contrast Louis Adrian Montrose's marginalization of Rosalind's relationship with Celia in his "'The Place of a Brother' in *As You Like It*: Social Process and Comic Form" (see Chapter 6 in this guide) with feminist readings of the play. She then assigns two early modern discussions of sisterhood and women's agency, the "Approbation" of Thomas Goad (1576–1638) to *The Mothers Legacie, To her unborne Childe* (1624) by Elizabeth Jocelin (1596–1622) and some of the letters of Dorothy Bacon (1597–1629), to illustrate that these texts foreground motherhood and comfortable sisterhood as the basis for female relationships. In short, Stirm's assignments and class discussions demonstrate how early modern women "constructed sisterhood around familiarity, similarity, pleasure, duty, and presence".[54]

Stirm then moves to *As You Like It*, and divides her analysis into three sections: "metaphoric sisterhood", where the class concentrates on the first act of the play; "siblinghood", where the focus shifts to Acts 2, 3, and 4; and "sisterhood through marriage", where consideration turns to Rosalind's and Celia's increasing silence. Stirm emphasizes Shakespeare's distinction between the "natural"[55] bonds between the "sisters" Rosalind and Celia and the unnaturalness between Oliver and Orlando and Frederick and Duke Senior. The unnaturalness inherent in the men's relationships implicitly suggests that the women's relationship provides an "alternative", a better "model" for the men.[56] Stirm softens considerably others' contentions that Act 5 negates any autonomy the women achieve; instead, she believes that by Act 5 the men have "absorbed the positive qualities associated with sisterhood", and have "made these qualities masculine", and finally "subordinated women and sisterhood into the revised patriarchy".[57] Stirm also explains how social class determines the strength of sisterhood, and illustrates her point through Rosalind's rejection of Phebe – not only as lover but as sister.

As these current studies illustrate, interest in *As You Like It* extends far beyond our acknowledgement of Shakespeare's stature as moral model, master manipulator of genre, or national hero. Despite our evolving interrogations of this play, we always pay close attention to its text and maintain a rapt awareness of its usefulness in understanding more clearly our own culture.

NOTES

INTRODUCTION

1. Quoted in Bernard F. Dukore (ed.) *The Drama Observed*, 4 vols. University Park: The Pennsylvania State University Press, 1991, p. 1062.
2. Quoted in ibid., pp. 1062–63.
3. For a discussion of rival companies and its influence on their selection of plays, see E.K. Chambers (ed.) *The Elizabethan Stage*, vol. 2. Oxford: Clarendon Press, 1923, pp. 6–7.
4. Both these allusions are provided in Stephen Greenblatt et al. (eds.), *The Norton Shakespeare*, 2nd edition. New York and London: W.W. Norton & Co., 2008. For discussions of dating, see Greenblatt et al (eds.) (2008), p. 1623; and James Shapiro, *A Year in the Life of William Shakespeare: 1599*. New York: HarperCollins, 2005, pp. 203–29.
5. For discussions of *As You Like It*'s performance history, see Heather Dubrow (ed.) *As You Like It*. Boston and elsewhere: Wadsworth Cengage Learning, 2012, pp. 55–69; and Cynthia Marshall, *As You Like It. Shakespeare in Production*. Cambridge: Cambridge University Press, 2004, pp. 1–95.
6. Stationers' Register entry for *As You Like It, Henry V,* and *Much Ado about Nothing*, 4 August 1600, shakespearedocumented.org (accessed 1 May 2018).
7. Stanley Wells and Gary Taylor (eds.) *William Shakespeare: A Textual Companion*. New York and London: W.W. Norton & Co., 1997, p. 392.
8. Many useful studies of the pastoral tradition are available, including Paul Alpers' *What Is Pastoral?* Chicago: University of Chicago Press, 1996.
9. Jean E. Howard, "Introduction to *As You Like It*", in Stephen Greenblatt et al. (eds.), *The Norton Shakespeare*, 2nd edition. New York and London: W.W. Norton & Co., 2008, p. 1617.

CHAPTER ONE

1. Michael Dobson, *The Making of the National Poet. Shakespeare, Adaptation and Authorship, 1660–1769*. Oxford: Clarendon Press, 1992, p. 3.
2. Charles Gildon, "An Essay on the Art, Rise and Progress of the Stage in *Greece, Rome* and *England*", in Nicholas Rowe (ed.), *The Works of Mr. William Shakespear*. London: 1710. Reprinted by Pickering & Chatto, 1999, p. viii.
3. Ibid., p. viii.
4. John Dryden, *Of Dramatic Poesy, The Works of John Dryden*, vol. 17. H.T. Swedenberg, Jr. (gen. ed.). Berkeley and elsewhere: University of California Press, 1971, p. 55.
5. Brian Vickers, *Returning to Shakespeare*. London and New York: Routledge, 1989, p. 198.
6. John Dryden, *Preface to All for Love, The Works of John Dryden*, vol. 13. H.T. Swedenberg, Jr. (gen. ed.). Berkeley and elsewhere: University of California Press, 1971, p. 10.
7. Vickers (1989), p. 202.
8. Dobson (1992), p. 12.
9. Ibid., p. 187.

10. Hugh Grady, *The Modernist Shakespeare. Critical Texts in a Material World*. Oxford: Clarendon Press, 1991, p. 166.
11. Nicholas Rowe (ed.) *The Works of Mr. William Shakespear; in Six Volumes*. London: Jacob Tonson, 1709, p. xix.
12. Ibid., pp. xx–xxi.
13. Ibid., p. xvii.
14. Jonathan Bate, *Shakespearean Constitutions. Politics, Theatre, Criticism 1730–1830*. Oxford: Clarendon Press, 1989, p. 145.
15. Charles Gildon, "Remarks on the Plays of Shakespear", in Nicholas Rowe (ed.), *The Works of Mr. William Shakespear*. London: 1710. Reprinted by Pickering & Chatto, 1999), p. 326.
16. Ibid., p. 258.
17. Ibid., p. 326.
18. Quoted in Vickers (ed.) *Shakespeare. The Critical Heritage*, 5 vols. London and elsewhere: Routledge & Kegan Paul, 1979, vol. 3, p. 234.
19. Ibid., pp. 381–82.
20. Samuel Johnson (ed.) *The Plays of William Shakespeare, in Eight Volumes, with the Corrections and Illustrations of Various Commentators; To which are added Notes by Sam. Johnson*. London, 1765, p. 62.
21. Johnson (1765) "Preface", p. 64.
22. Ibid., p. 63.
23. Johnson (1765) "Notes", p. 264.
24. Ibid., p. 257.
25. Ibid., p. 264.
26. Johnson (1765) "Preface", p. 66.
27. Richard Hurd, *Epistula ad Pisones* (1766), *The Works of Richard Hurd*, vol. 1. London: T. Cadell and W. Davies, 1811, p. 216.
28. Ibid., p. 217.
29. Ibid., p. 217.
30. Francis Gentleman, *The Dramatic Censor; Or, Critical Companion*: Volume 1 London: J. Bell, 1770, p. 478.
31. Ibid., p. 462.
32. Ibid., p. 461.
33. Ibid., p. 475.
34. Ibid., p. 475.
35. Ibid., p. 475–76.
36. Ibid., p. 465.
37. Ibid., p. 468.
38. Ibid., p. 477.
39. Ibid., p. 469.
40. Ibid., p. 473.
41. Ibid., p. 465.
42. Ibid., p. 475.
43. Ibid., p. 472.
44. Marianne Novy (ed.) *Women's Re-Visions of Shakespeare. On the Responses of Dickinson, Woolf, Rich, H.D., George Eliot, and Others*. Urbana and Chicago: University of Illinois Press, 1990, p. 7.
45. (Mrs) Elizabeth Griffith, *The Morality of Shakespeare's Drama Illustrated*. London: T. Cadell, 1775, p. v.

46. Ibid., p. vi.
47. Ibid., p. ix.
48. Ibid., p. xii.
49. Ibid., p. xi.
50. Ibid., p. 69.
51. Ibid., p. 87.
52. Ibid., p. 85.
53. Ibid., pp. 71–72.
54. Ibid., p. 72.
55. Ibid., p. 74.
56. Ibid., p. 86.
57. Ibid., p. 82.
58. Vickers (1989), p. 197.
59. Ibid., p. 198.
60. William Richardson, *A Philosophical Analysis and Illustration of Some of Shakespeare's Remarkable Characters*. London: J. Murray, 1780. Reprint New York: AMS Press, 1966, p. 24.
61. Ibid., p. 8.
62. Ibid., p. 146.
63. Ibid., p. 146.
64. Ibid., p. 147.
65. Ibid., p. 157.
66. Ibid., p. 166.
67. Ibid., p. 170.
68. Ibid., p. 172.
69. Walter Whiter, *A Specimen of a Commentary on Shakespeare. Containing Notes on 'As You Like It'. An Attempt to Explain and Illustrate Various Passages, on a New Principle of Criticism, Derived from Mr. Locke's Doctrine of the Association of Ideas*. London: T. Cadell, 1794. Reprint, Alan Over and Mary Bell (eds.). London: Methuen & Co., 1967, p. 63.
70. Ibid., p. 64.
71. Ibid., p. 63.
72. Ibid., p. 64.
73. Ibid., p. 60.
74. Ibid., p. 64.
75. Ibid., p. 65.
76. Alan Over and Mary Bell (eds.), reprint of Walter Whiter, *A Specimen of a Commentary on Shakespeare. Containing Notes on 'As You Like It'. An Attempt to Explain and Illustrate Various Passages, on a New Principle of Criticism, Derived from Mr. Locke's Doctrine of the Association of Ideas*. London: Methuen & Co., 1967, p. l.
77. Whiter (1967 reprint), p. 35.
78. Ibid., p. 34.
79. Ibid., p. 42.
80. Ibid., p. 42.
81. Ibid., p. 18.

CHAPTER TWO

1. Hugh Grady, *The Modernist Shakespeare. Critical Texts in a Material World*. Oxford: Clarendon Press, 1991, p. 36.
2. Ibid., p. 65.

3. Ibid., p. 28.
4. Ibid., p. 82.
5. Ibid., p. 36.
6. Augustus William Schlegel, Lecture XXIII (c. 1811). *A Course of Lectures. Dramatic Art and Literature*. Rev. A.J.W. Morrison (ed.); John Black (trans.) London: Henry G. Bohn, 1846, p. 368.
7. Charles Cowden Clarke, *Shakespeare-Characters; Chiefly Those Subordinate*. London: Smith, Elder & Co.; Edinburgh: James Nichol, 1863, pp. 102–03.
8. Marianne Novy (ed.) *Women's Re-Visions of Shakespeare. On the Responses of Dickinson, Woolf, Rich, H.D., George Eliot, and Others*. Urbana and Chicago: University of Illinois Press, 1990, p. 3.
9. Uttara Natarajan, "William Hazlitt", in Adrian Poole (ed.), *Lamb, Hazlitt, Keats*, Volume IV Great Shakespeareans. London and New York: Continuum, 2010, p. 68.
10. Grady (1991), p. 65.
11. C.L. Barber, *Shakespeare's Festive Comedy. A Study of Dramatic Form and Its Relation to Social Custom*. Princeton: Princeton University Press, 1959. Reprint 1972, p. 4.
12. Samuel Taylor Coleridge, *The Collected Works of Samuel Taylor Coleridge*: Volume IV. H.J. Jackson and George Whalley (eds.). Princeton: Princeton University Press, 1998, p. 817.
13. Ibid., p. 697.
14. Ibid., p. 784.
15. Ibid., p. 697.
16. Ibid., p. 698.
17. Schlegel (1846), p. 361.
18. Ibid., p. 355.
19. Ibid., p. 359.
20. Ibid., p. 359.
21. Ibid., p. 391.
22. Ibid., pp. 391–92.
23. Ibid., p. 391.
24. Jonathan Bate, *Shakespearean Constitutions. Politics, Theatre, Criticism 1730–1830*. Oxford: Clarendon Press, 1989, p. 144.
25. Ibid., p. 151.
26. William Hazlitt, *Characters of Shakespear's Plays & Lectures on the English Poets* (1817). London: Macmillan and Co., 1920 (Reprint of 1903 ed.), p. 275.
27. Ibid., p. 187.
28. Ibid., p. 188.
29. Ibid., p. 188.
30. Ibid., p. 189.
31. Ibid., p. 189.
32. Bate (1989), p. 155.
33. Cheri Lin Larsen Hoeckley, "Anna Jacobson", in Gail Marshall (ed.), *Jameson, Cowden Clarke, Kemble, Cushman*. Volume VII Great Shakespeareans. London and New York: Continuum, 2011, pp. 16–17.
34. Russell Jackson, "'Perfect Types of Womanhood': Rosalind, Beatrice and Viola in Victorian Criticism and Performance", *Shakespeare Survey* 32 (1979), p. 15.
35. Hoeckley (2011), p. 13.
36. Anna Brownell Jameson, *Shakespeare's Heroines. Characteristics of Women Moral, Poetical, and Historical* (1832). London: George Bell & Sons, 1898, p. 74.
37. Ibid., p. 75.
38. Ibid., p. 78.

39. Ibid., p. 79.
40. Ibid., pp. 79–80.
41. Ibid., p. 80.
42. William Maginn, *The Shakespeare Papers*. New York: Redfield, 1856, pp. 48–49.
43. Ibid., p. 60
44. Ibid., p. 50.
45. Ibid., p. 56.
46. Ibid., p. 55.
47. Ibid., pp. 50–51.
48. Ibid., p. 59.
49. Hermann Ulrici, *Shakespeare's Dramatic Art: And His Relation to Calderon and Goethe* (1839). Rev. A.J.W. Morrison (trans.). London: Chapman, Brothers, 1846, p. 79.
50. Ibid., p. 94.
51. Ibid., p. 103.
52. Ibid., pp. 104–05.
53. Ibid., p. 118.
54. Ibid., p. 123.
55. Ibid., p. 246.
56. Ibid., p. 253.
57. Ibid., p. 255.
58. Ibid., p. 254.
59. Ibid., p. 256.
60. Ibid., p. 256.
61. Ibid., p. 257.
62. Ibid., p. 257.
63. Ibid., p. 258.
64. Grady (1991), p. 44.
65. G.G. Gervinus, *Shakespeare Commentaries* (1849–50), F.E. Bunnett (trans.). London: Smith, Elder & Co. Revised edition, 1877, Preface p. xiii.
66. Ibid., p. 386.
67. Ibid., p. 387.
68. Ibid., p. 388.
69. Ibid., p. 389.
70. Ibid., p. 390.
71. Ibid., p. 391.
72. Ibid., p. 394.
73. Ibid., p. 394.
74. Ibid., p. 394.
75. Ibid., p. 396.
76. Ibid., p. 395.
77. Ibid., p. 395.
78. Ibid., p. 396.
79. Ibid., p. 398.
80. Ibid., p. 402.
81. Ibid., pp. 403–04.
82. Ann Thompson and Sasha Roberts, "Mary Cowden Clarke: Marriage, Gender and the Victorian Woman Critic of Shakespeare", in Gail Marshall and Adrian Poole (eds.), *Victorian Shakespeare, Volume 2*. Basingstoke: Palgrave Macmillan, 2003, p. 177.
83. Cowden Clarke (1863), Preface p. v–vi.

84. Thompson and Roberts (2003), p. 174.
85. Cowden Clarke (1863), p. 60.
86. Ibid., pp. 42–43.
87. Ibid., p. 36.
88. Ibid., p. 36.
89. Ibid., p. 43.
90. Ibid., pp. 43–44.
91. Ibid., p. 45.
92. Ibid., p. 35.
93. Ibid., pp. 46–47.
94. Ibid., p. 46.
95. Ibid., pp. 49–50.
96. Ibid., pp. 49–50.
97. Ibid., pp. 54–55.
98. Ibid., p. 38.
99. Ibid., p. 43.
100. Ibid., p. 42.
101. Ibid., p. 37.
102. Hippolyte A. Taine, *History of English Literature* (1863), H. Van Laun (trans.). New York: T.Y. Crowell, 1873, p. 215.
103. Ibid., p. 232.
104. Ibid., p. 234.
105. Ibid., p. 235.
106. Ibid., p. 234.
107. Rev. H[enry].N. Hudson, *Shakespeare: Life, Art, and Characters*, vol. 1. Boston and elsewhere: Ginn & Co., 1872, p. 337.
108. Ibid., p. 339.
109. Ibid., p. 340.
110. Ibid., p. 344.
111. Ibid., p. 345.
112. Ibid., p. 346.
113. Ibid., p. 343.
114. Ibid., p. 341.
115. Denton J. Snider, *The Shakespearian Drama. A Commentary. The Comedies.* St. Louis: Sigma Publishing, 1887, p. 11.
116. Ibid., p. 19.
117. Ibid., p. 40.
118. Ibid., p. 14.
119. Ibid., pp. 40–41.
120. Ibid., pp. 41–42.
121. Ibid., p. 44.
122. Ibid., p. 42.
123. Ibid., pp. 48–49.
124. Ibid., pp. 360–61.
125. Ibid., p. 361.
126. Ibid., p. 343.
127. Ibid., p. 358.
128. Helena Faucit Martin (or, Helen Faucit, Lady Martin), *On Some of Shakespeare's Female Characters*. Edinburgh and London: William Blackwood & Sons, 1893, p. 236.

129. Ibid., p. 237.
130. Ibid., p. 240.
131. Ibid., p. 252.
132. Ibid., p. 273.
133. Ibid., p. 267.
134. Ibid., p. 236.
135. Ibid., p. 229.
136. Frederick S. Boas, *Shakespeare and His Predecessors* (1896). Reprinted, New York: Gordian Press, 1968, p. 330.
137. Ibid., p. 332.
138. Ibid., p. 338.
139. Ibid., pp. 333–34.
140. Ibid., p. 339.
141. Ibid., pp. 340–41.
142. Ibid., pp. 336–37.
143. Quoted in Bernard F. Dukore (ed.) *The Drama Observed*, 4 vols. University Park: The Pennsylvania State University Press, 1991, pp. 715–16.
144. Quoted in ibid., p. 912.
145. Quoted in ibid., p. 587.
146. Quoted in ibid., p. 715.
147. Quoted in ibid., pp. 714–15.
148. Quoted by Edwin Wilson (ed.) *Shaw on Shakespeare. An Anthology of Bernard Shaw's Writings on the Plays and Production of Shakespeare*. New York: E.P. Dutton, 1961, p. 27.

CHAPTER THREE

1. J.B. Priestley, *The English Comic Characters* (1925). Reprint, New York: Phaeton Press, 1972, pp. 29–30.
2. Hugh Grady, *The Modernist Shakespeare. Critical Texts in a Material World*. Oxford: Clarendon Press, 1991, pp. 69–70.
3. Ibid., p. 71.
4. Elmer Edgar Stoll, "Shakespeare, Marston, and the Malcontent Type". *Modern Philology* 3.3 (January 1906), p. 4.
5. Ibid., pp. 1–2.
6. Elmer Edgar Stoll, *Shakespeare's Young Lovers*. London and elsewhere: Oxford University Press, 1937, p. 58.
7. Ibid., pp. 46–47.
8. P.V. Kreider, "Genial Literary Satire in the Forest of Arden". *Shakespeare Association Bulletin* 10.4 (October 1935), pp. 212–13.
9. Ibid., p. 212.
10. Ibid., pp. 214–15.
11. E.K. Chambers, *Shakespeare: A Survey*. London: Sidgwick & Jackson, 1925. Reprint New York: Hill and Wang, n.d., p. 158.
12. Ibid., pp. 155–56.
13. Ibid., p. 156.
14. Ibid., p. 156.
15. Ibid., pp. 157–58.
16. Ibid., p. 161.
17. Ibid., pp. 162–63.

18. H.B. Charlton, *Shakespearean Comedy.* London: Methuen & Co., 1938, p. 266.
19. Ibid., p. 266.
20. Ibid., p. 269.
21. Ibid., p. 293.
22. Ibid., p. 282.
23. Ibid., p. 287.
24. Ibid., p. 283.
25. Ibid., p. 277.
26. Ibid., pp. 277–78.
27. Ibid., p. 281.
28. C.L. Barber, "The Use of Comedy in *As You Like It*". *Philological Quarterly* 21.4 (October 1942), p. 353.
29. Ibid., p. 367.
30. Ibid., p. 355.
31. Ibid., p. 354.
32. Ibid., p. 356.
33. Ibid., p. 357.
34. Ibid., p. 359.
35. Ibid., p. 364.
36. Ibid., p. 362.
37. Ibid., p. 365.
38. Harold Jenkins, "*As You Like It*". *Shakespeare Survey* 8 (1955), pp. 47–48.
39. Ibid., pp. 40–41.
40. Ibid., p. 43.
41. Ibid., p. 41.
42. Ibid., p. 50.
43. Ibid., p. 43.
44. Ibid., pp. 46–47.
45. Ibid., p. 45.
46. Ibid., p. 49.
47. Marco Mincoff, "What Shakespeare Did to Rosalynde". *Shakespeare Jahrbuch* 96 (1960), p. 82.
48. Ibid., p. 79.
49. Ibid., p. 81.
50. Ibid., p. 79.
51. Ibid., p. 82.
52. Ibid., pp. 84–85.
53. Jay L. Halio, "'No Clock in the Forest': Time in *As You Like It*". *Studies in English Literature* 2 (1962), p. 197.
54. Ibid., p. 204.
55. Ibid., p. 200.
56. Ibid., p. 202.
57. Ibid., pp. 200–01.
58. Ibid., p. 202.
59. Ibid., pp. 202–03.
60. Ibid., p. 206.
61. Ibid., p. 207.
62. Madeleine Doran, "Yet am I Inland Bred". *Shakespeare Quarterly* 15.2 (Spring 1964), p. 99.
63. Ibid., p. 100.

64. Ibid., p. 102.
65. Ibid., pp. 102–03.
66. Ibid., pp. 104–05.
67. Ibid., p. 106.
68. Ibid., p. 106.
69. Ibid., p. 108.
70. Ibid., pp. 111–12.
71. Sylvan Barnet, "Strange Events: Improbability in *As You Like It*". *Shakespeare Studies* 4 (1968), p. 120.
72. Ibid., p. 126.
73. Ibid., p. 121.
74. Ibid., pp. 128–29.
75. Ibid., p. 128.
76. David Young, *The Heart's Forest: A Study of Shakespeare's Pastoral Plays*. New Haven and London: Yale University Press, 1972, p. 40.
77. Ibid., pp. 42–43.
78. Ibid., pp. 45–46.
79. Ibid., p. 50.
80. Ibid., pp. 51–52.
81. Ibid., p. 55.
82. Ibid., p. 57.
83. Ibid., p. 59.
84. Ibid., pp. 59–60.
85. Ibid., pp. 61–62.
86. Ibid., pp. 62–63.
87. Ibid., p. 66.

CHAPTER FOUR

1. Northrop Frye, "The Argument of Comedy". *English Institute Essays* (1948–49). Reprinted in Leonard F. Dean (ed.), *Shakespeare: Modern Essays in Criticism*. New York: Oxford University Press, 1961, p. 89.
2. Ibid., p. 86.
3. Ibid., p. 82.
4. Ibid., p. 86.
5. Ibid., p. 85.
6. Ibid., p. 87.
7. Ibid., p. 81.
8. Northrop Frye, *A Natural Perspective*. New York and London: Columbia University Press, 1965, p. 61.
9. Ibid., p. 142.
10. Ibid., p. 86.
11. Ibid., pp. 142–43.
12. Ibid., p. 141.
13. Ibid., p. 123.
14. Ibid., p. 103.
15. Ibid., p. 101.
16. Peter Erickson, "C.L. Barber", in Hugh Grady (ed.), *Empson, Wilson Knight, Barber, Kott*. Volume XIII Great Shakespeareans. London and New York: Continuum, 2012, p. 93.

17. Ibid., p. 94.
18. C.L. Barber, *Shakespeare's Festive Comedy. A Study of Dramatic Form and Its Relation to Social Custom*. Princeton: Princeton University Press, 1959. Reprint 1972, p. 4.
19. Ibid., p. 6.
20. Ibid., p. 12 (footnote).
21. Ibid., p. 7.
22. Ibid., p. 9.
23. Ibid., pp. 223–24.
24. Ibid., p. 225.
25. Ibid., p. 230.
26. Ibid., p. 230.
27. Ibid., p. 235.
28. Quoted in ibid., p. 236.
29. Ibid., p. 13.
30. Ibid., p. 229.
31. Ibid., p. 232.
32. Ibid., p. 229.
33. Jan Kott, *Shakespeare Our Contemporary*, Boleslaw Taborski (trans.). Garden City: Anchor Books, 1966, p. 326.
34. Ibid., p. 333.
35. Ibid., p. 325.
36. Ibid., pp. 332–33.
37. Ibid., p. 328.
38. Ibid., p. 333.
39. Ibid., p. 318.
40. Ibid., p. 340.
41. Ibid., p. 342.
42. Ibid., p. 320.
43. Ibid., p. 320.
44. Ibid., p. 331.
45. Anne Barton, "*As You Like It* and *Twelfth Night*: Shakespeare's Sense of an Ending", in Malcolm Bradbury and David Palmer (gen. eds.), *Shakespearean Comedy*. Stratford-Upon-Avon Studies 14; London: Edward Arnold, 1972, pp. 161–62.
46. Ibid., p. 161.
47. Ibid., pp. 163–64.
48. Ibid., p. 166.
49. Ibid., p. 169.
50. Ibid., pp. 168–69.
51. Ibid., p. 170.
52. Peter Erickson, *Patriarchal Structures in Shakespeare's Drama*. Berkeley and elsewhere: University of California Press, 1985, p. 15.
53. Ibid., p. 16.
54. Ibid., p. 25.
55. Ibid., p. 19.
56. Ibid., p. 23.
57. Ibid., p. 25.
58. Ibid., p. 22.
59. Ibid., p. 23.
60. Ibid., p. 30.

61. Ibid., pp. 27–28.
62. Ibid., p. 29.
63. Ibid., p. 31.
64. Ibid., p. 32.
65. Ibid., p. 25.
66. Ibid., p. 34.
67. Ibid., p. 17.
68. Terry Eagleton, *William Shakespeare*. Oxford: Blackwell, 1986, p. 90.
69. Ibid., pp. 91–92.
70. Ibid., p. 92.
71. Ibid., p. 93.
72. Brian Gibbons, "Amorous Fictions and *As You Like It*", in John W. Mahon and Thomas A. Pendleton (eds.), *"Fanned and Winnowed Opinions". Shakespearean Essays Presented to Harold Jenkins*. London and New York: Methuen, 1987, p. 54.
73. Ibid., p. 57.
74. Ibid., p. 52.
75. Ibid., p. 53.
76. Ibid., p. 56.
77. Ibid., p. 57.
78. Ibid., pp. 57–58.
79. Ibid., p. 58.
80. Ibid., p. 59.
81. Ibid., p. 59.
82. Ibid., p. 62.
83. Ibid., pp. 67–68.
84. Ibid., p. 69.
85. Ibid., pp. 70–71.
86. Martha Ronk, "Locating the Visual in *As You Like It*". *Shakespeare Quarterly* 52 (2001), pp. 255–56.
87. Ibid., p. 255.
88. Ibid., p. 274.
89. Ibid., p. 256.
90. Ibid., p. 257.
91. Ibid., p. 258.
92. Ibid., p. 259.
93. Ibid., pp. 259–60.
94. Ibid., p. 261.
95. Ibid., p. 262.
96. Ibid., pp. 263–64.
97. Ibid., p. 267.
98. Ibid., p. 268.
99. Ibid., p. 269.
100. Ibid., p. 274.
101. Robert N. Watson, "As You Liken It: Simile in the Wilderness", *Shakespeare Survey* 56 (2003), p. 79.
102. Ibid., p. 79.
103. Ibid., p. 80.
104. Ibid., p. 81.
105. Ibid., p. 83.

106. Ibid., p. 84.
107. Ibid., p. 85.
108. Ibid., p. 86.
109. Ibid., p. 87.
110. Ibid., p. 89.
111. Ibid., p. 89.
112. Ibid., p. 91.
113. Wolfgang Iser, "The Dramatization of Double Meaning in Shakespeare's *As You Like It*". *Theatre Journal* 35.3 (October 1983), pp. 307–08.
114. Ibid., p. 308.
115. Ibid., p. 309.
116. Ibid., p. 310.
117. Ibid., p. 311.
118. Ibid., p. 312.
119. Ibid., p. 313.
120. Ibid., p. 322.
121. Ibid., p. 323.
122. Ibid., p. 323.
123. Ibid., p. 325.
124. Ibid., p. 326.
125. Ibid., p. 327.
126. Ibid., pp. 329–30.
127. Ibid., pp. 313–14.
128. Ibid., pp. 314–15.
129. Ibid., p. 316.
130. Ibid., pp. 317–18.

CHAPTER FIVE

1. Walter Cohen, "Political Criticism of Shakespeare", in Jean E. Howard and Marion F. O'Connor (eds.), *Shakespeare Reproduced. The Text in History and Ideology*. New York and London: Methuen, 1987, p. 18.
2. Jean E. Howard and Marion F. O'Connor (eds.) *Shakespeare Reproduced. The Text in History and Ideology*. New York and London: Methuen, 1987, p. 3.
3. Jonathan Bate, *Shakespearean Constitutions. Politics, Theatre, Criticism 1730–1830*. Oxford: Clarendon Press, 1989, p. 3.
4. Judy Z. Kronenfeld, "Social Rank and the Pastoral Ideals of *As You Like It*". *Shakespeare Quarterly* 29.3 (Summer 1978), p. 335.
5. Ibid., p. 336.
6. Ibid., pp. 336–37.
7. Ibid., p. 343.
8. Ibid., p. 344.
9. Ibid., p. 338.
10. Ibid., p. 345.
11. Ibid., p. 348.
12. Elliott Krieger, *A Marxist Study of Shakespeare's Comedies*. London: Macmillan, 1979; New York: Harper & Row, 1979, p. 88.
13. Ibid., pp. 74–75.
14. Ibid., pp. 76–77.

15. Ibid., p. 80.
16. Ibid., p. 77.
17. Ibid., p. 81.
18. Ibid., pp. 83–84.
19. Ibid., p. 88.
20. Ibid., p. 90.
21. Ibid., p. 92.
22. Ibid., p. 94.
23. Ibid., p. 95.
24. Martha Ronk Lifson, "Learning by Talking: Conversation in *As You Like It*". *Shakespeare Survey* 40 (1988), p. 91.
25. Ibid., p. 92.
26. Ibid., p. 92.
27. Ibid., p. 93.
28. Ibid., p. 94.
29. Ibid., pp. 98–99.
30. Ibid., p. 102.
31. Ibid., p. 104.
32. Grace Tiffany, "'That Reason Wonder May Diminish': *As You Like It*, Androgyny, and the Theater Wars". *Huntington Library Quarterly* 57.3 (Summer 1994), p. 215.
33. Ibid., p. 217.
34. Ibid., p. 216.
35. Ibid., p. 219.
36. Ibid., p. 223.
37. Ibid., p. 226.
38. Ibid., p. 219.
39. Ibid., pp. 224–25.
40. Ibid., p. 228.
41. Ibid., p. 230.
42. Ibid., p. 232.
43. Andrew Barnaby, "The Political Conscious of Shakespeare's *As You Like It*". *Studies in English Literature, 1500–1900* 36.2 (Spring, 1996), pp. 374–75.
44. Ibid., p. 374.
45. Ibid., p. 391.
46. Ibid., p. 379.
47. Ibid., p. 380.
48. Ibid., p. 381.
49. Ibid., p. 383.
50. Ibid., p. 384.
51. Ibid., p. 390.
52. Ibid., p. 391.
53. Louise Schleiner, "Voice, Ideology, and Gendered Subjects: The Case of *As You Like It* and *Two Gentlemen*". *Shakespeare Quarterly* 50 (1999), p. 285.
54. Ibid., p. 286.
55. Ibid., p. 300.
56. Ibid., p. 308.
57. Ibid., p. 302.
58. Peter Milward, "Religion in Arden". *Shakespeare Survey* 54 (2001), p. 116.
59. Ibid., p. 121.

60. Nathaniel Strout, "*As You Like It, Rosalynde*, and Mutuality". *Studies in English Literature, 1500–1900* 41.2 (Spring 2001), p. 278.
61. Ibid., p. 278.
62. Ibid., p. 279.
63. Ibid., p. 281.
64. Ibid., p. 281.
65. Ibid., p. 287.
66. Ibid., p. 285.
67. Ibid., p. 288.
68. Ibid., pp. 289–90.
69. Ibid., p. 291.
70. Linda Woodbridge, "Country Matters: *As You Like It* and the Pastoral-Bashing Impulse", in Evelyn Gajowski (ed.), *Re-Visions of Shakespeare: Essays in Honor of Robert Ornstein*. Dover: University of Delaware Press: 2004, p. 189.
71. Ibid., pp. 194–95.
72. Ibid., p. 192.
73. Ibid., p. 195.
74. Ibid., p. 191.
75. Ibid., p. 210.
76. Ibid., p. 207.
77. Ibid., p. 210.
78. Ibid., p. 208.
79. Ibid., p. 209.
80. Ibid., pp. 210–11.
81. Ibid., p. 202.
82. Ibid., pp. 204–05.
83. Chris Fitter, "Reading Orlando Historically: Vagrancy, Forest, and Vestry Values in Shakespeare's *As You Like It*". *Medieval and Renaissance Drama in England: An Annual Gathering of Research, Criticism and Reviews* 23 (2010), p. 114.
84. Ibid., p. 115.
85. Ibid., p. 115.
86. Ibid., p. 115.
87. Ibid., p. 115.
88. Ibid., p. 118.
89. Ibid., p. 116.
90. Ibid., p. 120.
91. Ibid., p. 120.
92. Ibid., pp. 120–21.
93. Ibid., p. 121.
94. Ibid., p. 122.
95. Ibid., p. 128. Fitter's italics.
96. Ibid., p. 122.
97. Ibid., p. 124.
98. Ibid., p. 127.
99. Ibid., p. 128.
100. Ibid., pp. 129–30.
101. Ibid., pp. 130–31.
102. Ibid., p. 132.
103. Ibid., pp. 133–34.

104. Ibid., pp. 134–35.
105. Ibid., p. 136.
106. Ibid., p. 136.

CHAPTER SIX

1. Stephen Greenblatt, *Renaissance Self-Fashioning. From More to Shakespeare*. Chicago and London: University of Chicago Press, 1980, p. 5.
2. Ibid., p. 5.
3. Stephen Greenblatt, *Shakespearean Negotiations. The Circulation of Social Energy in Renaissance England*. Berkeley and Los Angeles: University of California Press, 1988, p. 88.
4. Ibid., p. 87.
5. Ibid., p. 88.
6. Ibid., pp. 89–90.
7. Ibid., p. 90.
8. Ibid., pp. 90–91.
9. Ibid., p. 91.
10. Louis Adrian Montrose, "'The Place of a Brother' in *As You Like It*: Social Process and Comic Form". *Shakespeare Quarterly* 32 (1981), p. 29.
11. Ibid., p. 28.
12. Ibid., p. 41.
13. Ibid., p. 28.
14. Ibid., p. 29.
15. Ibid., pp. 30–31.
16. Ibid., p. 31.
17. Ibid., p. 32.
18. Ibid., p. 33.
19. Ibid., pp. 33–34.
20. Ibid., pp. 34–35.
21. Ibid., pp. 35–36.
22. Ibid., p. 37.
23. Ibid., p. 38.
24. Ibid., pp. 39–40.
25. Ibid., p. 40.
26. Ibid., p. 41.
27. Ibid., p. 43.
28. Ibid., p. 45.
29. Ibid., p. 48.
30. Ibid., pp. 48–49.
31. Ibid., p. 51.
32. Ibid., p. 51.
33. Ibid., pp. 52–53.
34. Richard Wilson, "Like the Old Robin Hood: *As You Like It* and the Enclosure Riots", *Will Power: Essays on Shakespearean Authority*. Hemel Hempstead: Harvester Wheatsheaf, 1993, p. 65.
35. Ibid., p. 66.
36. Ibid., p. 67.
37. Ibid., p. 69.
38. Ibid., p. 68.

39. Ibid., pp. 69–70.
40. Ibid., pp. 70–71.
41. Ibid., p. 72.
42. Ibid., p. 73.
43. Ibid., p. 76.
44. Ibid., p. 80.
45. Ibid., p. 78.
46. Cynthia Marshall, "Wrestling as Play and Game in *As You Like It*". *Studies in English Literature, 1500–1900* 33.2 (Spring 1993), p. 265.
47. Ibid., pp. 266–67.
48. Ibid., p. 272.
49. Ibid., p. 270.
50. Ibid., p. 274.
51. Ibid., p. 274.
52. Ibid., p. 277.
53. Ibid., p. 278.
54. Ibid., p. 279.
55. Ibid., p. 279.
56. Ibid., p. 279.
57. Ibid., p. 282.
58. A. Stuart Daley, "Calling and Commonwealth in *As You Like It*: A Late Elizabethan Political Play". *The Upstart Crow* 14 (1994), p. 29.
59. Ibid. p. 28.
60. Ibid., p. 28.
61. Ibid., p. 31.
62. Ibid., p. 32.
63. Ibid., p. 32.
64. Ibid., pp. 33–34.
65. Ibid., p. 35.
66. Ibid., p. 36.
67. Ibid., pp. 37–38.
68. Ibid., pp. 39–40.
69. Ibid., p. 41.
70. Susanne L. Wofford, "'To You I Give Myself, for I Am Yours': Erotic Performance and Theatrical Performatives in *As You Like It*", in Russ McDonald (ed.), *Shakespeare Reread. The Texts in New Contexts*. Ithaca and London: Cornell University Press, 1994, p. 149.
71. Ibid., p. 149.
72. Ibid., p. 153.
73. Ibid., p. 155.
74. Ibid., p. 156.
75. Ibid., p. 158.
76. Ibid., p. 161.
77. Ibid., pp. 162–63.
78. Ibid., p. 165.
79. Catherine Belsey, *Shakespeare and the Loss of Eden: The Construction of Family Values in Early Modern Culture*. New Brunswick: Rutgers University Press, 1999, Preface p. xv.
80. Ibid., p. 23.
81. Ibid., p. 6.
82. Ibid., pp. 5–6.

83. Ibid., p. 25.
84. Ibid., pp. 28–29.
85. Ibid., p. 30.
86. Ibid., pp. 30–31.
87. Ibid., pp. 46–47.
88. Ibid., p. 46.
89. Ibid., pp. 46–47.
90. Ibid., p. 48.
91. Ibid., p. 50.
92. Ibid., pp. 47–48.
93. Ibid., p. 53.
94. Ibid., p. 50.
95. Ibid., p. 53.
96. Ibid., p. 48.
97. Ibid., p. 54.
98. Mary Thomas Crane, *Shakespeare's Brain: Reading with Cognitive Theory*. Princeton: Princeton University Press, 2001, p. 233.
99. Ibid., p. 224.
100. Ibid., pp. 233–34.
101. Ibid., p. 215.
102. Ibid., p. 219.
103. Ibid., p. 226.
104. Ibid., p. 221.
105. Ibid., p. 226.
106. Ibid., p. 227.
107. Ibid., p. 217.
108. Ibid., p. 218.
109. Ibid., p. 223.
110. Ibid., p. 224.
111. Ibid., p. 215.
112. Matthew Kendrick. "The Carnivalesque and Class Hybridization in *As You Like It*". *Explorations in Renaissance Culture* 36.2 (Winter 2010), p. 241.
113. Ibid., p. 230.
114. Ibid., p. 229.
115. Ibid., p. 230.
116. Ibid., p. 230.
117. Ibid., p. 231.
118. Ibid., p. 234.
119. Ibid., p. 235.
120. Ibid., pp. 237–38.
121. Ibid., p. 238.
122. Ibid., p. 240.

CHAPTER SEVEN

1. Carolyn Ruth Swift Lenz, Gayle Green, and Carol Thomas Neely (eds.) *The Woman's Part: Feminist Criticism of Shakespeare*. Urbana: University of Illinois Press, 1980.
2. Marianne Novy (ed.) *Women's Re-Visions of Shakespeare. On the Responses of Dickinson, Woolf, Rich, H.D., George Eliot, and Others*. Urbana and Chicago: University of Illinois Press, 1990, p. 5.

3. Nancy K. Hayles, "Sexual Disguise in *As You Like It* and *Twelfth Night*". *Shakespeare Survey* 32 (1979), p. 63.
4. Ibid., pp. 66–67.
5. Ibid., p. 64.
6. Ibid., p. 65.
7. Ibid., pp. 65–66.
8. Clara Claiborne Park, "As We Like It: How a Girl Can Be Smart and Still Popular", in Carolyn Ruth Swift Lenz, Gayle Green, and Carol Thomas Neely (eds.), *The Woman's Part. Feminist Criticism of Shakespeare*. Urbana and elsewhere: University of Illinois Press, 1980, p. 101.
9. Ibid., p. 103.
10. Ibid., p. 104.
11. Ibid., p. 105.
12. Ibid., p. 102.
13. Ibid., p. 107.
14. Ibid., p. 108.
15. Barbara J. Bono, "Mixed Gender, Mixed Genre in Shakespeare's *As You Like It*", in Barbara Kiefer Lewalski (ed.), *Renaissance Genres. Essays on Theory, History, and Interpretation*. Harvard English Studies, vol. 14. Cambridge and London: Harvard University Press, 1986, p. 190.
16. Ibid., p. 194.
17. Ibid., p. 194.
18. Ibid., p. 196.
19. Ibid., p. 199.
20. Ibid., pp. 198–99.
21. Ibid., p. 201.
22. Ibid., p. 202.
23. Ibid., p. 203.
24. Ibid., p. 204.
25. Ibid., p. 210.
26. Marjorie Garber, "The Education of Orlando", in A.R. Braunmuller and J.C. Bulman (eds.), *Comedy from Shakespeare to Sheridan. Change and Continuity in the English and European Dramatic Tradition*. Newark: University of Delaware Press; London and Toronto: Associated University Presses, 1986, p. 104.
27. Ibid., p. 104.
28. Ibid., p. 105.
29. Ibid., pp. 105–06.
30. Ibid., p. 107.
31. Ibid., p. 106.
32. Ibid., p. 109.
33. Ibid., p. 110.
34. Phyllis Rackin, "Androgyny, Mimesis, and the Marriage of the Boy Heroine on the English Renaissance Stage", *Publications of the Modern Language Association of America* 102.1 (January 1987), p. 29.
35. Ibid., p. 31.
36. Ibid., p. 32.
37. Ibid., p. 33.
38. Ibid., p. 33.
39. Ibid., p. 35.

40. Ibid., pp. 36–37.
41. Jean E. Howard, "Crossdressing, The Theater, and Gender Struggle in Early Modern England". *Shakespeare Quarterly* 39.4 (Winter 1988), p. 418.
42. Ibid., p. 421.
43. Ibid., p. 422.
44. Ibid., p. 423.
45. Ibid., pp. 424–25.
46. Ibid., p. 428.
47. Ibid., p. 429.
48. Ibid., p. 430.
49. Ibid., pp. 434–35.
50. Ibid., p. 435.
51. Ibid., p. 435.
52. Carol Rutter, *Clamorous Voices: Shakespeare's Women Today.* New York: Routledge, 1989, Introduction p. xi.
53. Quoted in ibid., p. 97.
54. Quoted in ibid., p. 97.
55. Quoted in ibid., p. 98.
56. Quoted in ibid., p. 99.
57. Quoted in ibid., p. 101.
58. Quoted in ibid., pp. 102–03.
59. Quoted in ibid., p. 104.
60. Quoted in ibid., p. 105.
61. Quoted in ibid., p. 107.
62. Quoted in ibid., pp. 108–09.
63. Quoted in ibid., p. 110.
64. Quoted in ibid., p. 111.
65. Quoted in ibid., p. 114.
66. Quoted in ibid., p. 115.
67. Quoted in ibid., pp. 116–17.
68. Kay Stanton, "Remembering Patriarchy in *As You Like It*", in Ronald Dotterer (ed.), *Shakespeare. Text, Subtext, and Context.* Selinsgrove: Susquehanna University Press; London & Toronto: Associated University Presses, 1989, p. 139.
69. Ibid., p. 140.
70. Ibid., p. 140.
71. Ibid., p. 140.
72. Ibid., p. 142.
73. Ibid., p. 140.
74. Ibid., p. 143.
75. Ibid., p. 145.
76. Ibid., p. 145.
77. Ibid., p. 147.
78. Ibid., p. 148.
79. Lesley Anne Soule, "Subverting Rosalind: Cocky Ros in the Forest of Arden". *New Theatre Quarterly* 7 (1991), p. 127.
80. Ibid., p. 127.
81. Ibid., p. 127.
82. Ibid., p. 128.
83. Ibid., p. 129.

84. Ibid., p. 130.
85. Ibid., p. 131.
86. Ibid., p. 131.
87. Ibid., p. 134.
88. Juliet Dusinberre. "As Who Liked It?" *Shakespeare Survey* 46 (1994), p. 21.
89. Ibid., p. 17.
90. Ibid., p. 21.
91. Ibid., p. 16.
92. Ibid., p. 21.
93. Ibid., p. 10.
94. Ibid., p. 11.
95. Ibid., p. 12.
96. Penny Gay, *As She Likes It. Shakespeare's Unruly Women*. London and New York: Routledge, 1994, Preface p. xi.
97. Ibid., p. 2.
98. Ibid., p. 3.
99. Ibid., p. 3.
100. Ibid., p. 10.
101. Ibid., p. 11.
102. Ibid., p. 49.
103. Ibid., p. 55.
104. Ibid., p. 55.
105. Ibid., p. 57.
106. Ibid., p. 61.
107. Ibid., p. 64.
108. Ibid., p. 71.
109. Ibid., p. 72.
110. Ibid., p. 73.
111. Ibid., p. 74.
112. Ibid., p. 76.
113. Ibid., p. 81.
114. Ibid., p. 82.
115. Ibid., p. 83.
116. Ibid., p. 85.
117. Ibid., p. 84.
118. Cynthia Lewis, "Horns, the Dream-Work, and Female Potency in *As You Like It*". *South Atlantic Review* 66.4 (Autumn 2001), p. 46.
119. Ibid., p. 48.
120. Ibid., p. 49.
121. Ibid., p. 50.
122. Ibid., pp. 47–48.
123. Ibid., p. 48.
124. Ibid., p. 50.
125. Ibid., p. 52.
126. Ibid., p. 57.
127. Ibid., p. 58.
128. Ibid., p. 62.
129. Ibid., p. 64.

CHAPTER EIGHT

1. Robert Kimbrough, "Androgyny Seen through Shakespeare's Disguise". *Shakespeare Quarterly* 33.1 (Spring 1982), p. 17.
2. Ibid., p. 19.
3. Ibid., p. 20.
4. Ibid., p. 23.
5. Ibid., p. 25.
6. Ibid., p. 26.
7. Ibid., p. 28.
8. Bruce R. Smith, *Homosexual Desire in Shakespeare's England. A Cultural Poetics*. Chicago and London: University of Chicago Press, 1991, p. 125.
9. Ibid., p. 146.
10. Ibid., p. 147.
11. Ibid., p. 122.
12. Ibid., p. 136.
13. Ibid., p. 136.
14. Ibid., p. 128.
15. Ibid., p. 123.
16. Ibid., p. 128.
17. Ibid., p. 130.
18. Ibid., p. 146.
19. Ibid., p. 150.
20. Ibid., p. 153.
21. Ibid., pp. 154–55.
22. Valerie Traub, "The Homoerotics of Shakespearean Comedy", in *Desire and Anxiety: Circulations of Sexuality in Shakespearean Drama*. London: Routledge, 1992, p. 117.
23. Ibid., p. 118.
24. Ibid., p. 118.
25. Ibid., p. 119.
26. Ibid., p. 121.
27. Ibid., p. 122.
28. Ibid., pp. 122–23.
29. Ibid., p. 123.
30. Ibid., p. 124.
31. Ibid., p. 126.
32. Ibid., p. 126.
33. Ibid., p. 127.
34. Ibid., p. 127.
35. Ibid., p. 127.
36. Ibid., p. 128.
37. Ibid., p. 130.
38. Ibid., p. 136.
39. Ibid., p. 139.
40. William Kerrigan, "Female Friends and Fraternal Enemies in *As You Like It*", in Valeria Finucci and Regina Schwartz (eds.), *Desire in the Renaissance. Psychoanalysis and Literature*. Princeton: Princeton University Press, 1994, p. 192.
41. Ibid., p. 191.

42. Ibid., p. 192.
43. Ibid., p. 189.
44. Ibid., p. 190.
45. Ibid., p. 190.
46. Ibid., pp. 186–87.
47. Ibid., p. 195.
48. Ibid., p. 196.
49. Ibid., p. 197.
50. Ibid., p. 197.
51. Ibid., p. 188.
52. Ibid., p. 198.
53. Ibid., p. 187.
54. Ibid., p. 199.
55. Cynthia Marshall, "The Doubled Jacques and Constructions of Negation in *As You Like It*". *Shakespeare Quarterly* 49.4 (Winter 1998), p. 376.
56. Ibid., p. 375.
57. Ibid., pp. 375–76.
58. Ibid., p. 376.
59. Ibid., p. 377.
60. Ibid., pp. 377–78.
61. Ibid., p. 378.
62. Ibid., p. 385.
63. Ibid., p. 379.
64. Ibid., p. 379.
65. Ibid., p. 380.
66. Ibid., p. 381.
67. Ibid., p. 386.
68. Ibid., p. 388.
69. Ibid., p. 388.
70. Ibid., p. 389.
71. Ibid., p. 391.
72. Jessica Tvordi. "Female Alliance and the Construction of Homoeroticism in *As You Like It* and *Twelfth Night*", in Susan Frye and Karen Robertson (eds.), *Maids and Mistresses, Cousins and Queens. Women's Alliances in Early Modern England*. New York and Oxford: Oxford University Press, 1999, p. 126.
73. Ibid., p. 116.
74. Ibid. pp. 114–15.
75. Ibid., p. 117.
76. Ibid., pp. 118–19.
77. Ibid., p. 115.
78. Ibid., pp. 116–17.
79. Ibid., pp. 118–19.
80. Ibid., pp. 120–21.
81. Ibid., p. 114.
82. Carol Thomas Neely, "Lovesickness, Gender, and Subjectivity: *Twelfth Night* and *As You Like It*", in Dympna Callaghan (ed.), *The Feminist Companion to Shakespeare*. Oxford and Malden: Blackwell Publishers, 2000, p. 276.
83. Ibid., p. 276.
84. Ibid., p. 277.

85. Ibid., p. 279.
86. Ibid., pp. 280–81.
87. Ibid., p. 283.
88. Ibid., p. 285.
89. Ibid., p. 285.
90. Ibid., p. 285.
91. Ibid., p. 286.
92. Ibid., p. 286.
93. Ibid., p. 291.
94. Ibid., p. 292.
95. Ibid., p. 292.
96. Ibid., pp. 292–93.
97. Ibid., p. 293.
98. Ibid., p. 293.
99. Ibid., p. 294.
100. Ibid., p. 295.
101. Valerie Rohy, "*As You Like It*: Fortune's Turn", in Madhavi Menon (ed.), *Shakesqueer. A Queer Companion to the Complete Works of Shakespeare*. Durham and London: Duke University Press, 2011, pp. 56–57.
102. Ibid., p. 57.
103. Ibid., p. 58.
104. Ibid., p. 58.
105. Ibid., p. 58.
106. Ibid., p. 59.
107. Ibid., p. 59.

CONCLUSION

1. Russell Jackson, "'Perfect Types of Womanhood': Rosalind, Beatrice and Viola in Victorian Criticism and Performance". *Shakespeare Survey* 32 (1979), pp. 15–16.
2. Ibid., p. 24.
3. Ibid., p. 25.
4. Richard Foulkes, "Touchstone for the Times: Victorians in the Forest of Arden", in Gail Marshall and Adrian Poole (eds.), *Victorian Shakespeare, Volume 1. Theatre, Drama and Performance*. Basingstoke: Palgrave Macmillan, 2003, p. 153.
5. Ibid., p. 149.
6. Ibid., p. 150.
7. Lina Perkins Wilder, "Playing Sodomites: Gender and Protean Character in *As You Like It*", in Yu Jin Ko and Michael W. Shurgot (eds.), *Shakespeare's Sense of Character. On the Page and From the Stage*. Farnham and Burlington: Ashgate, 2012, p. 190.
8. Ibid., p. 191.
9. Ibid., p. 192.
10. Ibid., p. 193.
11. Ibid., p. 194.
12. Ibid., p. 196.
13. Ibid., p. 197.
14. Ibid., p. 201.
15. Ibid., p. 203.
16. Ibid., p. 205.

17. Ibid., p. 206.
18. Indira Ghose, "'Better Days': Cultural Memory in *As You Like It*", in Graham Bradshaw and Tom Bishop (gen. eds.), *The Shakespearean International Yearbook Volume 8: Special Section, European Shakespeares*. Aldershot and Burlington: Ashgate, 2008, p. 204.
19. Ibid., p. 205.
20. Ibid., p. 209.
21. Ibid., p. 206.
22. Ibid., p. 209.
23. Foulkes (2003), p. 158.
24. Inga-Stina Ewbank, "As They Liked It: Shakespearean Comedy Goes Continental", in Gail Marshall and Adrian Poole (eds.), *Victorian Shakespeare, Volume 1. Theatre, Drama and Performance*. Basingstoke: Palgrave Macmillan, 2003, p. 131.
25. Leah S. Marcus, "Anti-Conquest and *As You Like It*". *Shakespeare Studies* 42 (2014), p. 173.
26. Ibid., pp. 170–71.
27. Ibid., p. 175.
28. Ibid., p. 175.
29. Ibid., p. 176.
30. Ibid., p. 179.
31. Ibid., p. 181.
32. Ibid., p. 180.
33. Ibid., p. 184.
34. Ibid., p. 186.
35. Ibid., p. 187.
36. Ibid., p. 188.
37. Ibid., p. 191.
38. Ryan Farrar, "*As You Like It*: The Thin Line between Legitimate Utopia and Compensatory Vacation". *Utopian Studies* 25.2 (2014), p. 362.
39. Ibid., p. 360.
40. Ibid., p. 360.
41. Ibid., p. 361.
42. Ibid., p. 361.
43. Ibid., p. 365.
44. Ibid., p. 367.
45. Ibid., p. 375.
46. Ibid., pp. 378–79.
47. Ibid., p. 381.
48. Elaine Hobby, "'My Affection Hath an Unknown Bottom': Homosexuality and the Teaching of *As You Like It*", in Lesley Aers and Nigel Wheale (eds.), *Shakespeare in the Changing Curriculum*. London and New York: Routledge, 1991, pp. 133–34.
49. Ibid., p. 134.
50. Ibid., p. 136.
51. Ibid., p. 137.
52. Ibid., p. 138.
53. Jan Stirm, "'For Solace a Twinne-like Sister': Teaching Themes of Sisterhood in *As You Like It* and Beyond". *Shakespeare Quarterly* 47.4 (Winter 1996), p. 374.
54. Ibid., p. 379.
55. Ibid., p. 381 and *passim*.
56. Ibid., p. 383.
57. Ibid., p. 384.

SELECT BIBLIOGRAPHY

Brown, Pamela Allen and Howard, Jean E. (eds.) *As You Like It. Texts and Contexts*. Boston and New York: Bedford, 2014.
Dubrow, Heather (ed.) *As You Like It*. Boston and elsewhere: Wadsworth Cengage Learning, 2012.
Furness, Horace Howard (ed.) *As You Like It. A New Variorum Edition*. Philadelphia: J.B. Lippincott Company, 1890.
Greenblatt, Stephen, Cohen, Walter, Howard, Jean E., and Maus, Katharine Eisaman (eds.), *The Norton Shakespeare*, 2nd edition. New York and London: W.W. Norton & Co., 2008.
Greenblatt, Stephen, Cohen, Walter, Gossett, Suzanne, Howard, Jean E., Maus, Katharine Eisaman and McMullan, Gordon (eds.), *The Norton Shakespeare*, 3rd edition. New York: W.W. Norton, 2015.
Johnson, Samuel (ed.) *The Plays of William Shakespeare, in Eight Volumes, with the Corrections and Illustrations of Various Commentators; To which are added Notes by Sam. Johnson*. London, 1765.
Knowles, Richard (ed.) *As You Like It. A New Variorum Edition*. New York: MLA, 1977.
Mowat, Barbara and Werstine, Paul (eds.) *As You Like It*. New York and elsewhere: Washington Square Press (Folger Shakespeare Library), 1997.
Rowe, Nicholas (ed.) *The Works of Mr. William Shakespear; in Six Volumes*. London: Jacob Tonson, 1709.
Taylor, Gary, Jowett, John, Bourus, Terri and Egan, Gabriel (gen. eds.), *The New Oxford Shakespeare. The Complete Works*. Oxford: Oxford University Press, 2016.
Warburton, William (ed.) *The Works of Shakespeare. In Eight Volumes. The Genuine Text (collated with all the former Editions, and then corrected and emended) is here settled: Being restored from the Blunders of the first Editors, and the Interpolations of the two Last: with a Comment and Notes, Critical and Explanatory*. London, 1747.

ANTHOLOGIES OF CRITICISM

Anthologies of general Shakespeare criticism which include key material on *As You Like It*

Vickers, Brian (ed.) *Shakespeare. The Critical Heritage*, 5 vols. London and elsewhere: Routledge & Kegan Paul, 1979.
Wells, Stanley and Gary Taylor (eds.) *William Shakespeare: A Textual Companion*. New York and London: W.W. Norton & Co., 1997.
Williamson, Marilyn L (ed.) *As You Like It, Much Ado About Nothing, and Twelfth Night, or, What You Will: An Annotated Bibliography of Shakespeare Studies 1673–2001*. Richard L. Nochimson, (gen. ed.). Fairview: Pegasus Press, 2003.

Anthologies of criticism specifically devoted to *As You Like It*

Bloom, Harold (ed.) *Rosalind*. New York and Philadelphia: Chelsea House, 1995.

Halio, Jay L. and Barbara Millard (eds.) *As You Like It: An Annotated Bibliography, 1940–1980*. New York: Garland, 1985.
Halio, Jay L. (ed.) *Twentieth Century Interpretations of As You Like It. A Collection of Critical Essays*. Englewood Cliffs: Prentice-Hall, 1968.
Scott, Mark W. (ed.) *As You Like It. Shakespeare Criticism: Excerpts from the Criticism of William Shakespeare's Plays and Poetry from the First Published Appraisals to Current Evaluations* series. New York: Garland, 1987.
Tomarken, Edward (ed.) *As You Like It from 1600 to the Present. Critical Essays*. London and New York: Garland Publishing, 1997.

INTRODUCTION
Alpers, Paul. *What Is Pastoral?* Chicago: University of Chicago Press, 1996.
Chambers, E.K. (ed.) *The Elizabethan Stage*, 4 vols. Oxford: Clarendon Press, 1923.
Dubrow, Heather (ed.) *As You Like It*. Boston and elsewhere: Wadsworth Cengage Learning, 2012.
Dukore, Bernard F. (ed.) *The Drama Observed*, 4 vols. University Park: The Pennsylvania State University Press, 1991.
Greenblatt, Stephen, Cohen, Walter, Gossett, Suzanne, Howard, Jean E., Maus, Katharine Eisaman and McMullan, Gordon (gen. eds.) *The Norton Shakespeare*. New York: W.W. Norton, 2015.
Howard, Jean E. "Introduction to *As You Like It*", in Stephen Greenblatt et al. (eds.), *The Norton Shakespeare*. New York: W.W. Norton, 2015, pp. 1615–24.
Marshall, Cynthia. *As You Like It. Shakespeare in Production*. Cambridge: Cambridge University Press, 2004.
Shapiro, James. *A Year in the Life of William Shakespeare: 1599*. New York: HarperCollins, 2005.
Stationers' Register entry for *As You Like It, Henry V*, and *Much Ado about Nothing*, 4 August 1600. shakespearedocumented.org (accessed 1 May 2018).
Wells, Stanley and Gary Taylor (eds.) *William Shakespeare: A Textual Companion*. New York and London: W.W. Norton & Co., 1997.

CHAPTER ONE: 1709–1800: "TO BREED ME WELL": DETERMINATIONS OF GENRE AND CHARACTER
Baker, David Erskine (ed.) *Biographia Dramatica, or, A Companion to the Playhouse*, vol. 1. Dublin: T. Henshall, 1782.
Bate, Jonathan. *Shakespearean Constitutions. Politics, Theatre, Criticism 1730–1830*. Oxford: Clarendon Press, 1989.
Dobson, Michael. *The Making of the National Poet. Shakespeare, Adaptation and Authorship, 1660–1769*. Oxford: Clarendon Press, 1992.
Dryden, John. *Of Dramatic Poesy, The Works of John Dryden*, vol. 17, H.T. Swedenberg, Jr. (gen. ed.). Berkeley and elsewhere: University of California Press, 1971.
———. *Preface to All for Love, The Works of John Dryden*, vol. 13. H.T. Swedenberg, Jr. (gen. ed.). Berkeley and elsewhere: University of California Press, 1971.
Gentleman, Francis. *The Dramatic Censor; Or, Critical Companion*, vol. 1. London: J. Bell, 1770.
Gildon, Charles. "An Essay on the Art, Rise and Progress of the Stage in *Greece, Rome* and *England*", in Nicholas Rowe (ed.), *The Works of Mr. William Shakespear*. London: 1710. Reprinted by Pickering & Chatto, 1999. pp. i–lxxii.

_____. "Remarks on the Plays of Shakespear", in Nicholas Rowe (ed.), *The Works of Mr. William Shakespear*. London: 1710. Reprinted by Pickering & Chatto, 1999. pp. 257–444.

Grady, Hugh. *The Modernist Shakespeare. Critical Texts in a Material World*. Oxford: Clarendon Press, 1991.

Griffith, (Mrs) Elizabeth. *The Morality of Shakespeare's Drama Illustrated*. London: T. Cadell, 1775.

Guthrie, William. *Critical Review* xx (November, December 1765), and xxi (January, February 1766), pp. 13–26, 81–88; excerpted in Vickers 5: 211–30.

Hurd, Richard. *Epistula ad Pisones* (1766). In *The Works of Richard Hurd*, vol. 1. London: T. Cadell and W. Davies, 1811.

Johnson, Samuel (ed.) *The Dramatick Works of William Shakespeare* (1765). Arthur Sherbo (ed.) *The Yale Edition of the Works of Samuel Johnson*, vol. 7. New Haven: Yale University Press, 1968.

Novy, Marianne (ed.) *Women's Re-Visions of Shakespeare. On the Responses of Dickinson, Woolf, Rich, H.D., George Eliot, and Others*. Urbana and Chicago: University of Illinois Press, 1990.

Richardson, William. *A Philosophical Analysis and Illustration of Some of Shakespeare's Remarkable Characters*. London: J. Murray, 1780. Reprint New York: AMS Press, 1966.

Rowe, Nicholas (ed.) *The Works of Mr. William Shakespear; in Six Volumes*. London: Jacob Tonson, 1709.

Vickers, Brian, *Returning to Shakespeare*. London and New York: Routledge, 1989.

_____ (ed.) *Shakespeare. The Critical Heritage*, 5 vols. London and elsewhere: Routledge & Kegan Paul, 1979.

Warburton, William (ed.) *The Works of Shakespeare. In Eight Volumes. The Genuine Text (collated with all the former Editions, and then corrected and emended) is here settled: Being restored from the Blunders of the first Editors, and the Interpolations of the two Last: with a Comment and Notes, Critical and Explanatory*. London, 1747.

Whiter, Walter. *A Specimen of a Commentary on Shakespeare. Containing Notes on 'As You Like It'. An Attempt to Explain and Illustrate Various Passages, on a New Principle of Criticism, Derived from Mr. Locke's Doctrine of the Association of Ideas*. London: T. Cadell, 1794. Reprint, Alan Over and Mary Bell (eds.). London: Methuen & Co., 1967.

CHAPTER TWO: 1800–1900: "DANCING MEASURES": ARRIVING AT CRITICAL CONSENSUS

Barber, C.L. *Shakespeare's Festive Comedy. A Study of Dramatic Form and Its Relation to Social Custom*. Princeton: Princeton University Press, 1959. Reprint 1972.

Bate, Jonathan. *Shakespearean Constitutions. Politics, Theatre, Criticism 1730–1830*. Oxford: Clarendon Press, 1989.

Boas, Frederick S. *Shakespeare and His Predecessors*. 1896. Reprinted, New York: Gordian Press, 1968.

Coleridge, Samuel Taylor. *The Collected Works of Samuel Taylor Coleridge*, vol. IV. H.J. Jackson and George Whalley (eds.). Princeton: Princeton University Press, 1998.

Cowden Clarke, Charles and Mary. *Shakespeare-Characters; Chiefly Those Subordinate*. London: Smith, Elder & Co.; Edinburgh: James Nichol, 1863.

Dukore, Bernard F. (ed.) *The Drama Observed*, 4 vols. University Park: The Pennsylvania State University Press, 1991.

Faucit Martin, Helena (or, Helen Faucit, Lady Martin). *On Some of Shakespeare's Female Characters*. Edinburgh and London: William Blackwood & Sons, 1893.

Gervinus, G.G. *Shakespeare Commentaries* (1849–50). F.E. Bunnett (trans.). London: Smith, Elder & Co. Revised edition, 1877.
Grady, Hugh. *The Modernist Shakespeare. Critical Texts in a Material World*. Oxford: Clarendon Press, 1991.
Hazlitt, William. *Characters of Shakespear's Plays & Lectures on the English Poets* (1817). London: Macmillan and Co., 1920 (reprint of 1903 ed.).
Hoeckley, Cheri Lin Larsen. "Anna Jacobson", in Gail Marshall (ed.), *Jameson, Cowden Clarke, Kemble, Cushman*. Volume VII Great Shakespeareans. London and New York: Continuum, 2011.
Hudson, Rev. H[enry].N. *Shakespeare: Life, Art, and Characters*, vol. 1. Boston and elsewhere: Ginn & Co., 1872.
Jackson, Russell. "'Perfect Types of Womanhood': Rosalind, Beatrice and Viola in Victorian Criticism and Performance". *Shakespeare Survey* 32 (1979), pp. 15–26.
Jameson, Anna Brownell. *Shakespeare's Heroines. Characteristics of Women Moral, Poetical, and Historical* (1832). London: George Bell & Sons, 1898.
Maginn, William. *The Shakespeare Papers*. New York: Redfield, 1856.
Natarajan, Uttara. "William Hazlitt", in Adrian Poole (ed.), *Lamb, Hazlitt, Keats*, Volume IV Great Shakespeareans. London and New York: Continuum, 2010.
Novy, Marianne (ed.) *Women's Re-Visions of Shakespeare. On the Responses of Dickinson, Woolf, Rich, H.D., George Eliot, and Others*. Urbana and Chicago: University of Illinois Press, 1990.
Schlegel, Augustus William. Lecture XXIII (c. 1811). *A Course of Lectures. Dramatic Art and Literature*. Rev. A.J.W. Morrison (ed.); John Black (trans.) London: Henry G. Bohn, 1846.
Shaw, George Bernard. *The Drama Observed*, 4 vols. Bernard F. Dukore (ed.), University Park: The Pennsylvania State University Press, 1991.
_____. "Various reviews, from 1890–1897", in Edwin Wilson (ed.), *Shaw on Shakespeare. An Anthology of Bernard Shaw's Writings on the Plays and Production of Shakespeare*. New York: E.P. Dutton, 1961.
Snider, Denton J. *The Shakespearian Drama. A Commentary. The Comedies*. St. Louis: Sigma Publishing, 1887.
Taine, Hippolyte A. *History of English Literature* (1863). H. Van Laun (trans.). New York: T.Y. Crowell, 1873.
Thompson, Ann and Sasha Roberts, "Mary Cowden Clarke: Marriage, Gender and the Victorian Woman Critic of Shakespeare", in Gail Marshall and Adrian Poole (eds.), *Victorian Shakespeare, Volume 2*. Basingstoke: Palgrave Macmillan, 2003.
Ulrici, Hermann. *Shakespeare's Dramatic Art: And His Relation to Calderon and Goethe* (1839). Rev. A.J.W. Morrison (trans.). London: Chapman, Brothers, 1846.
Wilson, Edwin (ed.) *Shaw on Shakespeare. An Anthology of Bernard Shaw's Writings on the Plays and Production of Shakespeare*. New York: E.P. Dutton, 1961.

CHAPTER THREE: 1906–72: "A GREAT RECKONING": NEW CRITICISM
Barber, C.L. "The Use of Comedy in *As You Like It*". *Philological Quarterly* 21.4 (October 1942), pp. 353–67.
Barnet, Sylvan. "Strange Events: Improbability in *As You Like It*". *Shakespeare Studies* 4 (1968), pp. 119–31.
Chambers, E.K. *Shakespeare: A Survey*. London: Sidgwick & Jackson, 1925. Reprint New York: Hill and Wang, n.d.
Charlton, H.B. *Shakespearean Comedy*. London: Methuen & Co., 1938.

Doran, Madeleine. "Yet Am I Inland Bred." *Shakespeare Quarterly* 15.2 (1964), pp. 99–114.
Grady, Hugh. *The Modernist Shakespeare. Critical Texts in a Material World*. Oxford: Clarendon Press, 1991.
Halio, Jay L. "'No Clock in the Forest': Time in *As You Like It*". *Studies in English Literature* 2 (1962), pp. 197–207. Reprinted in Jay L. Halio (ed.), *Twentieth Century Interpretations of As You Like It*. Englewood Cliffs: Prentice-Hall, 1968.
Jenkins, Harold. "*As You Like It*". *Shakespeare Survey* 8 (1955). Allardyce Nichol, (ed.), pp. 40–51. Reprinted in Kenneth Muir (ed.), *Shakespeare: The Comedies, A Collection of Critical Essays*. Englewood Cliffs: Prentice-Hall, 1965, and in Jay Halio (ed.), *Twentieth Century Interpretations of As You Like It*. Englewood Cliffs: Prentice-Hall, 1968.
Kreider, P.V. "Genial Literary Satire in the Forest of Arden". *Shakespeare Association Bulletin* 10.4 (October 1935), pp. 212–31.
Mincoff, Marco. "What Shakespeare Did to Rosalynde". *Shakespeare Jahrbuch* 96 (1960), pp. 78–89.
Priestley, J.B. *The English Comic Characters* (1925). Reprint, New York: Phaeton Press, 1972.
Stoll, Elmer Edgar. "Shakespeare, Marston, and the Malcontent Type". *Modern Philology* 3.3 (January 1906), pp. 281–303.
_____. *Shakespeare's Young Lovers*. London and elsewhere: Oxford University Press, 1937.
Young, David. *The Heart's Forest: A Study of Shakespeare's Pastoral Plays*. New Haven: Yale University Press, 1972.

CHAPTER FOUR: 1948–83: "NOT FOR ALL MARKETS": MOVEMENTS AWAY FROM NEW CRITICISM AND THE AUTHORITY OF THE TEXT

Barber, C.L. *Shakespeare's Festive Comedy. A Study of Dramatic Form and Its Relation to Social Custom*. Princeton: Princeton University Press, 1959. Reprint 1972.
Barton, Anne. "*As You Like It* and *Twelfth Night*: Shakespeare's Sense of an Ending", in Malcolm Bradbury and David Palmer (gen. eds.), *Shakespearean Comedy* (Stratford-Upon-Avon Studies 14). London: Edward Arnold, 1972, pp. 160–80.
Eagleton, Terry. *William Shakespeare*. Oxford: Blackwell, 1986.
Erickson, Peter. "C.L. Barber", in Hugh Grady (ed.), *Empson, Wilson Knight, Barber, Kott*. Volume XIII Great Shakespeareans. London and New York: Continuum, 2012.
_____. *Patriarchal Structures in Shakespeare's Drama*. Berkeley and elsewhere: University of California Press, 1985.
Frye, Northrop. *A Natural Perspective*. New York and London: Columbia University Press, 1965.
_____. "The Argument of Comedy". *English Institute Essays* (1948–49), pp. 58–73. Reprinted in Leonard F. Dean (ed.), *Shakespeare: Modern Essays in Criticism*, New York: Oxford University Press, 1961, pp. 79–89.
Gibbons, Brian. "Amorous Fictions and *As You Like It*", in John W. Mahon and Thomas A. Pendleton (eds.), "*Fanned and Winnowed Opinions*". *Shakespearean Essays Presented to Harold Jenkins*. London and New York: Methuen, 1987, pp. 52–78.
Iser, Wolgang. "The Dramatization of Double Meaning in Shakespeare's *As You Like It*". *Theatre Journal* 35.3 (October 1983), pp. 307–32.
Kott, Jan. *Shakespeare Our Contemporary*. Boleslaw Taborski (trans.). Garden City: Anchor Books, 1966.
Ronk, Martha. "Locating the Visual in *As You Like It*". *Shakespeare Quarterly* 52 (2001), pp. 255–76.
Watson, Robert N. "As You Liken It: Simile in the Wilderness". *Shakespeare Survey* 56 (2003), pp. 79–92.

CHAPTER FIVE: 1978–PRESENT: "ALL THE WORLD'S A STAGE": CULTURAL STUDIES

Barnaby, Andrew. "The Political Conscious of Shakespeare's *As You Like It*". *Studies in English Literature, 1500–1900* 36.2 (Spring, 1996), pp. 373–95.

Bate, Jonathan. *Shakespearean Constitutions. Politics, Theatre, Criticism 1730–1830*. Oxford: Clarendon Press, 1989.

Cohen, Walter. "Political Criticism of Shakespeare", in Jean E. Howard and Marion F. O'Connor (eds.), *Shakespeare Reproduced. The Text in History and Ideology*. New York and London: Methuen, 1987.

Fitter, Chris. "Reading Orlando Historically: Vagrancy, Forest, and Vestry Values in Shakespeare's *As You Like It*". *Medieval and Renaissance Drama in England: An Annual Gathering of Research, Criticism and Reviews* 23 (2010), pp. 114–41.

Howard, Jean E. and Marion F. O'Connor (eds.) *Shakespeare Reproduced. The Text in History and Ideology*. New York and London: Methuen, 1987.

Krieger, Elliott. *A Marxist Study of Shakespeare's Comedies*. London: Macmillan, 1979; New York: Harper & Row, 1979.

Kronenfeld, Judy Z. "Social Rank and the Pastoral Ideals of *As You Like It*". *Shakespeare Quarterly* 29.3 (Summer 1978), pp. 333–48.

Lifson, Martha Ronk. "Learning by Talking: Conversation in *As You Like It*". *Shakespeare Survey* 40 (1988), pp. 91–105.

Milward, Peter. "Religion in Arden". *Shakespeare Survey* 54 (2001), pp. 115–21.

Schleiner, Louise. "Voice, Ideology, and Gendered Subjects: The Case of *As You Like It* and *Two Gentlemen*". *Shakespeare Quarterly* 50 (1999), pp. 285–309.

Strout, Nathaniel. "*As You Like It, Rosalynde*, and Mutuality". *Studies in English Literature, 1500–1900* 41.2 (Spring 2001), pp. 277–95.

Tiffany, Grace. "'That Reason Wonder May Diminish': *As You Like It*, Androgyny, and the Theater Wars". *Huntington Library Quarterly* 57.3 (Summer 1994), pp. 213–39.

Woodbridge, Linda. "Country Matters: *As You Like It* and the Pastoral-Bashing Impulse", in Evelyn Gajowski (ed.), *Re-Visions of Shakespeare: Essays in Honor of Robert Ornstein*. Dover: University of Delaware Press: 2004, pp. 189–214.

CHAPTER SIX: 1980–PRESENT: "TO MUTINY AGAINST THIS SERVITUDE": NEW HISTORICISM

Belsey, Catherine. *Shakespeare and the Loss of Eden: The Construction of Family Values in Early Modern Culture*. New Brunswick: Rutgers University Press, 1999.

Crane, Mary Thomas. *Shakespeare's Brain: Reading with Cognitive Theory*. Princeton: Princeton University Press, 2001.

Daley, A. Stuart. "Calling and Commonwealth in *As You Like It*: A Late Elizabethan Political Play". *The Upstart Crow* 14 (1994), pp. 28–46.

Greenblatt, Stephen. *Renaissance Self-Fashioning. From More to Shakespeare*. Chicago and London: University of Chicago Press, 1980.

———. *Shakespearean Negotiations. The Circulation of Social Energy in Renaissance England*. Berkeley and Los Angeles: University of California Press, 1988.

Kendrick, Matthew. "The Carnivalesque and Class Hybridization in *As You Like It*". *Explorations in Renaissance Culture* 36.2 (Winter 2010), pp. 229–44.

Marshall, Cynthia. "Wrestling as Play and Game in *As You Like It*". *Studies in English Literature, 1500–1900* 33.2 (Spring 1993), pp. 265–87.

Montrose, Louis Adrian. "'The Place of a Brother' in *As You Like It*: Social Process and Comic Form". *Shakespeare Quarterly* 32 (1981), pp. 28–54.

Wilson, Richard. "Like the Old Robin Hood: *As You Like It* and the Enclosure Riots". *Will Power. Essays on Shakespearean Authority*. Hemel Hempstead: Harvester Wheatsheaf, 1993. Originally published in *Shakespeare Quarterly* 43 (1992), pp. 1–19.

Wofford, Susanne L. "'To You I Give Myself, for I Am Yours': Erotic Performance and Theatrical Performatives in *As You Like It*", in Russ McDonald (ed.), *Shakespeare Reread. The Texts in New Contexts*. Ithaca and London: Cornell University Press, 1994.

CHAPTER SEVEN: 1965–PRESENT: "IF I WERE A WOMAN": FEMINISM AND GENDER

Bono, Barbara J. "Mixed Gender, Mixed Genre in Shakespeare's *As You Like It*", in Barbara Kiefer Lewalski (ed.), *Renaissance Genres: Essays on Theory, History, and Interpretation*. Harvard English Studies, vol. 14. Cambridge and London: Harvard University Press, 1986, pp. 189–212.

Dusinberre, Juliet. "As Who Liked It?" *Shakespeare Survey* 46 (1994), pp. 9–21.

Garber, Marjorie. "The Education of Orlando", in A.R. Braunmuller and J.C. Bulman (eds.), *Comedy from Shakespeare to Sheridan. Change and Continuity in the English and European Dramatic Tradition*. Newark: University of Delaware Press; London and Toronto: Associated University Presses, 1986, pp. 102–12.

Gay, Penny. *As She Likes It. Shakespeare's Unruly Women*. London and New York: Routledge, 1994.

Hayles, Nancy K. "Sexual Desire in *As You Like It* and *Twelfth Night*". *Shakespeare Survey* 32 (1979), pp. 63–72.

Howard, Jean E. "Crossdressing, the Theater, and Gender Struggle in Early Modern England". *Shakespeare Quarterly* 39.4 (Winter 1988), pp. 418–40.

Lenz, Carolyn Ruth Swift, Gayle Green, and Carol Thomas Neely (eds.), *The Woman's Part: Feminist Criticism of Shakespeare*. Urbana: University of Illinois Press, 1980.

Lewis, Cynthia. "Horns, the Dream-Work, and Female Potency in *As You Like It*". *South Atlantic Review* 66.4 (Autumn 2001), pp. 45–69.

Novy, Marianne (ed.) *Women's Re-Visions of Shakespeare. On the Responses of Dickinson, Woolf, Rich, H.D., George Eliot, and Others*. Urbana and Chicago: University of Illinois Press, 1990.

Park, Clara Claiborne. "As We Like It: How a Girl Can Be Smart and Still Popular". *The American Scholar* 42 (Spring 1973), pp. 262–78. Reprinted in Carolyn Ruth Swift Lenz, Gayle Green, and Carol Thomas Neely (eds.), *The Woman's Part. Feminist Criticism of Shakespeare*. Urbana and elsewhere: University of Illinois Press, 1980, pp. 100–16.

Rackin, Phyllis. "Androgyny, Mimesis, and the Marriage of the Boy Heroine on the English Renaissance Stage". *Publications of the Modern Language Association of America* 102.1 (January 1987), pp. 29–41.

Rutter, Carol. *Clamorous Voices: Shakespeare's Women Today*. New York: Routledge, 1989.

Soule, Lesley Anne. "Subverting Rosalind: Cocky Ros in the Forest of Arden". *New Theatre Quarterly* 7 (1991), pp. 126–36.

Stanton, Kay. "Remembering Patriarchy in *As You Like It*", in Ronald Dotterer (ed.), *Shakespeare. Text, Subtext, and Context*. Selinsgrove: Susquehanna University Press; London & Toronto: Associated University Presses, 1989, pp. 139–49.

CHAPTER EIGHT: 1981–PRESENT: "SHE PHEBES ME": HOMOEROTICS, QUEER THEORY AND IDENTITY

Kerrigan, William. "Female Friends and Fraternal Enemies in *As You Like It*", in Valeria Finucci and Regina Schwartz (eds.), *Desire in the Renaissance. Psychoanalysis and Literature*. Princeton: Princeton University Press, 1994, pp. 184–203.

Kimbrough, Robert. "Androgyny Seen through Shakespeare's Disguise". *Shakespeare Quarterly* 33.1 (Spring 1982), pp. 17–33.

Marshall, Cynthia. "The Doubled Jacques and Constructions of Negation in *As You Like It*". *Shakespeare Quarterly* 49.4 (Winter 1998), pp. 375–92.
Neely, Carol Thomas. "Lovesickness, Gender, and Subjectivity: *Twelfth Night* and *As You Like It*", in Dympna Callaghan (ed.), *The Feminist Companion to Shakespeare*. Oxford and Malden: Blackwell Publishers, 2000, pp. 276–98.
Rohy, Valerie. "*As You Like It*: Fortune's Turn", in Madhavi Menon (ed.), *Shakesqueer. A Queer Companion to the Complete Works of Shakespeare*. Durham and London: Duke University Press, 2011, pp. 55–61.
Smith, Bruce R. *Homosexual Desire in Shakespeare's England. A Cultural Poetics*. Chicago and London: University of Chicago Press, 1991.
Traub, Valerie. *Desire and Anxiety: Circulations of Sexuality in Shakespearean Drama*. London: Routledge, 1992.
Tvordi, Jessica. "Female Alliance and the Construction of Homoeroticism in *As You Like It* and *Twelfth Night*", in Susan Frye and Karen Robertson (eds.), *Maids and Mistresses, Cousins and Queens. Women's Alliances in Early Modern England*. New York and Oxford: Oxford University Press, 1999, pp. 114–30.

CONCLUSION

Ewbank, Inga-Stina. "As They Liked It: Shakespearean Comedy Goes Continental", in Gail Marshall and Adrian Poole (eds.), *Victorian Shakespeare, Volume 1. Theatre, Drama and Performance*. Basingstoke: Palgrave Macmillan, 2003, pp. 128–45.
Farrar, Ryan. "*As You Like It*: The Thin Line between Legitimate Utopia and Compensatory Vacation". *Utopian Studies* 25.2 (2014), pp. 359–83.
Foulkes, Richard. "Touchstone for the Times: Victorians in the Forest of Arden", in Gail Marshall and Adrian Poole (eds.), *Victorian Shakespeare, Volume 1. Theatre, Drama and Performance*. Basingstoke: Palgrave Macmillan, 2003, pp. 146–60.
Ghose, Indira. "'Better Days': Cultural Memory in *As You Like It*," in Graham Bradshaw and Tom Bishop (gen. eds.), *The Shakespearean International Yearbook Volume 8: Special Section, European Shakespeares*. Aldershot and Burlington: Ashgate, 2008, pp. 204–15.
Hobby, Elaine. "'My Affection Hath an Unknown Bottom': Homosexuality and the Teaching of *As You Like It*", in Lesley Aers and Nigel Wheale (eds.), *Shakespeare in the Changing Curriculum*. London and New York: Routledge, 1991, pp. 125–42.
Jackson, Russell. "'Perfect Types of Womanhood': Rosalind, Beatrice and Viola in Victorian Criticism and Performance". *Shakespeare Survey* 32 (1979), pp. 15–26.
Marcus, Leah S. "Anti-Conquest and *As You Like It*". *Shakespeare Studies* 42 (2014), pp. 170–95.
Stirm, Jan. "'For Solace a Twinne-like Sister': Teaching Themes of Sisterhood in *As You Like It* and Beyond". *Shakespeare Quarterly* 47.4 (Winter 1996), pp. 374–86.
Wilder, Lina Perkins. "Playing Sodomites: Gender and Protean Character in *As You Like It*", in Yu Jin Ko and Michael W. Shurgot (eds.), *Shakespeare's Sense of Character. On the Page and From the Stage*. Farnham and Burlington: Ashgate, 2012, pp. 189–207.

INDEX

Abbey of Thelema   113
Adam   6, 22, 81, 98, 110
   analogues   xiv
   friendship   91
   frugality   80, 96
   loyalty   8, 34, 40, 75, 78, 91, 136
   proponent of the pastoral   22
   servitude   80
Adam on Stage   29
Adrian, Max   115
Alexander, George   28–29
Allen, William   76
All's Well that Ends Well   35
Althusser, Louis   66, 93
Amphion   41
Anderson, Mary   133
Androgyne   105, 106
Anti-theatricality   133
Antony and Cleopatra   2
Archetype   45–46, 51, 59, 61
Arden, Edward   75
Ariosto, Ludovico   113
Aristophanes   46, 112
Aristotle   2, 17
Armin, Robert   xiii, 95
Arnold, Matthew   12, 31
As You Like It, stage versions
   16 November 1896: Alexander   28–29
   2 October 1897: Daly   29
   1952: Shaw   114
   1961: Elliot   114–115
   1967 (re-staged 1968): Jones   115
   1967: Williams   115
   1973: Goodbody   115
   1977: Nunn   115
   1980: Hands   115
   1985: Noble   108–109, 115–116
As You Like It, topics
   androgyny   51, 53–54, 72–73, 105–106, 119, 121
   animal inhabitants   6, 22, 36, 40, 61, 78, 91, 110, 117, 123, 135
   audience   8, 43, 72, 74–75, 77, 85, 86, 91, 94, 111, 113, 114, 120, 134
   boys playing women   52, 54–55, 62, 108, 111–112, 119, 120, 122
   capitalism   61, 75, 78, 80, 87, 95–96, 97–98
   character studies   xv, 8–9, 12, 14, 21–23, 24–25, 26–27, 32–33
      Adam   6
      Celia   6, 15, 22–23, 27
      Duke Senior   6, 22, 24, 27
      Jacques   6, 8, 15, 23, 25, 27
      Oliver   12–13
      Orlando   12, 22, 24, 27
      Rosalind   6, 15, 25, 27
      Silvius   15
      Touchstone   6, 15, 23, 25, 32–33
   Christian influences   42
   churl, churlishness   95–96
   cooperation, mutuality   xv, 50, 77, 91, 100–101
   courtship   123–124
   cross-dressing   xvii, 98, 108, 121
   dating   xii–xiii, 19
   "doubleness"   123–124
   "doubling"   63–64
   education   7
   empathy   111
   enclosure laws   xv, 41, 57, 73–74, 87–88

172 INDEX

As You Like It, topics (*Continued*)
  eroticism 72, 83–84, 91–93, 112, 133
  fairies 6
  family 42, 74, 84–85, 86, 90, 93–95, 137
  fatherhood 70, 84–85
  fear 116–117, 135
  female friendship 8, 109
  feminism vii
  "festive comedy" 46–50, 87–88, 96, 115
    rejection of the festive 96–97
  folly 49–50
  friendship xiv, 8, 34, 86, 91
  gender xiv, 132, 133, 137
    androgyny 51, 54, 119, 121
    biology 62
    control 102, 107, 109
    domesticity 78
    gender fluidity 54–55, 70, 92–93, 128–129
    identity 52, 62, 84, 109, 111–112
    male dominance 53–54, 106–108
    sexuality 120–121
    social class 106–107, 119–120
    subjectivity 128–130
    unity of male and female 51, 77, 119
  genre xv, 3, 59, 120
    comedy 3, 5, 18, 25–26, 32, 35–36, 36–37, 38–39, 46–47, 52, 96–97
    fairy tale 6, 38
    masque 19, 112
    "mythic comedy" 72–73
    pastoral 5, 15, 20, 27, 32, 33, 34, 38–39, 51–52, 59, 63, 68–69, 87, 102–103
    romance 32, 34, 35, 86
    "romantic courtship" 93
    satire 33–34
  homoeroticism xiv, 70, 92, 118, 121–123, 127–129

homosexual desire 120–121
homosexuality xiv, 120–121, 124, 130, 137
honor 52
human falsity 52
identity xiv, 52, 61–62, 83–84, 94, 97, 99, 100, 102, 102–103, 109, 132
illusion and reality 43–44, 52
improbability of plot 6, 13, 19, 24, 36, 38, 42, 53, 59, 87
kindness xiv
love xiv, 7, 20, 36, 94, 109, 118
loyalty xiv, 88
male friendship 8, 53
marginalization 52, 87–88
marriage xiv, 92, 97–98, 114, 117, 129, 131
memory, remembrance 40, 110–111, 134
metatheatricality 133
migration 88
misogyny 117, 119, 127, 129
morality 5, 6–7, 20, 74, 78, 91
mortality 53, 93
myth 41, 51, 52
nationalism 27, 135
nature 69
patience 20
patriarchy xiv, 48, 53–56, 74, 84–87, 99–100, 102, 104, 107, 110–111, 114, 116
pedagogy 137
performance 132
  of civility 94
  of class 56–57, 74, 75, 91
  of eroticism 91–93
  of family dynamics 74
  of gender 51–52, 54–55, 89–90, 92, 105, 108, 120–121, 133–134
  of identity 94
  of love 89–90
  of marriage 124
  of merit 98

INDEX   173

of transgression   78–81, 92
of wrestling   89–90
primogeniture   xiv, 12, 51, 85–86, 90–91
proper women's behavior   7
reconciliation   51, 85
representation
   difficulties of stage representation   59–60
   of anarchy   93
   of the carnivalesque   97–98
   of class   73–74, 85, 87–88, 95–97, 97–98
   of cruelty   93
   of culture   36–37, 51, 87–88
   of family   93–95
   of Ganymede/Rosalind   60, 112
   of gender   105–106
   of homoeroticism   122
   of human relationships   52
   of individuality   85–87
   of love   129
   of marriage   91–93
   of political, social ills   51–52, 78–81, 87–88, 90–91
   of Rosalind's and Orlando's wedding   91–92
   of self   56, 102
   of subjectivity   75
   of violence   89–90
   of women   101–102
   tensions between visual and verbal representation   59–60
self-discovery   53
self-will   20, 77, 86, 97
semantics   95–96
"Separation, Mediation, Return"   26
sexuality   133, 137
sibling rivalry   86, 90, 124, 137
singing, song   24
social class   56–57, 68–69, 69–70, 73–74, 78–81, 97–98, 106–108, 120–121, 138

social mobility   73–74, 87–88, 95–96
source studies   xiii–xiv, 3, 4, 5, 39, 42
stage performances   28–30, 108–109, 112, 113–116, 132–133
suffering   20, 22, 24–25, xiv, 28, 71
transformation   59, 87
transgression
   female transgression 53, 112–113, 114–115, 129–130, 132, 137
   homoerotic transgression   126
   political transgression   78–81, 87–88, 113–114
   sexual, social transgression   121–123
text   xiii, 27–28
trust   xiv, 47
vagrancy   78–81, 88, 96
villain, villainy   95–96
violence   61, 88–89, 90, 109, 110
virtue   20, 24, 91
vocation   91
wrestling   88–89, 97, 110; *see also* names of individual characters
"Association of Ideas"   9–10
Audrey   53, 111
   analogues   xiv, xv
   and the pastoral tradition   28, 34, 37, 39, 51
   and Touchstone   15, 23, 37, 39, 44, 62, 69, 129
   love   37
Ayscough, Samuel   12

Bacon, Dorothy   138
Bakhtin, Mikhail   24, 48, 62, 63, 66, 68, 81, 88, 97, 102
Bannen, Ian   115
Barber, C.L.   12, 24, 33, 36–37, 48–50, 52, 54, 65, 66, 82, 86, 100, 102, 115, 129
Barnaby, Andrew   73–74
Barnet, Sylvan   42
Barthes, Roland   vii, 47, 48, 81

Barton, Anne 52–53
Bate, Jonathan 3, 14, 15, 67
Beaumont, Francis 120
Belsey, Catherine 93–95
Benjamin, Walter 81
Bentley's Miscellany 16
The Bible xv
Blackwood's Magazine 27
Boas, Frederick S. 27–28, 30, 32
Bono, Barbara J. 102–103
Brooks, Cleanth 31

Caird, John 116
Calhoun, Eleanor 133
Campion, Edmund 76
Canterbury Tales xv
Carey, Henry 95
Celia 13, 24, 99
  aggression 127–128
  Aliena 34, 88
  analogues xii, xiv
  devotion 22–23, 42
  friendship 5, 8, 91
  homoeroticism 92, 118, 127, 131
  in Arden 51, 135
  lack of imagination 27
  matriarchy, patriarchy 110–111
  morality 5, 20
  patience 21, 23
  privilege 68, 70
  proper women's behavior 7
  relationship with Oliver 5, 77, 110
  relationship with Rosalind 4, 7, 10, 34, 85, 100, 109, 115, 123–124, 127–128, 137–138
  speech 6, 15, 16, 22, 28, 64
  transgressor 127
Celia on Stage 108–109, 115
Censorship 79–81, 82
Chambers, E.K. 34–35
Charivari 88
Charles the Wrestler 3, 6, 19, 22, 88
Charlton, H.B. 35–36

Chettle, Henry xii
Churchwardens 87–89
Cleopatra 10
"Cocky Ros" 111–112
Cognitive Theory 95, 96, 100
Cohen, Walter 66
Coleridge, Samuel Taylor 11, 12–13, 14, 31
Colonization, Colonialism xvii, 11, 61, 134–136
Comedy of Errors 3
Conversion Therapy 131
Cooper, Thomas 41
Copjec, Joan 126
Corin
  analogues xiv
  and love 37
  and the pastoral tradition 28, 34, 37, 39
  as proponent of the pastoral 22
  friendship 91, 96
  interactions with Touchstone 6, 8, 44, 62, 69
  manners 38
  social class 68, 70
Cowden Clarke, Charles 11
Cowden Clarke, Charles and Mary 21–23
Cowden Clarke, Mary xvi, 100
Crane, Mary Thomas 95–97
Cross-Dressing 98, 106–108
Cuckoldry 116
"Cultural History" 93–95
Cultural Materialism 81
Cultural Studies xvi, 45, 52, 81, 82, 93, 99, 112
  defined 66–68
Cycle Plays 112

Daly, A. Stuart 90–91
Daly, Augustin 29
Darwin, Charles 19
Debdale, Robert 76

de Certeau, Michel   48
Deconstruction   55–56, 59, 60–61, 81, 96
Dekker, Thomas   72
Derrida, Jacques   55, 61, 66
de Saussure, Ferdinand   47, 55
"Dialectic of Irony"   18–19
"Dialogue"   62–63, 64
Dobson, Michael   1, 2
Doran, Madeleine   40–42
Douai   76
"Doubling"   63–64
Dream Analysis   116–117
Dryden, John   2
Duke Senior
  and Christian behavior   22, 24, 68, 80–81
  and Shakespeare's relations   75–76
  as double   63–65
  analogues   xiv
  benevolence   22, 27, 35, 42, 54, 78, 88, 103
  conflict with Frederick   19, 40, 91, 103, 111
  discussion of the Forest   7, 10, 22, 29, 47, 61
  misrepresenting the Forest   62, 69, 136
  optimism   38
  primogeniture   90
  relationship with Rosalind   99, 136
  relationship with Orlando   40–41, 53, 54, 88, 110
  relationships with other foresters   10, 68, 135, 136
  resilience   6, 20, 22, 23, 35
Duke Senior on Stage   29
Duke Senior's Feast   80–81
Dusinberre, Juliet   112–113

Eagleton, Terry   56–57
Ekphrasis   59
Eliot, T.S.   17, 50

Elizabeth I   87, 112
Elyot, Thomas   41
Erickson, Peter   48, 53–55
Every Man in His Humor   xiii
Every Man Out of His Humor   72
Ewbank, Inga-Stina   134

Farrar, Ryan   136
"Female Potency"   116–117
Feminism   xvii, 56, 66, 81, 84, 98, 101, 110, 112, 113, 115, 117, 118, 138
  defined   99–100
First Folio   2, 136
Fitter, Chris   78–81
Fleetwood, Susan   115
Fletcher, John   5
Florio, John   41
Folger Shakespeare Library   137
Forest of Arden   xiv, 29, 33, 41
  and class   97
  and doubling   63
  and England 88, 135
  and gender   97, 124
  and love   14
  and religion   75–76
  and sibling rivalry   124
  artificiality of   43, 46–47
  as colony   135
  as mirror   43, 52, 64
  edenic qualities   32, 42, 5552, 61, 134
  expression of the hidden   64
  liberating qualities   14, 49, 51, 53, 64, 113, 99
  melding of animal and human   135
  patriarchal qualities   54, 86, 124
  permanence   69
  real-world qualities   22, 28, 40, 51, 53, 54, 88, 95, 100, 136
  Rosalind's acclimation   35
  Rosalind's control while there   86–87, 114
  transformative qualities   10, 35, 39–40, 42, 46–47, 78, 86

INDEX

"Fort / Da" 125
Fortune 6, 49, 70
Foucault, Michel xvii, 66, 81, 88
Foulkes, Richard 132, 134
Frederick
  analogues xiv
  as double 63–65
  as incompletely drawn character 19, 20
  banishment of Rosalind 42, 70, 104, 136
  conflict with Duke Senior 6, 19, 40, 41, 91, 111, 136
  conversion 4, 35, 42, 50, 76, 86, 129
  his court 32, 40, 47, 51, 53, 78, 110
Freud, Sigmund 66, 70, 123, 125, 126
Frith, John 76
Frye, Northrop 45–47, 48, 52, 54, 65, 66, 129

Garber, Marjorie 104
Gay, Penny 113–116
Geertz, Clifford xvii, 66, 81
"Gender Roles" 105
Gender Studies xvii, 81, 98, 117, 118
  defined 99–100
Gentleman, Francis 5–6
Gervinus, G.G. 19–21
Ghose, Indira 134
Gibbons, Brian 57–59
Gildon, Charles 1, 3
Goad, Thomas 138
Goodbody, Buzz 115
Grady, Hugh 2, 11, 12, 19, 33
Gramsci, Antonio 66, 67
Greek Comedy 46
Green (or Golden) World xiii-xiv, 40, 42, 46–47, 51, 54
Greenblatt, Stephen vii, 81, 82, 83–84, 135
Griffith, Mrs. Elizabeth 6–7

Halio, Jay L. 39–40
Hamlet xi, 109, 133
Hands, Terry 115
Harrington, Sir John 113
Harvey, Laurence 114
Hathaway, Anne 76
Hayles, Nancy K. 100–101
Hazlitt, William 12, 14–15
Henry V xiii, 57
Henslowe, Philip xii
Hermaphrodites 84, 98, 105
Hesketh, Sir Thomas 76
Hobby, Elaine 137
Hoeckley, Cheri Lin Larsen 15
Hoghton, Alexander 76
Howard, Jean E. xv, 106–108
Howard, Jean E. and Marion F. O'Connor 67
Hudson, Rev. H[enry] N. 24–25
Humanism 61
Hurd, Richard 5
Hymen 24, 59, 70, 71, 122, 126, 134, 136

Ideology xvi, 2, 45–46, 56, 66, 68, 70, 75, 79, 95, 103, 107, 108, 111, 128
  defined 67
"Inherited Narratives" 113
"Inland Bred" 40–42, 88
Iser, Wolfgang 62–65

Jackson, Russell 15, 132–133
Jacques
  analogues xii, xiv, xv
  and the pastoral tradition 22, 28, 37, 39
  as clown, fool 23, 50
  as colonizer 135–136
  as idiotes 47
  as social critic 33, 91, 137
  as transgressor 113
  as wastrel 27
  contemplative nature 15, 25

INDEX   177

"ducdame"   56, 135–136
feminine qualities   110
isolation at conclusion   46, 94
melancholic nature   2, 3, 8, 9,16–17,
  18, 20, 33, 38, 65, 125–127
narcissism   61
object of scorn   136
Seven Ages of Man   xii, 3, 6, 17, 29
speech   5, 62, 77, 126, 135
views on love   23, 72
unchanging nature   44, 53
Jacques on Stage   29, 115
Jacques de Boys   59, 76, 125–127
Jakobsen, Roman   47
Jameson, Anna Brownell   xvi, 15–16,
  100
Jauss, Hans Robert   62, 63
Jenkins, Harold   33, 38–39
Jocelin, Elizabeth   138
Johnson, Charles   xiii
Johnson, Samuel   4–5
Jones, David   115
Jones, Richard   4
Jonson, Ben   2, 72
Jonsonian Satire   72

Kempe, Will   xiii, 95, 96
Kendrick, Matthew   97–98
Kerrigan, William   123–124
Kimbrough, Robert   119
King Lear   35
Kott, Jan   50–52, 65, 66
Kreider, P.V.   32, 33–34
Krieger, Elliott   69–70
Kronenfeld, Judy Z.   68–69

Lacan, Jacques   66, 124, 126
Lamb, Charles   12
Langtry, Lillie   133
Leighton, Margaret   114
Lennox, Charlotte   2
Lenz, Carolyn Ruth Swift, Gayle
  Green, and Carol Thomas
  Neely   100, 113

Lévi-Strauss,Claude   47, 48
Lewis, Cynthia   116–117
Lodge, Thomas   xii
  Rosalynde   xii, xiv-xv, 39, 42, 57,
  76–77, 85
Lord Chamberlain's Men   xii, xiii, 95, 96
Loue Labours Wonne   xii
Love's Labours Lost   49, 53
Love Story   102
Lovesickness   128–130
Lyly, John   xii

Maginn, William   16–17
Marcus, Leah S.   134–136
Marlowe, Christopher   34, 120
Marshall, Cynthia   88–89, 125–127
Marston, John   72
Martin, Helena Faucit   xvi, 26–27,
  100, 133
Marx, Karl   66
Marxism   66, 68, 69–70, 81, 84, 93,
  95, 99
Measure for Measure   16
Menander   46
Merchant of Venice   16, 102, 108
Meres, Francis   xii
Merry Wives of Windsor   3
Metatheatricality   43
Milward, Peter   83–84
Mincoff, Marco   39
Misogyny   72
Montrose, Louis Adrian   77, 84–87,
  90, 138
Much Ado About Nothing   xiii, 16, 35, 102
Munday, Anthony   xii
Myth   48

Natarajan, Uttara   12
Neely, Carol Thomas   128–130
Negation   125–126
Nelligan, Kate   115
Neoclassicism   2, 12
New Criticism   xvi, 30, 52, 62, 66, 81
  defined   31–32

New Historicism   xvii, 24, 41, 45, 49, 54, 56, 66, 73, 93, 98, 99, 112
  defined   81–83
  resistance to New Historicism   73, 77–78, 90, 95, 97
Noble, Adrian   109, 115
Novy, Marianne   6, 12, 100
Nunn, Trevor   115

Oliver   104, 111
  analogues   xiv, xv
  and male rivalry   89, 100
  and masculinity   123
  and social class   87–88
  as double   63–65
  as incompletely drawn character   19, 20
  conflict with Orlando   3, 19, 24, 38, 40, 41, 42, 74, 79, 86, 89, 90, 96, 117, 136
  conversion   6, 35, 42, 50, 86, 116, 117, 124, 129
  hatred   12–13, 20, 41, 42, 74, 78, 86
  relationship with Celia   4, 77, 110, 128
  relationship with Orlando   12–13, 19, 21, 22, 40, 84–85, 86, 100, 103, 117
  speech   28, 96, 117
Orlando   6, 76
  aggression   21, 40, 61, 88, 89–90, 101, 103, 109, 117
  analogues   8, xiv, xv
  as double   63–65
  as role model   81
  behavioral transformation   26, 39, 40, 42, 50, 54, 73, 81, 88, 94, 104, 117
  class, privilege   24, 27, 41, 69–70, 74, 75, 79–81, 86, 87–88, 89, 95–96, 97
  goodness   20, 21, 22, 24, 38, 40, 54, 58, 75, 87–88, 110, 124
  homoeroticism   vii, 70, 92, 118, 121, 122, 126
  in Arden   51, 135
  intelligence   29, 53–54, 104
  interactions with Duke Senior   40, 53
  male rivalry   100
  masculinity   102–103
  memory   110
  miscomprehension of Rosalind   7, 61–62, 93, 103, 110, 117
  Ovidean / Petrarchan leanings   72, 73
  physique   12, 22, 29, 86
  poems   10, 29, 60, 61–62, 71, 94, 110
  power over Rosalind   99
  primogeniture   86, 90
  reaction to love   26, 34, 35, 38, 93, 104, 109
  relationship with Adam   8
  relationship with Duke Senior   40–41, 53, 84–85
  relationship with Jacques   15
  relationship with Oliver   3, 12–13, 19, 40, 78, 84–85, 86, 96, 100, 103, 136
  relationship with Rosalind   4, 6, 7, 26, 37, 53–54, 79, 80, 93, 97–98, 100, 111
  resilience   23
  self-pity   34, 41, 77, 79
  self-will   69, 86, 97
  speech   28, 60, 70–71, 77, 94, 116–117, 120, 122, 124
  understanding of women   102–103, 117
Orlando on Stage   29, 115
Orlando Furioso   113
Orpheus   41
Over, Alan, and Mary Bell   10
Ovid   xv, 41, 72, 73, 94, 120, 121

Parks, Clara Claiborne   101–102
Pastoral Tradition   32, 61
  and As You Like It   8, 5, 15, 20, 27–28, 33, 34, 36–37, 39, 39–40, 43–44, 59, 69
  and doubling   63–64
  and enclosure   87

and festive comedy   49
and Rosalind   16
and social criticism   64, 69, 74, 77–78, 90, 102–103
and the theatre   57–58
critical resistance to pastoral tradition   20, 77–78
defined   xiii-xiv
origins   5
Shakespeare's attack on pastoral tradition   33–34, 38–39, 51–52, 60, 68–69
Paul the Apostle   42
Pen Warren, Robert   31
Performance Theory   132–134
Petrarchanism   39, 62, 64, 72, 73, 103, 118
Phebe   15, 99, 111
  analogues   xiv
  and homoeroticism   118, 122
  and love   20, 37, 77, 93
  and the pastoral tradition   16, 28, 34, 35, 37, 38, 49, 51
  and Petrarchanism   39
  as caricature   28
  interactions with Rosalind   xvii, 70, 73, 119
Poetomachia   72
Pope, Alexander   3
Priestley, J.B.   32–33
Prodigal Son   42, 74
Prometheus   41
Protestant Reformation   60, 61, 75
Proteus   133
Psychoanalysis   81, 84, 99, 102, 115, 123–124, 125
Puritanism   75, 81

Queer Theory   xvii, 81, 100, 131
  defined   118

Rabelais, Francois   113
Rackin, Phyllis   105–106
Ransom, John Crowe   31
Reader Response Criticism   62–63, 99

"Reality Principle"   105
Redgrave, Vanessa   114–115
Rehan, Ada   133
Richardson, William   8
Robin Hood   xii, xiv, xv, 40, 87, 88, 120, 134
Rohy, Valerie   130–131
Romanticism   12, 13, 14, 22, 34
Ronk, Martha   59–60
Ronk Lifson, Martha   70–71
Rosalind   24, 61, 76, 108
  analogues   xiv, xv
  androgyny   51, 53, 72–73
  and reconciliation   51, 73
  as Ganymede
    and feigned masculinity   53–54, 93, 100–101, 123
    and gender indeterminacy   122, 134, 137
    and the pastoral tradition   34
    and Phebe   vii, 39, 122
    control over others   86, 117, 122, 133
    egoticism   71
    homoeroticism   70
    identity   43, 62, 64–65, 109, 118, 124, 126, 134
    liberation through disguise   97–98, 99, 108, 126, 133
    representations   vii, 99, 112
    speech   vii, 56, 64, 71
    teaching Orlando   71, 94, 104
    testing Orlando   64, 103
    threat to men   86–87
    transformative qualities   72–73
    transgressive qualities   86, 88, 97–98, 102–103, 104, 122–123, 128
    unification of male and female   72–73, 119
  as teacher   21, 28, 88, 104, 130
  beauty   10
  class, privilege   68, 69–70, 97
  clear view of love   38, 39, 40, 50, 73
  clothing   10, 29, 97, 108

Rosalind (*Continued*)
  commentary on women 119
  commentary on love 49–50
  erotic acts, language vii, 70, 72–73, 84
  fear 117
  female desire vii, 112–113, 117
  gender fluidity 118
  homoeroticism viii, 92, 121–123
  ideal female 8, 111–112
  identity 97, 103
  in Arden 35–36, 51, 64, 86, 104, 113, 114, 117, 135
  independence 86, 97–98, 109, 111, 113, 117, 119, 133, 136
  intellect 24, 26–27, 28, 33, 34, 35–36, 37, 38, 40, 44, 53–54, 77, 96, 119
  kindness 6, 42
  language, speech 8, 6, 13, 15, 16, 28, 56, 60, 64, 69–71, 72, 84, 92–93, 94, 103, 112, 116–117, 120, 132
  memory 110
  modesty 5, 12, 13, 25, 36, 132
  morality 20–21
  playfulness 103
  primogeniture 90
  reaction to love 4, 36, 53–54
  relationship with Celia 4, 7, 10, 22–23, 34, 85, 100, 109, 115, 123–124, 127–128, 137–138
  relationship with Jacques 8, 135–136
  relationship with Orlando vii, 7, 21, 37, 38, 62, 73, 79, 80, 92, 97–98, 109, 111, 117
  relationships with men 110
  response to banishment 70
  role model 8, 10, 16, 23, 36, 49–50, 69–71, 81, 111, 135–136, 138
  self-will 69–70, 109
  submission 53–54, 77, 84–87, 92–93, 96, 99, 101, 102, 108, 111, 122, 132

  testing Orlando's love 26, 27, 28, 100, 103
  transgressive qualities 72–73, 88, 97, 102–103, 108–109, 112–113
Rosalind on Stage 29, 108–109, 111, 114–115, 116, 132–133
Rose Theater xii
Rowe, Nicholas 3
"Ruling Character" 12
Rutter, Carol 108–109
Rymer, Thomas, 2

Satire 72
Saturnalian Ritual 48–49
Saviolo, Vincentio 4
Schlegel, Augustus William 13–14
Schleiner, Louise 74–75
Senex 46
Shakespeare, John and Mary Arden 75
Shakespeare, William
  and actors 106, 108, 111, 121, 132, 133
  and art 33, 105–106
  and audience 14, 57–59, 76–77, 78–81, 87–88, 101–102, 105, 119
  and capitalism 12, 95
  and civility 41
  and clothing 107, 121
  and culture xiv, 11–12, 13, 25–26, 27, 30, 33–34, 40–42, 45–46, 51–52, 56–57, 61–62, 65, 72–74, 77–78, 84–87, 87–88, 91–93, 97–98, 100–101, 134, 136
  and domestic life 7
  and domesticity 7
  and dramatic structure 2, 5–6, 7, 10, 11, 14, 18, 20, 24, 25–26, 31, 35–37, 38–39, 48–49, 52, 57–60, 85–86
  and dreams 23, 47
  and education 2, 7, 11, 12, 13, 41, 134

INDEX   181

and the festive   24, 46, 48–50, 54, 79–81, 83, 86–87, 95, 96, 97–98
and free will   18
and gender   15, 74–75, 99, 106–108, 121–122
and homoeroticism   121–122
and industrialization   12
and liberation   49
and love   7, 12, 14, 26, 36, 37, 39, 49–50, 71, 77, 78, 89, 93–95, 104
and marriage   6, 37, 70, 76, 78, 84–87, 94, 97
and meditation   25–26
and misogyny   17, 72
and moderation   20
and morality   2, 5, 8, 12, 17, 21, 24, 69, 74, 88
and nationalism   2–3
and nature   1–2, 3, 4, 13, 14, 17, 18, 20, 28, 47, 49, 51, 52, 56, 69
and parish oligarchies   79–81
and positive images of women   21
and psychology   8, 15, 37
and religion   18, 22, 24, 25–26, 68, 75–76, 81, 91
and self-improvement   8, 19, 20
and sexuality   83
and social mobility   95
and his theatre   95–97, 105–106, 106–107
  theatrical representation
  of cross-dressing   106–107
  of eroticism   83
  of individuality   83
and textual indeterminacy   56
and time   39–40
and Tudor politics   90–91
and vagrancy   88, 98
and virtue   2, 8
and women   26–27, 33, 53–54, 61, 72–73, 73, 100, 101–102, 105, 113, 119
and women's behavior   7, 15

as national poet   2, 28
as role model   7, 12, 19, 134
Shakespeare Concordances   21
Shakespeare Criticism   xv—xvii, 9, 31–32, 45, 47–48, 55–56
  Eighteenth-century criticism   xv, 1–2, 8
  Nineteenth-century criticism   xvi, 12, 13, 19, 27, 100, 134, 135, 136
  Romantic criticism   12, 13, 14, 22
  Twentieth-Century criticism   27, 32–33
  Victorian criticism   19, 132
Shakespeare Editions   3, 4, 9, 21
Shakespeare in Performance   51–52, 54–55, 67–68, 88–89, 108–109, 111, 114
Shakespeare's Catholicism   75–76
Shaw, Fiona   108–109, 115
Shaw, Glen Byam   114
Shaw, George Bernard   8, 28–30
Showalter, Elaine   102
Sidney, Sir Philip   xv, 57, 58, 106
Silvius   xiv, 122
  and love   15, 20, 37, 73, 77
  and the pastoral tradition   28, 34, 37, 38, 49
  and Petrarchanism   39
  as caricature   28
  interactions with Rosalind   70
  masculinity   77
Sir Clyomon and Sir Clamydes   xv
Sir Oliver Martext   xiv, 19, 40, 76
Skimmington Raids   88
Smith, Bruce R.   120–121
Snider, Denton J.   25–26
"Social Reconciliation"   45–47, 129
Somerville Plot   75
Soule, Lesley Anne   111–112
Stanton, Kay   110–111
Stevenson, Juliet   108–109, 115
Stirm, Jan   137–138
Stoll, Elmer Edgar   32, 33, 35

Strout, Nathaniel   76–77
Structuralism   47–48, 55–56, 57, 79, 93, 99, 125
Subjectivity   69, 74–75, 86

Taine, Hippolyte A.   23–24, 30
Tale of Gamelyn   xv
Tasso, Torquato   5
Tate, Allen   31
Taylor, Gary   xiii
The Taming of the Shrew   3
The Tempest   104
Theobald, Lewis   9, 12
Theocritus   xv, 34
Thomas, Thomas   41
Thompson, Ann and Sasha Roberts   21, 22
Thompson, Sophie   116
Tiffany, Grace   72–73
Touchstone   32, 63, 119
  analogues   xiii, xiv
  and Audrey   15, 18, 23, 39, 44, 62, 69, 116, 129
  and gender relations   86
  chorus   35
  clown   15, 21, 25, 35, 37, 50, 134
  critic of the pastoral   28, 33, 34, 37, 39
  dueling   4
  honor   23
  "if"   123
  interactions with Corin   8, 44, 62, 69
  interaction with William   69
  love   18–19, 86, 95
  lying   71
  mirror   33, 43
  proponent of the pastoral   22
  self-control   19

social class   70
speech   6, 21, 62, 65, 69, 123
transgressor   113
wit   15, 38
Touchstone on Stage   29, 115
Transvestitism   84
Traub, Valerie   121–123
Tvordi, Jessica   127–128
Twelfth Night   35, 49, 52, 83, 108, 127, 128
Two Gentlemen of Verona   xvii

Ulrici, Hermann   17–19
Utopia   136

"Venus and Adonis"   120
Vice Figure   112
Vickers, Brian   2, 8
Virgil   xv, 41

Warburton, William   3–4
Watson, Robert N.   60–62
Wells, Stanley   xiii
Whiter, Walter   9–10
Wilder, Lina Perkins   133
William
  abandoned by Audrey   129
  analogues   xiv, xv
  and the pastoral tradition   34, 39, 53
  interaction with Touchstone   6, 69
Williams, Clifford   115
Williams, Raymond   66, 67
Wilson, Richard   79, 87–88
Winter's Tale   vii
Woffard, Susan   91–93
Woodbridge, Linda   77–78

Young, David   43–44